WASHINGTON STATE RISING

BLACK POWER SERIES

General Editors: Ibram X. Kendi and Ashley D. Farmer

Fight the Power: African Americans and the Long History of Police Brutality in New York City
Clarence Taylor

We Are Worth Fighting For: A History of the Howard University Student Protest of 1989
Joshua M. Myers

Pasifika Black: Oceania, Anti-Colonialism, and the African World
Quito Swan

The Tuskegee Student Uprising: A History
Brian Jones

Washington State Rising: Black Power on Campus in the Pacific Northwest
Marc Arsell Robinson

Washington State Rising

Black Power on Campus in the Pacific Northwest

Marc Arsell Robinson

NEW YORK UNIVERSITY PRESS

New York

NEW YORK UNIVERSITY PRESS
New York
www.nyupress.org

Please contact the Library of Congress for Cataloging-in-Publication data.
ISBN: 9781479810406 (hardback)
ISBN: 9781479810420 (library ebook)
ISBN: 9781479810413 (consumer ebook)

New York University Press books are printed on acid-free paper, and their binding materials are chosen for strength and durability. We strive to use environmentally responsible suppliers and materials to the greatest extent possible in publishing our books.

Manufactured in the United States of America

10 9 8 7 6 5 4 3 2 1

Also available as an ebook

This book is dedicated to all the Black activists, freedom fighters, and revolutionaries of the state of Washington (and beyond) who struggled for greater justice and equity during the late 1960s. This book would not have been possible without their courage, actions, sacrifices, and victories.

CONTENTS

Introduction: Evergreen "Ungawa" and the
Black Power Movement   1

1. Seattle and the Foundations of the Black Student Union,
   1940s–1960s   21

2. "You Done *Really* Changed": The BSU at the University of
   Washington, Fall 1967–Spring 1968   57

3. "We Tired of Y'All's Half-Stepping": The BSU's May 1968
   Sit-In and Its Aftermath   86

4. "Never Just a Tea Party": The BSU and Black Power
   at Washington State University, 1967–1968   116

5. "Well, Glenn-Baby, What's Up Now?": The BSU and Black
   Studies at Washington State University, 1968–1970   133

Conclusion: "Fighting for Our Freedom Was Exhilarating"   159

Acknowledgments   169

Notes   173

Index   199

About the Author   211

Introduction

Evergreen "Ungawa" and the Black Power Movement

In 1967 the Black Power movement arrived at the University of Washington. In April, Stokely Carmichael visited Seattle and addressed large audiences on and off campus. In November, Black students at the University of Washington (UW) established a chapter of the Black Student Union, inspired by Carmichael and many others, along with broader developments in local and national black politics. By the following February, the organization garnered the attention of the campus newspaper. The organization's first major profile, titled "New Black Image Emerging," provides an enlightening window into the BSU's attitude and thinking. At the top of the piece, E. J. Brisker, BSU vice president, is quoted as saying, "Today's black students are defining for themselves what their cultural values will be." Brisker continued, "For this very reason we would like to see incorporated into the University a black curriculum of studies, a department planned, controlled, and influenced by the black community." Another officer of the organization, Larry Gossett, described in the article as the BSU's regional coordinator for Oregon and Washington, added, "'Black is beautiful' is not just a catchy phrase." This underscored the importance of Black pride for the students. Along with a new "Black curriculum" or Black Studies, the BSU also outlined aspirations to increase the numbers of Black students and faculty at the university. When asked whether they might eventually adopt more confrontational and militant tactics akin to other Black student organizations around the nation, Gossett answered, "Our militancy is entirely dependent on the white reaction to the concrete proposals that we make. It's the white communities' responsibility."[1] This article marked the beginning of a new phase in race relations at UW, and the university was profoundly transformed as a result.

A few months later, in May 1968, Black students at Washington State University (WSU) established their own Black Student Union, operating in a vastly different sociopolitical climate. Unlike the urban landscape of Seattle, Washington State University is in eastern Washington, approximately three hundred miles from Seattle, on the state's eastern border with Idaho. The rural conservatism and minuscule Black population on campus and in the surrounding area made the environment especially inhospitable to Black Power organizing. Nevertheless, the Black Student Union there also agitated for racial justice. In May, speaking through an open letter in the campus newspaper, Black students launched their group to the forefront of campus politics by denouncing their fellow white students and the entire university. During the prior weekend, a contingent of approximately fifty-four Black high school students from Seattle visited Washington State University as part of a statewide tour of colleges and universities. At WSU the adolescents experienced several incidents of bigotry and discrimination, including racial slurs. As the letter summarized, "The boys started back to Orton Hall where they were staying. The [white] 'college men' that reside in Orton and Rogers Halls yelled that age-old cliché, 'Nigger.'"[2] Due to this verbal attack and related abuses, the entire group abruptly left in protest, cutting short the planned visit.

In the aftermath of the incident, the Black college students expressed their dismay to the campus community. They wrote, "We as black students are truly ashamed at this performance put on by various students. We again state that we demand an explanation as to why Washington State University treated a group of black students in this manner?"[3] Just like the activism of their counterparts in Seattle and around the nation, the activism of Black students at Washington State University ushered in a new era of activism and racial reckoning. *Washington State Rising* chronicles the history of these two intrepid Black Student Unions at the University of Washington and Washington State University.

This monograph details the history of the Black Student Union in the state of Washington during the late 1960s. This research identifies these Black Student Unions as critical loci of Black Power organizing and protest. Consequently, it shows that the Black student engagement in the state of Washington was a significant node in the larger, nationwide struggle for Black equality during the decade. This project uncovers new details and coalesces shards of existing knowledge to illuminate the distinctive forms of activism of the BSU that led to successful campaigns for racial reform at the University of Washington, Washington State University, and beyond. At both universities, the BSU quickly became influential champions for institutional reform. Constituting a local manifestation of the national student wing of the Black Power movement, the BSU provides a window on the impact of Black Power in the Pacific Northwest, thereby adding new depths to scholarly understandings of mid-twentieth-century Black politics.

The phrase "Evergreen 'Ungawa'" in this introduction's subtitle references this Black Power activism of the Pacific Northwest. A popular nickname for the state of Washington is the "Evergreen State," a moniker that references the state's large forests of evergreen trees. "Ungawa" was a popular rallying cry within the Black Power movement. For example, in December 1967 supporters of Stokely Carmichael chanted, "Ungawa, Black Power!" when he arrived in New York City after international travel.[4] More specifically for this project, "ungawa" was adopted as a rallying cry for the BSU in Seattle. For instance, in May 1968 the BSU at UW held a sit-in protest in the university president's office, detailed later in the book, and at the end of the action left chanting, "Beep-Beep, Bang-Bang, Ungawa, Black Power!"[5] Similarly, earlier in the same school year, Black students at Garfield High School allied with the BSU at UW used a nearly identical chant during a demonstration to pressure school officials to allow a Black Student Union at the high school. Garfield student Elmer Dixon remembered leading the shout in a call-and-response style: "It went something like this: I'd say, 'bing-bing.' And they would echo, 'bing-bing.' I would say, 'bang-bang.' They would echo, 'bang-bang.' I'd say, 'ungawa.' They would echo, 'ungawa.' I would say, 'Black Power.' They would echo, 'Black Power.' And the whole auditorium erupted in this cheer, and this clapping."[6] Within a few weeks the principal relented and the BSU was established at Garfield, after continued pressure from students. However, the point here is that BSU members in Seattle, like other Black Power militants elsewhere, embraced "ungawa" as a mantra, often sung or chanted, to express an assertive demeanor, an ethos of empowerment, and a celebration of Black pride and African cultures. The exact origins and meaning of "ungawa" as a Black Power slogan are unclear; some suggest that it derived from Swahili. As with many instances of youth slang and vernacular culture, the precise etymology might never be known, but ungawa, sometimes spelled "ungowa," clearly connected with Black Power adherents' need to express themselves. Hence, "evergreen" and "ungawa" aptly capture the subject of this text.

Washington State Rising puts forth a number of significant arguments, including two overarching main points. The first assertion is that the state of Washington, especially its largest city, Seattle, was an important nexus of political organizing during the Black Power movement. The second assertion is that the study of late 1960s BSU actions in Washington broadens and complicates conventional understandings of the Black Power movement. Moreover, given that this book focuses on two different BSU chapters at two significantly different higher education institutions, there are additional arguments specific to each institution. A third point is that the BSU at the University of Washington highlights how Black Power activists utilized community organizing and interracial coalitions to achieve groundbreaking reforms. Finally, the fourth assertion is that the BSU at Washington State University illuminates both Black student protest and the existence of Jim Crow conditions in the northern and western region of the United States.

Expanding on point one, this monograph documents an inspiring episode of Black history in the Pacific Northwest by chronicling the groundbreaking activism of the Black Student Union therein. As a starting point, it challenges popular notions of the 1960s that underestimate the national scope of the Black Power movement (BPM) and the presence of Black protest in the northwestern corner of the country. In popular memory and existing scholarship, the Pacific Northwest region is usually rendered irrelevant in accounts of the civil rights and Black Power movements. Some published work has helped to address this misconception. Relevant texts that highlight Black activism in Seattle and nearby communities during the 1960s include *The Forging of a Black Community: Seattle's Central District from 1870 through the Civil Rights Era* (1994), by Quintard Taylor; *Seattle in Black and White: The Congress of Racial Equality and the Fight for Equal Opportunity* (2011), by Joan Singler et al.; *My People Are Rising: Memoir of a Black Panther Party Captain* (2012), by Aaron Dixon; and *The Portland Black Panthers: Empowering Albina and Remaking a City* (2016), by Lucas Burke and

Judson Jeffries. There have also been several dissertations and master's theses.[7] The University of Washington produced a documentary on the 1960s BSU, *In Pursuit of Social Justice: An Oral History of the Early Years of Diversity Efforts at the Unive..ity of Washington* (2007).[8] Additionally, relevant details are available in the Seattle Civil Rights and Labor History Project website, and in the memoir of Samuel E. Kelly, the inaugural vice president of minority affairs at UW, titled *Dr. Sam, Soldier, Educator, Advocate, Friend: An Autobiography* (2010).[9]

Washington State Rising is the first monograph to detail 1960s Black student activism in the Pacific Northwest, or anywhere north of California. This is significant as a project of additive revisionism, uncovering little-known Black history in a heretofore understudied locale. As a Black person who was born and raised in Washington State, I was personally inspired by this history when I first began researching the BSU as an undergraduate at the University of Washington. Having learned nothing of this history from kindergarten through high school, I heard only snippets from my mother and other members of my family and community. Later, in college, I found a new sense of connection to my hometown, and a new sense of empowerment, when I encountered a fuller picture of the Black Student Union's actions and influence. Therefore, one of the positives I hope readers take from this book is some piece of the affirmation and pride I felt when I learned that the Black freedom struggle extended to the northwestern corner of the nation.

Yet there is also a deeper significance beyond pointing out that "it happened here too." This is because this history reveals insights that would otherwise be missed if scholars examined only well-known and well-chronicled sites of Black unrest. Expressing a similar point, historian Robert Cohen made a relevant observation when advocating for research on student protest in the South:

> If we want to determine how major an impact the student movement of the 1960s had in changing America, the way to determine that is not to round up the usual suspects in the traditional northern centers of dissent but to see how well the movement penetrated an area like the South, which has historically been less amenable to left organizing. Much as you would tend not to assess a minister's oratorical abilities by judging only

by the reaction of the choir, one ought not judge a national student insurgency by probing only its northern epicenters.[10]

Of course, the state of Washington is not in the South, but Cohen's larger point is relevant to this project. He is stating that important insights can be gained from research that steps outside the epicenters of a movement. All the settings of this study are not among the "usual suspects" of Black Power politics; therefore, examining the movement in these locations enables us to appreciate the true extent of the movement's dynamism, malleability, and national impact.

As the second overarching argument, *Washington State Rising* contributes new evidence in support of a nuanced assessment of the Black Power movement, which contrasts to early interpretations that often demonized Black Power in relation to the civil rights movement (CRM). In particular, this text will document the BSU as representative of how some Black Power organizations pursued tangible gains and won meaningful reforms all across the nation. Moreover, their effective campaigns spanned the months and years following the assassination of Dr. Martin Luther King Jr., which is sometimes taken as the endpoint of the era's productive Black protests. In particular, *Washington State Rising* shows how during the late 1960s the BSUs at UW and WSU confronted discrimination, articulated a vision of institutional transformation, organized demonstrations, lobbied officials, formed alliances, and achieved many breakthroughs. In sum, the student activists forced their respective institutions to respond to the needs of African Americans like never before, proffering evidence of how Black Power reshaped and improved American higher education.

In addition to the overarching arguments just described, this monograph offers additional, site-specific assessments. One unique feature of *Washington State Rising* is that it chronicles Black student activism at two very different public universities in the same state, allowing for particular comparative analysis. As noted previously, the first of two BSUs examined here was at the University of Washington in Seattle. Located in a major city with a significant off-campus Black community, the BSU at UW showcases how some in Black Power embraced the strategies of interracial coalitions and community organizing. Regarding community organizing, the BSU's most relevant project was a dynamic outreach effort involving Black high school and middle school students in the area. This not only increased the BSU's support among local youth, many of whom were already favorably disposed toward the rebellious spirit and cool image of Black Power, but it also won support from older members of the Black community, namely, the parents and families of the adolescents. Undoubtably, the forging of these relational networks between the campus and community was essential to the BSU's success in Seattle, and it is significant for understanding the broader movement. This insight expands contemporary understandings of the range of Black Power tactics, provides a window into the quotidian work of building grassroots support, and provides potential tools for current and future social justice projects.

The other Black Student Union chronicled in *Washington State Rising* was at Washington State University in the small, eastern Washington town of Pullman. Getting to Pullman from Seattle in the 1960s, when the interstate highways were still being built, took an entire day of driving on country roads. Even today, with modern freeways, it takes five hours by car. Yet it was more than just a question of geographical distance; Pullman was virtually a world away from Seattle socially and politically. Pullman was in a conservative, rural, agricultural region called the Palouse, and had more in common with northern Idaho than western Washington. Pullman's population, like that of Whitman County as a whole, where Pullman is located, was overwhelmingly white, and there was no sizable off-campus Black community. Likewise, on campus, the population of Black students, staff, and faculty remained very small throughout the 1960s. No official record of student enrollment by race was kept until the 1970s, but one source estimated that by 1968 WSU had approximately two hundred Black students out of a total student body of about fourteen thousand.[11] Moreover, this total was very likely an all-time high for Black enrollment, and still amounted to less than 1 percent of the total student body. Given these circumstances, it is not surprising that the BSU at Washington State University faced greater threats and intimidation, as compared to its Seattle counterpart. This included numerous death threats and at least one potentially violent confrontation with local townsfolk. These conditions amounted to what scholars have termed Jim Crow North, which refers to conditions in the northern United States that mimicked the anti-Black oppression of the

South. Pullman and Whitman County were not as repressive as rural
Alabama or Mississippi, of course, but the story of the BSU in Pullman
extends literature on the Jim Crow North by locating "up South" conditions in the Pacific Northwest. Consequently, studying the BSU at WSU
also offers fascinating insights into the larger movement. We see how
Black Power was adaptable and compelling enough to take root in an
especially hostile, isolated, predominantly white campus. In addition,
we see the contrasting conditions, corresponding tactics, and differential
outcomes of the BSU in Pullman, vis-à-vis the chapter in Seattle.

Washington State Rising contributes to several scholarly fields, especially research that documents the history of the civil rights and Black
Power movements. A significant debate within this literature centers on
how to demarcate the two movements. Generally, scholars agree that the
civil rights movement (CRM) started in 1954 or 1955, with the *Brown* decision or the Montgomery bus boycott, respectively; and ended in 1965
or 1966, with the Voting Rights Act or Stokely Carmichael's Black Power
speech. Consequently, the Black Power movement (BPM) is commonly
dated as 1966 to 1975, which corresponds to the period of ascendance for
several prominent Black Power groups: Black Panther Party, Congress
of African Peoples, National Black Assembly, League of Revolutionary
Black Workers, National Welfare Rights Organization, and others.[12]
Complicating this basic understanding of mid-twentieth-century Black
politics, several prominent scholars over the past three decades have
posited a "long civil rights movement" framework that de-emphasizes
distinctions between the CRM and BPM. In varying degrees, scholars
Jeanne Theoharis, Komozi Woodard, Matthew Countryman, Robert O.
Self, Nikhil Pal Singh, Jacquelyn Dowd Hall, and others have argued
this position, which in essence holds that civil rights and Black Power
are more accurately conceptualized as two parts of one larger movement
rather than separate phenomena.[13] At its best, the "long movement"
framework constructively challenged earlier scholarship that treated the
civil rights movement as uniquely noble, anomalous, and disconnected
to earlier and later Black freedom struggles. Therefore, *Washington State
Rising* concurs with the "long movement" scholars in advocating for a
reappraisal of the BPM and the contextualization of the CRM in a longer
arc of Black history.

Yet, despite these strengths, critics such as historians Sundiata Keita Cha-Jua and Clarence Lang have articulated a dissenting view. They charge that "long movement" scholars "bend the stick too far in the opposite direction" and have described the CRM and BPM with excessive continuity. Explaining the point, Cha-Jua and Lang wrote that the long movement analysis at times posits "an unbroken chain of insurgency from the 1930s–1940s to the 1970s–1980s," and obscures important ideological shifts and methodological disjunctures. This includes the transformation in thought, vision, and rhetoric that marked the transition from civil rights to Black Power in the late 1960s. Indeed, there is also merit to this contention, given that the CRM and BPM were animated by very different visions of progress and liberation, even if the two at times overlapped in terms of participants, organizations, and strategies, such as sit-ins or boycotts. The civil rights movement was focused on integration and individual rights as US citizens, whereas Black Power coalesced around visions of self-reliance, independence, and collective empowerment. The rhetoric and vision of civil rights framed African Americans as eager to participate in the American mainstream. On the other hand, Black Power advocated an insurgent identity that was profoundly skeptical of Americanness, embraced Pan-Africanism, and allied with the Global South or Third World. Cha-Jua and Lang rightly point out that blurring together the CRM and BPM, as some of the long movement scholarship does, obfuscates the complex topography of influential Black intellectual and political debates.[14]

Consequently, my analysis in *Washington State Rising* proceeds with a synthesis of both sides of this debate. Concurring with Cha-Jua, Lang, Peniel Joseph, and others, this study focuses on the Black Power movement as a distinct historical phenomenon. However, given the merits of the long movement framework, this project also proceeds with an understanding that Black Power, like civil rights, was connected to a larger tradition of Black politics spanning the twentieth century and beyond. As historian Ashley Farmer put it, Black Power "evolved from a grassroots murmur into a national movement" in the mid-1960s, and that that earlier "murmur" was the product of avant-gardists like Malcolm X, Victoria (Vicki) Garvin, Robert F. Williams, and Audley Moore who were politically active as early as the 1940s and 1950s.[15] Moreover, in Peniel Joseph's succinct phrasing, the CRM and BPM were "two branches of the same tree," interrelated while also distinct.[16]

Further extending the scholarship of the "long movement" advocates, this project also contends that the Black Power movement deserves continued reevaluation to promote more nuanced and instructive notions of the past. The erroneous alternative is usually the framing of Black Power as the undoing of all productive protests of the era and equating it with ghetto rioting, white backlash, and aborted social reforms.[17]

Shifting to a different terrain of scholarship and historiography, *Washington State Rising* also contributes to a debate on regionalism in US and African American history. One influential argument against regionalism was articulated by Matthew Lassiter and Joseph Crespino in *The Myth of Southern Exceptionalism* (2010). In their evaluation of regional studies on the American South, they contend that these works could promote the inaccurate conception that white supremacy and racial injustice were principally southern characteristics. By contrast, they assert that anti-Black prejudice and institutional racism were present throughout the United States.[18]

I share Lassiter and Crespino's concern for the way regional studies could be taken to absolve the rest of the nation from culpability, yet I also contend that this does not negate the value of regional histories. Moreover, regional histories can also help uncover the degree to which racial injustice is ingrained in the American past. *Washington State Rising* joins the work of Lassiter and Crespino, and other scholars such as Donna Murch, Matthew Countryman, Josh Sides, Genevieve Carpio, Brett Gadsden, Jeanne Theoharis, and Brian Purnell, who highlight "Jim Crow North."[19] For instance, in *Up South: Civil Rights and Black Power in Philadelphia* (2006), Matthew Countryman wrote, "Racial oppression was, of course, not the same in Philadelphia as it was 'Down South.' . . . But to live 'Up South' was to confront structures of racial inequality and exclusion on a daily basis."[20] As we'll see here, "Up South" also extended to the Pacific Northwest, and regional studies need not produce the ill-effects that Lassiter and Crespino caution against. Elaborating on this point in defense of regionalism, history of education scholars Nancy Beadie and her coauthors wrote, "The problem it seems is the notion of *exceptionalism* rather than of region per se."[21] These scholars rightly contend that exceptionalism, or the idea that something is entirely unlike all others, can be avoided even as we pursue studies that explore aspects of a given region.

In addition, I join with Beadie et al. in arguing that there is a particular value in regionalist histories on the West, and by extension the Pacific Northwest. As Beadie et al. describe it, the West has a "distinctive history of race, racism(s), and racialization" stemming from the specific colonial projects and labor migrations of western history.[22] One result of these developments is that the demographics of the West have never fit into a simple Black/white racial binary. Instead, the region has always had a complex racial-ethnic landscape that includes peoples of numerous indigenous nations, and people with ancestry in Mexico, China, Japan, Hawaii, Europe, Africa, and elsewhere. In contrast to racism in other regions of the United States, "racism in much of the West was neither binary nor stable, but multiple, malleable, and shifting."[23] Consequently, the West provides a unique social environment within which to study how individuals, organizations, and institutions constructed and contested hierarchies of power and privilege. *Washington State Rising* engages the multifaceted racial-ethnic landscape of the West through its examination of late 1960s Black college students in Washington State. The text's concentration on *Black* collegians could be criticized as reproducing the typical Black-white racial frame, which obscures the presence and impacts of other people of color. Admittedly, a weakness of this work is that it does not say much about late 1960s student activism by non-Black marginalized groups. Hopefully, future scholarship will address this point more fully. Yet readers of *Washington State Rising* will find that it does reflect the West's complex racial-ethnic landscape. As demonstrated in the coming chapters, the Black Student Union chronicled herein welcomed the involvement of other people of color, and pursued reforms that would benefit them too. Like the West overall, the BSU challenged an uncomplicated white-Black binary and was responsive to the racial-ethnic diversity of the region, insights that confirm the value of regional studies, and the unique contributions of this text.

Returning to the concept of Jim Crow North, the introduction of the anthology *The Strange Careers of the Jim Crow North: Segregation and Struggle outside the South* (2019) provides a useful elaboration. There, Brian Purnell and Jeanne Theoharis outlined Jim Crow North as both overt acts of racism and more subtle institutional racism. While some white northerners screamed racial epithets and attacked African Americans, others "employed the levers of policy, law, and bureaucracy to maintain segregation and racial privilege."[24] This, of course, interrupts the popular belief that the North was characteristically tolerant and progressive, relative to the South.[25] *Washington State Rising* contributes to this point, demonstrating that "Jim Crow North" constrained the lives, and hindered the ambitions, of the Black students profiled in this study, even if that oppression was less ferocious than southern Jim Crow. Confronting this status quo was the *raison d'être* of the BSU.

This monograph is also in conversation with the literature on national student activism of the 1960s.[26] More specifically, *Washington State Rising* engages work on Black Power student activism across the country. This project understands the Black Student Union as part of a larger network of struggle, both on and off campus. The BSU was part of the student wing of Black Power, which featured African American pupils at colleges and universities around the nation. They organized, demonstrated, and demanded that their institutions address the systemic exclusions of Black people and other marginalized groups. Providing an estimate of the scope and impact of these efforts, African American studies scholar Martha Biondi found that "black students organized protests on nearly two hundred campuses" in 1968 and 1969 alone.[27] Most prominently, these decentralized campaigns demanded new and more socially relevant curricula, expanded enrollments of students like themselves, and greater Black representation among the faculty, staff, and administration at their respective schools.

Ibram X. Kendi outlined a crucial framework for this wave of Black campus activism in his text *The Black Campus Movement: Black Students and the Racial Reconstitution of Higher Education, 1965–1972* (2012). There, he differentiates the Black campus movement from other related, and at times overlapping, activist thrusts of the decade. In contrast to the larger Black student movement of the era, the Black campus movement focused largely on campus-based campaigns for change. Moreover, the Black campus movement was also distinct from concurrent activism by white students. As Kendi put it, even though Black and white students at times "battled the same structure in the same place with similarities in their ideas and tactics, and were sometimes allies," the Black campus movement and the white campus movement "must be conceptualized as independent from each other."[28] *Washington State Rising* broadens the scholarship of Kendi, Biondi, and others by documenting the presence and significance of the Black campus movement in the Pacific Northwest.[29] This in turn responds to, and qualifies, the hyper-focus on white student activists found in earlier scholarship.[30]

Washington State Rising carries forward Kendi's assessment that the Black campus movement transformed higher education. Kendi stated that the movement specifically challenged four facets of colleges and universities nationwide. The Black collegians confronted (1) a "moralized contraption," or the systemic disciplining of behavior and expression at historically Black colleges and universities, (2) "standardization of exclusion" that omitted Black people from the student body, the faculty, and the curriculum, (3) a "normalized mask of whiteness" that championed Eurocentrism, and (4) "ladder altruism," which encouraged Black students to seek individual achievement in white society.[31] *Washington State Rising* advances this analysis, particularly in regard to the "standardization of exclusion" and "normalized mask of whiteness." Through bold actions like insurgent classroom teach-ins, the Black Student Unions at the University of Washington and Washington State University challenged white domination in the curriculum, and populations, of their campuses, and carried forward the Black campus movement.

Community organizing is another topic discussed in scholarship on Black Power and student activism, which is also addressed in this text. Interestingly, the BSUs in Washington, especially the chapter in Seattle, employed grassroots outreach efforts as part of their activism. This strategic choice challenges reductive notions of Black Power, as BSU members were directly engaged in serving local people and addressing community needs. This point, therefore, elaborates existing scholarship such as *Neighborhood Rebels: Black Power at the Local Level* (2010), edited by Peniel Joseph.[32] The BSU at times worked within existing initiatives, and at other times it created new programs of its own. This was a prominent feature of the BSU at UW, and others like the original BSU at San Francisco State University, detailed in the next chapter. Notably, this off-campus outreach was not a prominent feature of the BSU at Washington State University, likely due to the campus being located in an area with no numerically significant off-campus Black community.

Education scholar Joy Ann Williamson-Lott described the Black Students Association at the University of Illinois at Urbana-Champaign in *Black Power on Campus: The University of Illinois, 1965–1975* (2003). There, the Black Students Association did contribute to university efforts to outreach to Black students at Chicago high schools, but the group was primarily focused on campus-based racial issues like access to university housing.[33] Offering another instructive comparison, historian Stefan M. Bradley profiled the Students' Afro-American Society (SAS) at Columbia University in *Harlem vs. Columbia University: Black Student Power in the Late 1960s* (2009). There, the SAS joined a community-initiated effort to prevent the construction of a ten-story gymnasium, cleverly termed "Gym Crow," in a public park beloved by the Black and Puerto Rican residents of Harlem and Morningside Heights. This ultimately successful campaign was the result of a laudable campus-community cooperation. Yet the fact was that the college students joined a struggle that was already underway.[34] By contrast, the Seattle BSU, like its San Francisco counterpart, deserves credit for initiating its community programs on its own, setting it apart from analogous student organizations.

Anyone who studies the Black Power movement knows that much scholarly attention has focused on one particular organization, the Black Panther Party for Self-Defense; therefore it is fitting that *Washington State Rising* is also in dialogue with literature on the Panthers. The Black Panther Party for Self-Defense, or Black Panther Party (BPP), was founded in Oakland, California, in 1966, and is the most well-remembered Black Power group today. It has also generated the largest body of literature, such as monographs and anthologies written and edited by Curtis J. Austin, Joshua Bloom and Waldo E. Martin Jr., Judson L. Jeffries, Charles E. Jones, Donna Jean Murch, Robyn C. Spencer, and others.[35] Along with the organization's prominence, the Black Panther Party is relevant to studies of the BSU because both groups started in the same year, 1966, and in the same metro area, the San Francisco Bay Area of northern California. The BSU started in March of that year at San Francisco State University and the Panthers were founded across the bay in October. Ideologically, the BSU and BPP had much in common and many individuals were members of both groups, either consecutively or simultaneously. This inter-organizational goodwill was significant, as not all Black Power groups were allies. Some were bitter rivals, as was true with the Black Panthers and Us, a cultural nationalist organization based in Los Angeles.

Comparing the Panthers and the BSU brings to light points that both confirm and counter existing scholarship. One correction pertains to *Black against Empire: The History and Politics of the Black Panther Party* (2016), by Joshua Bloom and Waldo E. Martin Jr., which mischaracterized the Black Student Union as an offshoot of the BPP.[36] As *Washington State Rising* shows, this was not the case in the Bay Area, and not so in the state of Washington. In both Oakland/San Francisco and Seattle, the BSUs therein existed before the Panthers and emerged from a trajectory of activism that did not involve BPP co-founders Huey Newton and Bobby Seale. In Seattle, Aaron Dixon was a BSU member before he was the inaugural "captain," or leader, of the Seattle Panthers; moreover, he was initially connected with Bobby Seale and the Panthers through his BSU activism, as he recounted in his 2012 memoir.[37] In Seattle, BSU organizing was a conduit for the Panthers, rather than the opposite, as Bloom and Martin stated. This is an important corrective that underscores the influence and significance of the Black campus movement and the Black Student Union. Perhaps in some locations, Panther chapters did foster and politicize Black student groups, but in general the Black Student Union and the Black campus movement were not auxiliaries of the Panthers. The BSU and the Black campus movement were forces for change in their own right, due to their own initiative and leadership, and therefore merit specific study and recognition.

One point of continuity between Black Panther scholarship and *Washington State Rising* is the critical role of first- and second-generation Black migrants from the South. As Donna Jean Murch and Robyn C. Spencer detailed in their respective texts, the Black Panther Party in Oakland was populated by activists with southern roots. Thus, the Panther organization, which expanded nationally, was directly connected to the Great Migration, when millions of African Americans moved from the South to the North and West between the 1910s and 1960s. In particular, Murch's *Living for the City: Migra-*

tion, Education, and the Rise of the Black Panther Party in Oakland, California (2010) highlights that not only were individual Panthers like Newton and Seale migrants or the children of migrants, but also Oakland itself was steeped in the cultural ways, traditions, and ethics of southern Black life.[38] Similarly, membership of the BSUs at the University of Washington and Washington State University featured the same pattern, in varying degrees. Although some members, such as Eddie Demmings, Larry Gossett, and Garry Owens, were born in Seattle, most had southern roots. Demmings's father was from Arkansas, Gossett's parents were from Texas, and Owens's father was from Missouri.[39] Likewise, in the BSU at WSU, Ernest Thomas was from Texas and Johnnetta Cole was from Florida.[40] Thus, like the Black Panthers, the BSU of *Washington State Rising* underscores how the Great Migration reshaped America and contributed to the Black Power movement.

Given the geographical proximity between Portland and Seattle, which are approximately 150 miles apart and connected by the Interstate 5 freeway, another counterpart to this work is Lucas Burke and Judson Jeffries's book *The Portland Black Panthers: Empowering Albina and Remaking a City*. Like *Washington State Rising*, Burke and Jeffries's work expands the spacial terrain of the Black Power movement and 1960s Black activism, bringing into relief the Pacific Northwest as a site of struggle. Moreover, the text offers probing reevaluations of northwestern cities, which have long enjoyed a reputation as liberal and tolerant. By contrast, the struggles of the Portland Panthers and the BSU in Washington underscore a different reality of racial discrimination, prejudice, and a corresponding struggle for justice that has often gone unacknowledged. Additionally, foregrounding the struggles of African Americans within the history of these northwestern cities helps modern observers appreciate the contribution of Black communities and provides context for current and future struggles.[41]

A final point of continuity between the Black Panthers and the Black Student Union was that both were targeted for surveillance by local and national law enforcement. The harassment of Black Panthers is well documented, including the arrests and prosecutions of countless Panthers, and the aggressive police raids that transpired across the country. Notoriously, one of these raids resulted in the police killing of

Fred Hampton and Marc Clark, Panther leaders in the Chicago area. Federal Bureau of Investigation files reveal that, by the final years of the sixties, the Panthers were a primary target of the bureau's Counterintelligence Program, also known as COINTELPRO. Yet, while the conflict between the Panthers and law enforcement is reasonably well known, many would be surprised to learn that the Black Student Union in Seattle was also under FBI surveillance.

Thanks to the research efforts of historian Trevor Griffey, the FBI file for the BSU in Seattle was published on the Internet Archive. The contents of the file show that the bureau began monitoring the Seattle BSU in November 1967, just as the organization was getting started, when an unnamed informant provided a flyer to an FBI agent.[42] The surveillance continued over the coming weeks and months, as the FBI kept records of BSU rallies and materials.[43] The FBI kept watch on the BSU with intelligence provided by unnamed informants, campus police, and others. Fortunately, the collegians were not subjected to the more extreme tactics of state repression, such as lethal force, predawn raids, and mass arrests. The college student organization was apparently spared the worst, but the bureau's attention further demonstrates the group's political significance.

Following this introduction, chapter 1 of *Washington State Rising* is the "foundations" chapter that examines threads of activism that constituted the precursors to the Black Student Union in the state of Washington. The chapter describes the political organizing of Black Seattle from the 1940s to 1960s and the first BSU at San Francisco State University, as both constitute vital forerunners of the BSU in Washington. The social, political, and racial history of Seattle is relevant to this study given the centrality of Seattle as a site of analysis. Hence, chapter 1 examines Seattle's World War II era Black population growth and the concomitant emergence of a Black political community, later encompassing local civil rights and Black Power movements. The last foundation covered in chapter 1 is the very first Black Student Union, founded at San Francisco State University in 1966. This group was directly responsible for inspiring the formation of the UW chapter and is therefore a key antecedent of the BSU in the Evergreen State.

Chapters 2 and 3 detail the actions of the Black Student Union at the University of Washington, spanning the years 1967 to 1970. Chapter

2 covers the group's founding and early campaigns, including a city-wide program to mentor local youth in high schools and junior high schools. Chapter 3 focuses on the BSU's sit-in and occupation of the UW president's office on May 20, 1968, and the productive aftermath of this climactic and unprecedented demonstration. Chapters 4 and 5 turn our attention to the BSU at Washington State University. Chapter 4 describes the social and demographic characteristics of the WSU campus, along with Pullman and the surrounding area. The chapter also uncovers the Black campus activism at the school that predated the BSU, and how an especially egregious racist incident involving Black high school students occasioned the emergence of the BSU at WSU. Chapter 5 chronicles the BSU's continued campaigning in Pullman during the 1968–1969 year, including its clashes with an array of opponents: white fraternity members, local law enforcement, hostile townsfolk, and campus officials. Despite it all, the group persevered and achieved its primary objective, the establishment of Black Studies. The final chapter concludes *Washington State Rising* by discussing ongoing legacies of late 1960s BSUs and other key findings for current and future activism.

While this monograph gives an in-depth account of two Black Student Unions in the state of Washington and offers larger insights into the time period, there are certainly limitations to this study and areas for future research. The discussion of the BSU at UW, WSU, and San Francisco State point to the need for a project that documents all late 1960s BSUs across the West Coast. Sibling BSUs were established at colleges and universities throughout California, Oregon, Washington, and beyond. There was no central command structure, but members of the various chapters stayed in communication through conferences, letter writing, travel, and other means. Consequently, an examination of BSUs across the West would undoubtedly illuminate new and important understandings of the Black campus movement.

Washington State Rising's focus on *Black* student activism, and temporal parameters of 1967 to 1970, both point out the need for continued study. Non-Black people of color are featured in this monograph, but additional scholarship is needed to fully unearth the breadth of their involvement in 1960s era politics. Organizations and campaigns launched by Asian and Pacific Islander, Native and Indigenous, and Chicano/a/x and Latinx protesters in the Pacific Northwest deserve in-depth study. Relevant sources for future research on Native activism in the Seattle metro area include the documentary film *As Long as the Rivers Run* (1971), and books *Where the Salmon Run: The Life and Legacy of Billy Frank Jr.* (2013), by Trova Heffernan; *Native Seattle: Histories from the Crossing-Over Place* (2017), by Coll Thrush; and *The River That Made Seattle: A Human and Natural History of the Duwamish* (2020), by B. J. Cummings.[44] For Chicano/a/x history, useful texts include *We Are Aztlán! Chicanx Histories in the Northern Borderlands* (2017), edited by Jerry García; and *Seattle's El Centro de la Raza: Dr. King's Living Laboratory* (2020), by Bruce E. Johansen.[45] Those interested in Asian/Pacific Islanders might consult two pertinent memoirs: *Hum Bows, Not Hot Dogs: Memoirs of a Savvy Asian American Activist* (2002), by Bob Santos; and *My Forgotten Seattle* (2020), by Ron Chew. Likewise, the monograph by Megan Asaka, *Seattle from the Margins: Exclusion, Erasure, and the Making of a Pacific Coast City* (2022), is also instructive.[46] Finally, for work that highlights interracial solidarity, one could start with *Gang of Four: Four Leaders, Four Communities, One Friendship* (2015), by Bob Santos and Gary Iwamoto; *Seattle in Coalition: Multiracial Alliances, Labor Politics, and Transnational Activism in the Pacific Northwest, 1970–1999* (2023), by Diana K. Johnson; and my article in *California History*, "Black Student Unions to the Gang of Four: Interracial Alliances and Community Organizing from San Francisco to Seattle."[47]

Likewise, there remains more to be written about the student politics of the 1970s, 1980s, and beyond, including on-campus fights over resources for minority studies programs, efforts to oppose South African apartheid, demands for multicultural course requirements, and calls for redoubled efforts to recruit and retain Black students, staff, and faculty. Moreover, the youth movement of hip hop in the 1970s and 1980s is relevant to analysis on late twentieth-century Black empowerment. A useful text for this line of inquiry is Daudi Abe's *Emerald Street: A History of Hip Hop in Seattle*.[48]

Even with its limitations, *Washington State Rising* makes significant contributions to several fields of research. Overall, it proves that the Black campus movement in Washington was a notable contributor to the nationwide wave of struggle, and it calls attention to a rich terrain for further scholarship. Furthermore, as we will see, many of the demands of the Black Student Union remain relevant today, such as greater educational equity and access, more faculty of color, and expanded curriculum that honors marginalized groups. Therefore, I write *Washington State Rising* with the goal of encouraging continued struggles for justice, in the form of both organizing and research.

1

Seattle and the Foundations of the Black Student Union, 1940s–1960s

Washington State Rising details the early years of the Black Student Union, a Black political student organization, in the state of Washington. Like any historically significant phenomenon, person, or organization, the Black Student Union (BSU) must be understood in the context in which it arose. It did not emerge from a vacuum, but from a particular set of circumstances and influences. This chapter will chart four threads of history and politics that created the foundation of the BSUs at the University of Washington and Washington State University. A focal point will be the immediate environs of Seattle, Washington, a crucial location because of its Black population and decades of Black activism.

The first section of the chapter covers Black Seattle from World War II to the end of the 1950s, an important period when African Americans became the largest non-white racial or ethnic group in the city. Moreover, the war years and their aftermath featured the beginning of Seattle's modern Black freedom struggle. The second section discusses Seattle's civil rights movement, which corresponded to the years 1960 to 1967. This was a period of major mobilizations toward the goals of racial integration and equal opportunity. Next, the chapter shifts to the early developments of the Black Power movement in Seattle, highlighting the local chapter of the Student Nonviolent Coordinating Committee and the crucial year of 1967.

Unlike the first three sections, the final segment of the chapter moves outside the Seattle area and details the first Black Student Union, founded at San Francisco State University. Although located approximately eight hundred miles apart, the West Coast cities of Seattle and San Francisco were connected by both the Interstate 5 freeway and similar patterns of World War II era expansion. Moreover, Seattle and San Francisco were two stops along a migratory route used by African Americans fleeing southern Jim Crow and attracted to war industry jobs in the West. Later, during the 1960s, linkages between the two cities fostered a strong connection between the BSUs at San Francisco State University (SF State) and the University of Washington, located in Seattle. The Black Student Union at SF State is the fourth crucial pillar in the foundation of the BSU in the state of Washington and is described in the final section of this chapter. What follows in each section is not meant to be comprehensive; rather, the brief overviews aim to illuminate the context of later chapters of *Washington State Rising*.

The Black Community and Politics in Seattle, 1940s–1950s

In 1941 the Japanese imperial military attacked Pearl Harbor in Hawaii, and the United States entered World War II. The military and political struggle between the Allied Powers (Great Britain, France, the Soviet Union, and the United States) and the Axis Powers (Germany, Italy, and Japan) had extraordinarily profound effects across the globe. For Seattle, World War II was a time of booming economies and populations that profoundly reshaped the city. Describing this transformational era, historian John M. Findlay dubbed this period "Seattle's second pandemonium moment," likening it to Seattle's initial population boom linked to the transcontinental railroad of 1883. Findlay wrote,

> After leveling off during the 1920s and 1930s, Seattle's population suddenly spiked again during the early 1940s, when the entire Pacific Coast mobilized for World War II. The war was actually a population drain on most states, but California, Washington and Oregon (in that order) led the nation in demographic increases.[1]

Census records show that "Seattle averaged 9,929 newcomers per year during the 1940s," and this growth continued during the 1950s with new arrivals totaling 8,950 per year.[2] In 1940 the population of Seattle was 368,302; by 1960 it was 557,087.[3]

In addition, the World War II era saw even higher rates of in-migration by African Americans. In 1940 Black Seattle totaled 3,789. By 1950, the African American population had grown over 400 percent, totaling 15,666. Then, by 1960, the population increased by another 71 percent, to 26,901. This expanding Black population would continue during the 1960s, even as Seattle's overall population growth leveled off.[4]

This was part of the Second Great Migration, when millions of African Americans left the southern United States for northern and western cities. As a result, Black Seattleites became the largest non-white group in the Emerald City (a colloquial name for Seattle) for the first time ever. From the late nineteenth century to the 1940s, Japanese and Japanese Americans were the largest community of color in Seattle, followed by African Americans, Chinese, Filipinos, and Native Americans in that order. In the 1940s, this changed due to African American in-migration and Japanese internment.[5]

A major draw for the Black sojourners to Seattle—like those who settled in Portland, San Francisco, Los Angeles, and other West Coast cities—was the prospect of defense industry employment and related economic opportunities. Specifically, in Seattle and the larger Puget Sound area, many of these jobs were offered by the Boeing Airplane Company. Supplying aircraft for the Allies, Boeing received government contracts totaling hundreds of millions of dollars during World War II, and the company expanded its production and staff. In 1939 Boeing had 4,000 workers. By 1944, at the peak of its wartime production, "Boeing employed nearly 50,000 workers."[6] Another thriving company was Pacific Car and Foundry Company, based in Renton, a city just south of Seattle. Pacific Car and Foundry shifted from producing logging trucks to making military tanks and expanded its workforce. Other sources of employment were the shipyards that dotted Puget Sound, including twenty-nine in Seattle alone, and the Navy facility in Bremerton, a town across the Sound. These shipyards and maritime facilities utilized a cumulative workforce of 150,000.[7] In total, "the city of Seattle by itself received $5.6 billion in war contracts during World War II," catapulting the local economy.[8]

Yet, as is often true in African American history, improved conditions for Black people came only because of their struggle and protest. The potential economic benefits of the wartime job market became real for Black Seattleites through socioeconomic activism, and these calls to end labor discrimination marked the start of the city's modern Black freedom struggle. This was a local iteration of the national "Double V" campaign, initiated by the *Pittsburgh Courier*, which called for resistance to fascism abroad and racism at home. The esteemed novelist and writer Richard Wright encapsulated this movement, stating, "If this is a war for democracy and freedom, then we fight in it, for democracy and freedom. We shall fight as determinedly against those who deny freedom at home as we shall fight against those who deny it to others abroad."[9] One front of the Double V movement pushed for Black access to defense jobs, led on a national level by A. Philip Randolph. Responding to pressure from Randolph and others, President Franklin D. Roosevelt eventually issued Executive Order 8802 on June 15, 1941, forbidding defense industry employment discrimination. With this victory, the struggle shifted to implementation.

Double V campaigners found much work to be done in Seattle, as Black workers there were initially barred from all defense industry jobs. For example, in the first ten weeks after Executive Order 8802, Boeing hired a thousand new employees per week, and none were African Americans. "In response, the black churches, fraternal organizations, and political and social clubs organized the Committee for the Defense of Negro Labor's Right to Work at Boeing Airplane Company."[10] Agitation by this committee, along with pressure from the federal government, national union leadership, and labor shortages, forced Boeing to change course and begin hiring African Americans in 1942. Interestingly, two women were the first Black Boeing employees. "Stenographer Florise Spearman was accepted as an office worker in January [1942]. Four months later, Dorothy West Williams, a sheet metal worker, became the first black production worker as well as the first black member of [International Association of Mechanics] Local 751."[11] However, Black women continued to face some of the worst labor discrimination.[12] Representing significant economic progress, Black workers would eventually make up a high of 7 percent of shipyard workers and 3 percent of aircraft construction workers. In addition, Seattle's Fort Lawton and other local military bases included 4,000 Black soldiers.[13] Consequently, Seattle's Black community experienced significant financial gains during World War II.

However, anti-Black racial injustice persisted in the Seattle metropolitan area. During the 1940s and 1950s, Black people continued to face prejudice and discrimination in various aspects of local society: social interactions, public accommodations, education, job prospects outside war industries, interactions with law enforcement, and more. Thus, Black organizing continued.

One prominent local group during the 1940s, 1950s, and beyond was the Seattle chapter of the National Association for the Advancement of Colored People (NAACP), whose existence predated World War II. Letitia A. Graves founded the Seattle NAACP in 1913, less than a decade after the national organization was established.[14] The Seattle NAACP was one of the earliest branches west of the Mississippi River, and it saw a major increase in membership during the 1940s. Prior to World War II, the group's largest membership had been 85; this increased to 1,550 by 1945. This new numerical strength ushered in new leadership and a new level of influence in local affairs. Black attorneys E. June Smith and Philip Burton were two prominent leaders of this revitalized NAACP and they "initiated suits against discriminatory practices and lobbied for strong state civil rights laws."[15] The Seattle NAACP also sponsored chapters in other locations throughout the state of Washington that saw increased Black populations during the war: Bremerton, Walla Walla, and the Tri-Cities community of Richland, Pasco, and Kennewick.[16]

Seattle's Urban League also experienced unprecedented growth in the forties, even though it was established in 1930.[17] Benefitting from the leadership of three successive executive secretaries between 1939 and 1950—Bernard Squires, Dean Hart, and Napoleon P. Dotson—the group doubled its membership and tripled its staff during the decade of World War II. Like the NAACP, the Urban League also used its newfound resources to initiate lawsuits and lobby for reform.[18]

Although largely forgotten today, the Christian Friends for Racial Equality (CFRE) was another noteworthy agent for social change in mid-century Seattle. On May 19, 1942, the CFRE was co-founded by "17 people from seven Christian denominations and the Jewish faith." The organization was most active from the 1940s to the mid-1960s, but continued until 1970.[19] The majority of the group's members and officers were women. One of the co-founders, Bertha Pitts Campbell, was a Black community leader who also co-founded the Seattle Urban League, and was a founding member of the national Delta Sigma Theta sorority.[20] Eschewing confrontation tactics, the CFRE aimed to ameliorate racial discrimination through persuasion and fellowship. It attracted many members and was "the largest civil rights organization in Seattle" by 1956.[21] As researcher Johanna Phillips summarized, the CFRE "aimed to create an enjoyable social environment in which interracial

and interfaith exchanges could take place" and "organized theater out-
ings, small teas and luncheons, picnics, nature walks, folk dances and art
classes." The Christian Friends for Racial Equality's other work included
letter writing, investigating businesses accused of discrimination, public
speaking, publishing a monthly newsletter called *Racial Equality Bulletin*, and successfully lobbying the Washington State legislature for a 1953
law banning white-only cemeteries.[22]

Community efforts also spurred municipal action, and Seattle mayor
William F. Devin established the city's Civic Unity Committee (CUC)
in 1944.[23] The initial fifteen-member committee included one representative of the Jewish community, Al Shemanski, one representative
of the Chinese community, Lew G. Kay, and two African Americans:
the Reverend Benjamin Davis, minister of Zion Baptist Church, and Dr.
Felix Cooper, a dentist. The other members were drawn from white Seattle's business, religious, and civic leadership, such as chairman George
Greenwood, president of Pacific National Bank.[24] The CUC's primary
tools were persuasion and public education; it had no enforcement
power. Consequently, its impact was limited. Yet the committee was still
significant as the city government's most prominent anti-discrimination
initiative of the time. As a case in point, the CUC worked to get African Americans hired as city bus drivers from March 1944 to April 1945.
Both the bus drivers' union and the bus company had long resisted integration.[25] To address this, the CUC negotiated with the Seattle Transit Company and partnered with the Seattle Urban League to identify
and train strong candidates. Eventually, after an extensive selection and
preparation process, seven men and one woman entered the bus company's driver training program, but all were eventually rejected for reasons like "illegible writing."[26] Despite the likely discrimination, the CUC
continued its patient prodding, and one Black bus driver was finally
hired in April 1945.[27] In the early 1960s, the Civic Unity Committee was
disbanded and its modest success shows the deeply entrenched racial
injustice that existed in Seattle. However, it reflects that Black activists
and their allies forced the city government to address their grievances,
even if meekly.[28]

Further indicating the mixed record of Black activism of the 1940s
and 1950s, organized pressure won passage of the Fair Employment
Practices Act of 1949 in the Washington State legislature. Modeled after

President Roosevelt's Executive Order 8802, the bill prohibited job discrimination "because of race, creed, color or national origin," and created the Washington State Board Against Discrimination to investigate violations.[29] Unfortunately, the new law and investigative board suffered from weak enforcement, and discrimination continued. Perhaps the most tangible and immediate outcome of the new law was the subsequent election of Charles M. Stokes in 1950. Stokes was voted in as the first African American from Seattle to serve in the state of Washington House of Representatives, and his rise to office was an outcome of his prominent role in lobbying for the new anti-discrimination law.[30] Thus, by the 1950s, African Americans and their allies could point to some victories, albeit limited, as evidence of their tireless efforts.

The following decade, the 1950s, was largely characterized by a continuation of discrimination and struggle for Black Seattleites, despite the gains of the 1940s. One bright spot was that many Black workers maintained their foothold at Boeing and in the shipyards after the war's end, partially due to pressure by Black civic and religious groups. Yet most other professions remained off limits to Black workers. These included other sectors of manufacturing like "newer electronics and chemical industries that sprang up after World War II"; likewise, African American applicants were largely barred from "rapidly growing service sectors such as retail sales, heath care facilities, and banking."[31] This employment inequality mirrored concurrent discrimination in other sectors like housing and education. During the 1940s and onward, Black residents were increasingly segregated into Seattle's Central District, also called the Central Area, and consequently schools in Seattle showed similar demographic patterns. As noted by historian Doris H. Pieroth, the racial distribution in Seattle schools in 1957 recorded that "black students were concentrated in six elementary schools and three secondary schools in the city's Central Area."[32] Due to persistent racial discrimination in Seattle, Black political protest continued into the 1960s.

The 1960s and Garry Owens

In the late 1960s, the era detailed in the following chapters of *Washington State Rising*, Garry Owens was an active member of the Black Student Union at the University of Washington. Yet his political consciousness began in the early 1960s. His recollections of growing up in Seattle provide an instructive window into the city during the era. Owens lived with his mother, father, and two younger siblings, first in the Rainier Vista Housing Projects, and later in a duplex in the Central District. His mother and maternal grandmother were born and raised in Ellensburg, a small town in central Washington State. His father was from St. Louis, Missouri. As a precocious high school student, Owens was deeply distressed by television reports of civil rights protesters being abused in the South, especially in places like Birmingham, Alabama. Owens's racial consciousness was also encouraged by his family and Seattle's Black community.

For instance, the barbershop frequented by Owens was a valuable communal space and incubator of his budding critique of racism. He recalled,

> On Saturdays or whatever, the barbershop was full of people. [For] a lot of young Black folks, that was the only day they could go, was on a Saturday, to get their haircut. And the barbers were all Black, and all of them were from the South. So they used to talk about it [life in the South and the Black protests] among themselves and they used to answer questions we had about what was it like. [We'd ask] why did they [civil rights activists] do this, or why didn't they do that, or whatever. So that piqued my interested to know, to get a bit closer [to the movement].[33]

Moreover, the Black barbers first alerted Owens to the insight that race relations in Seattle were not that different from conditions in the South. This was a shocking revelation, as Owens recalled:

> They said that, in their own words, that, in its own way, Seattle was no different from Alabama. And that was kind of startling to me because I'm thinking, man, I'm watching these violent things happening to Black people in Alabama and they're saying there's not too much difference.[34]

Around this time, Owens joined the Seattle chapter of the Congress of Racial Equality (CORE). By his graduation from Franklin High School in 1963, Owens has attended several CORE meetings and participated in campaigns to challenge job discrimination. With his self-described "boyish look," he listened during CORE meetings and learned more about the need for a movement in Seattle:

> I learned a lot because a lot of the people in the organization [CORE] were from the South and experienced some of the high-level discrimination and racism that existed in the South. In Seattle it wasn't the South, but they let us know in various ways discrimination was here. And it might not be the same kind of process or manifestation, the way it worked, but the outcome was the same. And the outcome was that, in many cases, Black people, be they [male] or female, younger or older, were not welcomed for jobs that white people had. So there were jobs available [for Blacks], but they weren't, I would say, they weren't the dignified jobs. They were the jobs that paid the least money and didn't provide very much self-esteem.[35]

Owens was one of many Seattleites who became politicized due to local and national race relations, and entered the movement through the Seattle chapter of CORE in the early 1960s. Founded in June 1961, Seattle CORE was one of the city's most prominent civil rights groups. Earlier that year, the national CORE organization garnered mainstream attention with its Freedom Rides campaign, wherein groups of activists violated southern segregation in interstate bus travel, and were subjected to arrests and brutality. In Seattle many individuals were inspired by the courage of the Freedom Riders; a few local activists decided to go join the campaign and others organized to support them, which led to the establishment of Seattle CORE.[36] Three individuals joined the Freedom Rides from Seattle: Ray Cooper, a twenty-year-old white resident of Seattle's University District, Widjonarko Tjokroadismarto, an Indonesian exchange student at the University of Washington, and Jon Schaefer, a young white man from Broadmoor, an elite, all-white community.[37] During the following months and years, Seattle CORE proceeded to launch a series of local campaigns challenging discrimination across the city, such as "selective buying campaigns" directed at area grocery stores that refused to hire Black applicants.[38] This effort to win jobs at grocery stores achieved some new hiring of African Americans, and CORE continued to lead protests regarding employment, housing, education, and more, into the late 1960s.

Another key organization of Seattle's civil rights movement was the Central Area Civil Rights Committee (CACRC), which began in 1962. The CACRC was a coalition organization that included representatives from local Black clergy, the NAACP, CORE, the Urban League, and similarly allied groups. Its leadership council included Walter Hundley of CORE, Charles V. Johnson of the NAACP, Edwin Pratt of the Urban League, and the Reverend John Adams of the First African Methodist Episcopal Church.[39] Two other influential ministers and members of CACRC leadership were the Reverend Mance Jackson of Bethel Christian Methodist Episcopal Church, and the Reverend Samuel B. McKinney, pastor of Mount Zion Baptist Church.[40] Throughout the decade, the CACRC and its chief spokesman, Adams, served as the leading voice and public face of Seattle's civil rights movement, while CORE often provided the shock troops.[41]

The clergy-led CACRC also buttressed linkages between the Emerald City's civil rights community and the national movement, the most prominent example being a two-day visit by Martin Luther King Jr. on November 9 and 10, 1961. The appearance was chiefly arranged by McKinney, who was a friend and former classmate of King at Morehouse College in Atlanta, Georgia. During this visit, his only trip to Seattle, King gave speeches at the University of Washington, Jewish Temple De Hirsch, Garfield High School, and the Eagles Auditorium. Yet King's trip was not without controversy, illuminating the state of race relations in the ostensibly liberal city and region. Before his arrival, an organized opposition petitioned school officials and religious leaders to prohibit King from speaking, claiming that he was too controversial. As a result, his invitation to speak at the First Presbyterian Church was rescinded and the address was moved to the Eagles Auditorium.[42] The controversy around King's appearance shows the opposition to Black protest that existed in Seattle. On the other hand, King's visit reflected, and no doubt bolstered, the sense of connectedness that Pacific Northwest activists felt with the national civil rights movement. Such linkages established Seattle as a node on the landscape of the nationwide movement, and helped local activists garner political capital.

Throughout the early to mid-1960s, Seattle's civil rights movement organized groundbreaking campaigns and demonstrations. At least three major milestones occurred in 1963. On June 15, the Reverend Mance

Jackson and other local leaders brought 1,000 people together for Seattle's first major civil rights march. Then, on August 28, another march of 1,500 participants demonstrated their solidarity with the concurrent March on Washington for Jobs and Freedom, the site of King's "I Have a Dream" speech.[43] That same day, the Seattle School Board announced a new Voluntary Racial Transfer Program, responding to years of organizing against school segregation. The new program allowed students to voluntarily transfer schools to address "racial imbalance." This was another hard-fought but limited victory, as the district declined to provide transportation for the program and small numbers of students would participate.[44]

During the following year, another key event was a citywide referendum on an open housing ordinance in Seattle, held on March 10. For years, at least from the 1940s population boom, activists had been pointing out the need to address housing discrimination, and in 1960 approximately "78 percent of all African Americans" were confined to "four census tracts in the Central Area."[45] In the run up to the vote, the CACRC, CORE, the NAACP, and other groups held an extensive outreach effort to urge support to win approval of the new ordinance. Despite their efforts, the measure was soundly rejected by Seattle voters. Motivated by racial prejudice that was encouraged by the local real estate industry, residents voted 115,627 against the ordinance, compared to 54,448 in favor.[46] The failure of this vote was a major disappointment for the civil rights community.

In the realm of education, the CACRC, CORE, and other groups coordinated a citywide boycott of public schools in 1966. This two-day mobilization, on March 31 and April 1, included a network of "Freedom Schools" that dramatized the need for change by providing integrated classrooms and curriculum on Black history and culture.[47] An ad hoc body of parents, educators, students, and activists worked together to plan the boycott and create the Freedom Schools. As described by historian Dale Soden, many religious institutions also supported the effort and provided meeting spaces:

> Freedom schools opened with approximately one hundred teachers and two principals at each site. Elementary schools opened at First AME [African Methodist Episcopal] Church, Madrona Presbyterian Church,

East Madison YMCA, Goodwill Baptist Church, St. Peter Claver Center, and Cherry Hill Baptist Church. Sites for junior high schools opened at Mount Zion Baptist Church and the Tabernacle Baptist Church. And senior high schools held classes at the Prince Hall Masonic Temple, the East Side YMCA, and Woodland Park Presbyterian Church.[48]

Once again, a vocal opposition emerged, including both of Seattle's daily newspapers and fifteen prominent ministers from "downtown churches" who publicly opposed the boycott. The school boycott went ahead anyway and attracted substantial cooperation from parents, and over three thousand students participated in the Freedom Schools each day. "In the Central Area public schools, absences increased from 824 the day before the boycott to 3,185 on its first day and 3,918 on the second."[49] As a direct connection to the Black Student Union, future member Eddie Demmings participated in the boycott as a high school senior. As he recalled, "I participated in it, not because I was an activist or I wanted to, but my mother ordered me to participate." Demmings added that his mother was not directly involved in the civil rights movement, but recognized the value of the school protest.[50]

Despite the success of the 1966 school boycott, the issue of school segregation and educational inequality remained largely unchanged in Seattle into the 1970s and beyond. This episode encapsulates a larger pattern of protest efforts in Seattle from the 1940s to the 1960s. In the city during these years, we see sustained effort and major campaigns, but concrete gains were often elusive. And such reforms that were achieved were insufficient to alter the larger, systemic patterns of racial inequality. The victories were largely token and symbolic, but the activists themselves merit commendation for their courageous efforts and for creating a foundation for future struggles. This lack of structural change led to the emergence of Seattle's Black Power movement by the late sixties.

Carl Miller, Seattle SNCC, and Black Power in Seattle

Another member of the Black Student Union was Carl Miller, and earlier he played a prominent role in launching Seattle's Black Power movement. Miller's experiences and recollections provide an instructive starting point for our brief look at early Black Power activism in the city. Reflecting on his younger self some fifty years later, Miller could not pinpoint a specific moment when he became politically conscious. Rather, it was an innumerable set of influences and understandings, combined with the zeitgeist, that drew him to activism. "I mean, it was just in the air," Miller recalled. "I wasn't born a radical. It was Watts [the Watts Riot of 1965] and it was various things like that that slowly changed my consciousness."[51] Miller grew up in Philadelphia, Pennsylvania, in an African American family that supported the civil rights movement but chose not to participate. Like many Black families of the time period, the Millers were well aware of the need to challenge American racism, yet they emphasized a cautious approach, stressing education over activism. Carl and his siblings were encouraged to pursue professional careers, and radical leaders like Malcolm X were to be avoided. Miller explained,

> My mom just wanted me to be careful. When I heard Malcolm X on the radio and asked her about the things he said, she said, "Don't listen to those Black supremacists. Keep a level head." My dad was more the, "The white man is gonna keep you down. You gotta be twice as good and get half the credit," kind of philosophy and he encouraged us to get all the education we could.[52]

During Miller's adolescence, Philadelphia had an active local civil rights movement that challenged employment discrimination and related inequality. As the historian Matthew J. Countryman detailed in *Up South: Civil Rights and Black Power in Philadelphia*, one example was a "selective buying" boycott between 1960 and 1964 that targeted companies such as Tastykake, Pepsi-Cola, and Gulf Oil, which had records of discrimination.[53] This was, of course, similar to the employment-related protests led by CORE in Seattle during the same time. Philadelphia activists also organized to support the national effort to challenge whites-only lunch counters in the South and picketed their local Woolworth department stores, supporting the national campaign initiated in 1960 by Black college students in Greensboro, North Carolina.[54] Miller remembered seeing one of the Woolworth protests in Philadelphia while working at a different downtown clothing store, but he declined to take part.[55]

After his 1963 high school graduation, Carl Miller volunteered for the US army, knowing that entering the military in this way rather than being drafted would give him better options in terms of deployment and location. Moreover, at this time, he was generally patriotic and believed in the righteousness of the American government, so he supported the war effort. As a result of his judicious decision to volunteer, Miller received professional training in dentistry and was stationed as a dental hygienist in Japan, a place he had long wanted to visit. Yet his stint in the army coincided with a shift in his politics. One set of transformational experiences related to bigotry Miller witnessed within the military, primarily directed at a fellow soldier who happened to be Jewish. The anti-Semitic harassment was so unrelenting that Miller tried to intervene, but was warned that he would be targeted next if he reported the abuse of the Jewish soldier. For Miller, this was a jarring contrast to the unity and camaraderie that the US military claimed to embody. Furthermore, Miller's budding consciousness was encouraged by national and international news, such as the Watts rebellion mentioned above. Consequently, as his time in the army ended, Miller's political orientation changed and he was looking to join a Black Power organization.

At the end of his service in 1966, Miller was discharged in Seattle and decided to make a home there, believing that the northwestern city offered better career and educational opportunities than his native Philadelphia. A year later, a fateful trip to wash his clothes provided the doorway into the movement that he was looking for. Miller recalled,

> I was at the laundromat one day in, like, February or March—no, January or February of 1967—and I was at a laundromat and I saw a little notice on the bulletin board—that's how people communicated in those days—a notice on the bulletin board about a SNCC meeting. Somebody wanted to talk about their experience in Mississippi. I wrote down the address and the phone number and went to the meeting. It was on a Sunday afternoon.[56]

The Student Nonviolent Coordinating Committee, or SNCC (commonly pronounced "snick"), was a prominent Black protest group of the era that particularly appealed to Miller because of the organization's reputation for bold and courageous actions in the South. SNCC was led by college-age activists who challenged segregation throughout the South, including in some of the most rural and repressive parts of states like Mississippi and Alabama. The organization's position on the cutting edge was confirmed by the Freedom Summer campaign of 1964, and later by SNCC chairman Stokely Carmichael's Black Power speech in 1966. Thus, Miller's interest in SNCC reflected his identification with the more militant wing of the Black political spectrum.

In the late 1960s, Seattle's chapter of SNCC was a crucial gateway for the emergence of the city's Black Power movement. Previously, there had been a "Friends of SNCC" chapter in Seattle, which primarily worked to garner funds and publicity for the national organization and its efforts in the South. In 1963 Seattle's Friends of SNCC began following a benefit concert by Harry Belafonte, the entertainer and activist. In a letter to Sandra "Casey" Hayden, SNCC's northern coordinator at the time, Seattle's Karen Stockham described the event: "It was a good way to introduce Seattle to SNCC. We received excellent press and radio time."[57] The Friends of SNCC chapter in Seattle continued during the following years, with varying degrees of activity.

In 1967 Seattle SNCC partially emerged from and eclipsed the city's Friends of SNCC chapter, as a new cohort of members emphasized local movement building. As Seattle SNCC reconstituted itself, it functioned for a time as a discussion group. During weekly meetings, members would gather together and debate Black Power and contemporary race relations. Miller recalled,

> It was a nascent organization, it was just the bare bones, we weren't even talking about organizing yet, just talking. Black Power, you know, what does Black Power mean? Why should we, you know, why should we protest? Black is beautiful. Those kinds of things were just [emerging, and being discussed].[58]

Furthermore, the dialogues soon attracted a large number of participants and grew to include two or three hundred attendees per meeting by April:

> We started having a series of meetings on Sunday afternoons and we kept outgrowing the space because people—we'd talk about SNCC—and peo-

ple, more and more people, would come to the meetings. It was just in the air. I wasn't the only one looking to get involved, people were looking for something to do.[59]

During this discussion group phase, Seattle SNCC encouraged meeting attendees to join demonstrations led by other groups in the city, aiming to maximize the number of people engaged in the movement for racial justice. In fact, even decisions about one's hairstyle and apparel, which may seem like benign style choices to modern readers, were potentially political and meaningful. Miller said, "And we encouraged people to grow their hair long" in an Afro and "wear a dashiki," an African-styled shirt associated with Black Power. "You'll make them think there's a million of us," Miller recalled thinking.[60]

Seattle SNCC also featured a multiracial membership. When asked to describe the group's white and Black demographics, Miller explained, "It was mixed. It was, at the first meeting, I'll say it was about half and half. . . . It didn't get all Black ever practically until after the Stokely speech and people, others wanted it to be all Black, but we never did [become all Black]." Many of the white members were college student activists and "liberals from Capitol Hill," a neighborhood adjacent to Seattle's largely Black Central District.[61]

As alluded to in the previous quote from Miller, the visit by Stokely Carmichael to Seattle on April 19, 1967, was a pivotal event for Seattle SNCC, and it had major ramifications for Black politics in Seattle.[62] Earlier that spring, SNCC headquarters contacted the Seattle chapter with an offer to help arrange an appearance by Carmichael (later known as Kwame Ture). The offer was that the national office would finance Carmichael's travel expenses if the local chapter arranged the speaking engagements and ensured a sizable audience. As Miller put it, the message from the SNCC main office in Atlanta was, "If you can guarantee us five hundred people, we can bring Stokely there." Miller and the others in Seattle SNCC enthusiastically agreed.[63] Carmichael traveled constantly during the late 1960s, giving speeches in cities and on college campuses all around the country. By April 1967, Carmichael had relinquished his post as chair of the national Student Nonviolent Coordinating Committee, but he continued to be an influential figure in the organization and a widely sought-after orator. For instance, the *Seattle Times* noted that

Carmichael arrived in Seattle after speaking engagements in Florida, and after visiting Seattle he would be going on to Central Washington University in Ellensburg.[64] Thus, his Seattle appearance was a part of a pattern of nationwide travel.

During this time, Carmichael was arguably the most famous advocate for Black militancy and unflinching critic of white America, a mantle Carmichael inherited following the death of Malcolm X in 1965 and the rise of Black Power to national prominence in 1966. Carmichael publicly denounced individual racism, institutional racism, and US policies like the war in Vietnam. He also was unabashed in urging Black people to take pride in themselves and seek self-determination. Many white Americans perceived these remarks as divisive, unpatriotic, anti-white, and tantamount to violence. In Seattle, some reactions to Carmichael's appearance reflected this mainstream hostility and fear, as civic authorities tried unsuccessfully to prevent Carmichael from speaking.[65] Two weeks before the eventual appearance, the Seattle School Board refused a request to rent the Garfield High School auditorium to Seattle SNCC and the Negro Voters League, the event co-sponsors.[66] The School Board justified its decision by claiming that "if Mr. Carmichael is permitted to speak a danger will be created in this community." In addition, the School Board argued that his appearance would undermine its integration efforts, saying that the event would "have an adverse effect upon their [the School Board's] program to achieve in Garfield High School a better proportion of white and black students."[67] To challenge the board's decision, two lawyers of the American Civil Liberties Union (ACLU) of Washington, Raymond E. Brown and Michael H. Rosen, filed a successful lawsuit in King County Superior Court, *Carmichael v. Bottomly*. Ruling in the case, Judge Frank D. James explained that he agreed with the Seattle School Board that Carmichael's statements were likely to be objectionable, but such concerns needed to be weighed against the importance of the First Amendment:

> What, in my judgment, the School Board has overlooked is the fact that the greater danger to the public would be the judicial sanction to their exercise of prior restraint upon Mr. Carmichael's constitutionally guaranteed right to speak, even though the things which he may say may be very offensive to most of us.[68]

Like the similar opposition to Martin Luther King Jr. earlier in the decade, described previously, the effort to thwart Carmichael's speaking engagements again indicates that many whites in the Emerald City were uncomfortable with 1960s Black protests.

On Wednesday, April 19, Carmichael delivered two speeches during his visit to Seattle, one at the University of Washington (UW) and the other at Garfield High School.[69] His midday speech at the university took place at the nine-thousand-seat Hec Edmundson Pavilion and was officially sponsored by the campus's Political Union, a student group.[70] The following day, the *Seattle Times* reported that "between 3,500 and 4,000 students and faculty members heard Carmichael at the university."[71] As the student newspaper at UW, the *Daily*, described him, "Stokely Carmichael, the fiery advocate of Black Power, presented a calm face yesterday afternoon in an 'intellectual appeal.'"[72] In his remarks, Carmichael addressed negative representations of Black Power in the "white press," arguing that such reports ignored how the movement was fostering "reasonable and productive dialogues" within the Black community and beyond. To illustrate the point, he noted a recent statement by the National Council of Churches affirming the call for Black empowerment.[73] Furthermore, he attempted to clarify the true aims of the Black Power movement: "No one is talking about the blacks taking over the country, but about taking over our communities."[74] He continued, "The people in the Negro community do not control the resources of that community, its political decisions, its law enforcement, its housing standards."[75] Therefore, "we must organize black community power to end abuses and to give the Negro community a chance to have its needs expressed."[76] When asked about white involvement, "he said that whites could participate in the Black Power Movement by either banding together to fight other whites that persecute Negroes" or speaking to and persuading hostile white people "to act 'in a civilized manner.'"[77]

By all accounts, Carmichael's evening speech was more passionate. There, he riveted the mostly Black audience that gathered to hear him. As a reporter wrote, "Carmichael was cool at the university and cold at the [UW] pavilion. . . . At Garfield he was warm, more smiling—theatrical at times—and he had an audience that was eager to hear him and didn't seem to be disturbed at waiting an hour to hear him."[78] Not surprisingly, given Carmichael's fame, the event attracted a very large crowd. Garfield's principal, Frank Hannawalt, estimated that 4,000 attendees were in the packed school auditorium, while another 2,500 heard Carmichael via a loudspeaker in the school's gymnasium.[79] The program began with Mattie Bundy, then chairperson of Seattle SNCC, leading the group in singing two freedom songs, "Everybody Wants Freedom" and "We Shall Not Turn Back." Cliff Hooper, head of the Negro Voters League, also gave opening remarks.[80]

Next, Carmichael took the podium and gave a speech that mixed bravado with political analysis. He said, "White people assume they can give freedom but nobody gives freedom. They can only deny it. We are all born free. We are enslaved by institutional racism. Our fight is to civilize white America." He also denounced the Vietnam War: "They put you in a uniform and send you 8,000 miles to shoot at someone who never called you 'nigger.'"[81] Reflecting common rhetorical elements of Black Power speechmaking of the time, Carmichael employed implied threats and combative statements to rally Black listeners. African Americans in attendance reportedly cheered when he said that Black people needed to fight the shackles imposed by "hunkies," and "the time has come that 'if anybody touches our black skin, he touches all of us, whether he wears a sheet by night or a badge.'"[82] Here, Carmichael was challenging badge-wearing police and the Ku Klux Klan, a violent white supremacist group known for wearing white sheets as robes.

Reflecting another rhetorical technique common to Black Power, Carmichael used humor to engage and entertain. At times, he made his listeners laugh as they also absorbed his sociopolitical critiques. For instance, in a segment on Black racial pride, he said, "You have tried so hard to be white. . . . You have gone to Tarzan movies and applauded as Tarzan beat up your black brothers [in Africa]. We have identified with white people. We have been brainwashed."[83] He continued, "Too long has the Negro been made to feel ashamed of himself. We have been taught we are lazy. . . . We are not lazy. We are the hardest working of Americans. In Mississippi Blacks pick cotton for $2 a day while whites sit on the porch and drink scotch and talk about us."[84] Both the reference to the fictional character Tarzan and the image of lazy white people could be both funny and thought-provoking.

Unsurprisingly, the reaction to Carmichael's remarks among mainstream, white Seattleites was apprehensive and antagonistic. In a telling statement, the *Seattle Post-Intelligencer* likened Carmichael's Garfield address to a knife attack. The journalist wrote, "Carmichael, tall, slender, with an engaging wit and smile to match, jabbed rapier-like stabs into the White Society and warned that the organized Negro would 'tear down' cities where the colored man's stature is curtailed." The violent imagery of this description reflects the alarm Black Power evoked in many white minds. Nevertheless, white Americans made up "at least 20 percent" of the audience at the Garfield speech, and cheered with the rest of the crowd, showing that white opinions were not monolithic.[85]

For many Black youth in attendance, Carmichael's speech was deeply affirming and life-changing. Yet, before elaborating on the address, it is worth noting that there is a danger of overstating the impact of any one speech, and an overemphasis on oratory can obscure other crucial organizing work: building relationships, crafting shared goals, distributing information, recruiting members, keeping records, mentoring, maintaining files, coordinating logistics, and so forth. Overlooking these critical tasks risks devaluing the contributions of women activists and others behind the scenes who commonly carried out these duties. However, while we may acknowledge this point, it is also true that Carmichael's visit was viewed by many in the burgeoning local Black Power movement as pivotal and galvanizing.

BSU member Larry Gossett remembered the following, which speaks to Carmichael's impact on his peer group:

> My friends when I got back said that they all went into Garfield on the morning that he [Carmichael] spoke referencing each other as Negros. And after he spoke that night, and they went back to Garfield and Franklin, the next morning all [of] them referenced themselves as Black. And were proud to be such. And started talking about Black Power immediately. That's the impact that he had on the 2,000 mostly black people assembled at Garfield on that evening.[86]

Although Gossett underestimated the crowd size, he provided an instructive assessment of the speech's influence. This shift in identification from "Negro" to "Black" signified the adoption of Black Power politics and an insurgent Black identity. "Negro" was associated with moderate to conservative, integration-oriented African Americans, while "Black" was the moniker of choice for those who embraced Black nationalism, African heritage, and cynicism toward the white mainstream. Hence, the new racial identity described by Gossett encapsulates a major political and ontological reorientation. Demonstrating that Carmichael's speech was particularly pivotal to the Black Student Union at UW, the BSU referenced the speech in its first newspaper interview almost a year after Carmichael's visit. The UW *Daily*'s extensive interview with BSU members was published on February 15, 1968, and several members credited Carmichael as an inspiration. BSU member Eddie Demmings recalled that Carmichael "had a profound effect on the black community." Demmings added, "He had something we could identify with. He told us that things could no longer stay the same." E. J. Brisker added, "He told us about rebellion against the white 'pig'; that's different from a riot."[87]

Beyond the nascent BSU, others in Seattle were prompted to action by Carmichael, and the local Black Power movement gained a newfound prominence. One indication was a Black Power forum organized on May 3 by Seattle SNCC. It brought together moderate and militant segments of Seattle's activist community to discuss the goals and importance of Black Power. Influential members of Seattle's civil rights establishment spoke on the program, including the Reverends John H. Adams and Samuel B. McKinney. Mount Zion Baptist, McKinney's church, was also the venue for the event. Characteristically, as a civil rights preacher, Adams expressed some reservations about Black Power. Yet he also affirmed Black Power's importance as "one of many youthful expressions of judgment upon the phoniness and emptiness" of America's purported values.[88] Another local leader on race issues who spoke was the Reverend Mineo Katagiri, the Japanese American minister of the United Church of Christ and member of the CACRC.[89] Katagiri said that the SNCC members and Black Power more broadly represented a "new phase in the struggle for social justice" and that the entire city needed to take notice. He added, "Seattle has always been considered 'a place where there was time to solve our problems. But now it is one minute to 12 o'clock.'"[90] These statements by Adams and Katagiri clearly show that the civil rights establishment in Seattle recognized the newfound influence of Black Power.

Representing Seattle SNCC at the forum, the other speakers were Mattie Bundy, Les McIntosh, and Carl Miller. Bundy called out African Americans for being too timid in the face of white prejudice. She admonished, "Negroes have been afraid of hurting the feelings of white people and they have always catered to the white man." McIntosh, Seattle SNCC's education committee chair, upended long-standing calls for school integration in Seattle and asserted that integration should be de-emphasized, describing how Black children in Seattle's Voluntary Racial Transfer Program were "subjected to ridicule and name calling at bus stops" and faced indifferent teachers at the transfer school. Instead, McIntosh outlined a Black Nationalist vision to improve schooling, saying that African Americans should "take over" predominately Black schools and install Black principals, teachers, and staff. Carl Miller, the group's housing committee chair, encapsulated Black Power's *raison d'être* by pointing to the alienation of many younger activists and the racial injustices that persisted despite the civil rights movement: "Young people feel leaders don't speak for them and they don't have a voice. When you can't get jobs or housing, it leaves a feeling of anger and frustration."[91]

Further demonstrating the ascendance of Black Power in Seattle, movement adherents won the attention of the state's governor, Dan Evans, during the following summer and successfully lobbied for meaningful reforms. This project was led by Les McIntosh, Infanta Spence, and other members of an ad hoc committee called We of the Grassroots, or simply We. In August, the committee organized a guided tour of the Central Area for Governor Evans to show him the urgent need for social services. "Following the tour Evans agreed to establish a multiservice center in the district which would include health, employment, and public assistance." Along with this notable achievement, the ad hoc committee would continue its work by challenging the Seattle mayor and school officials, and it soon developed into a new organization, the Central Area Committee for Peace and Improvement (CAPI), also headed by McIntosh.[92]

Similarly, the Black Power movement was evident in the shifting philosophy of Seattle CORE. In the late 1960s, after spearheading civil rights campaigns earlier in the decade, Seattle CORE was challenged by the attrition of long-standing members and the upsurge of Black Power. Both factors contributed to an intra-organizational dispute and ultimate reorganization in the summer of 1967, when a prominent faction led the chapter to embrace the goals and philosophy of Black Power. This was, of course, in sharp contrast to CORE's earlier iteration, characterized by white leadership, integrationist goals, and a polite style of politics. Yet this change reflected the rise of Black Power in the national CORE organization.[93]

As shown in the preceding examples, Seattle's Black Power movement mushroomed in 1967 following the visit of Stokely Carmichael. From that point to the mid-1970s, a network of individuals and groups embraced Black Power and took up leading roles in local race politics. By the end of the sixties, Seattle was home to numerous militant groups, including the Black Student Union, the Negro Voters League, Seattle SNCC, Seattle CORE, the Seattle Central Area Registration Program, the Central Area School of the Performing Arts, Black Arts West, the Central Area Committee for Peace and Improvement, and the Seattle chapter of the Black Panther Party.[94] This proliferation of Black Power groups illuminates the sociopolitical context for the Black Student Union in the late 1960s. Without this larger body of like-minded political organizing and support, the college students would have been less likely to be as successful in their campaigns for reform at the University of Washington and beyond.

James Garrett and the Black Student Union at San Francisco State

The final antecedent of the Black Student Union at UW outlined in this chapter is the BSU at San Francisco State University.[95] Despite the distance between the two campuses, Black student activists at San Francisco State (SF State) and UW had a direct and ongoing relationship during the late 1960s. Members of the BSU at SF State introduced the Seattle students to the BSU concept; also, James Garrett, a key student leader at SF State, was personally involved in BSU actions at UW. Thus, the final section of this chapter will profile the BSU at SF State as another crucial predecessor of the BSU in Seattle. Throughout the remainder of this section, San Francisco State *University* will often be referenced as San Francisco State *College*, as the school was known in the 1960s.[96]

The first Black Student Union was established at SF State, and it started with a bet. The wager was between two friends, James "Jimmy"

Garrett and Charlie Cobb.[97] Both were experienced organizers and veterans of the Student Nonviolent Coordinating Committee. Their wager was on who could build a campus-based Black student movement the fastest. In March 1965 the idea came up as Garrett drove Cobb and Bob Moses, another SNCC member, from Los Angeles to the San Francisco Bay Area. At the time, Garrett headed the Los Angeles SNCC office, a post he held from November 1964 to November 1965. Yet, instead of concentrating on his official duties to host events and raise funds, he was drawn to strategizing about the potential for Black student activism at predominately white college campuses. Garrett remembered,

> I was learning my craft of fundraising and mounting house parties and gatherings and then large auditorium things [in Los Angeles], and this and that and the other. But I was always going back, once a month or more, I would go back to SNCC staff meetings [in Atlanta, Georgia]. And people in SNCC were already discussing the contradictions that had been raised from the Mississippi Summer Project and among those was the great increase in the number of whites who were involved and a contraction or flattening out of the number of young Blacks, especially from colleges in the South, that were coming into the movement. And so those contradictions were just beginning to, or they evolved over that next year that I was running the SNCC office in LA.[98]

This period, midway through the sixties, was a time of shifting strategies for many in SNCC and throughout the movement. In consultation with other SNCC staff, Garrett became convinced that Black students in the North could be mobilized to create a new arm of the Black freedom struggle. Charlie Cobb had reached the same conclusion. Garrett settled on organizing Black students at predominately white institutions, while Cobb opted to focus on Black students at historically Black colleges and universities. At stake was ten dollars, one-fourth of their monthly SNCC salary. Ultimately, Garrett won the bet with a groundbreaking campaign that created a network of Black Student Unions, first at SF State and then across the West Coast.[99] Cobb, who launched his initial efforts at Howard University, was unsuccessful and soon shifted to other projects.

At San Francisco State, the direct predecessor of the Black Student Union was the Negro Student Association (NSA), which was formally established on September 19, 1963.[100] Dikran Karagueuzian, a Syrian American SF State student during the 1960s and former editor of the student newspaper, the *Golden Gater*, provided a sketch of the group, writing that it was founded "mainly in order to link the blacks on campus through social activities. Many of the organization's members were militant, but they rarely voiced their feelings, perhaps because the liberal college community would not have approved a black militant stance."[101] The 1964 edition of *Franciscan*, the SF State yearbook, included the NSA with a description of its activities. The unnamed author wrote that the Negro Student Association, "one of the youngest members of STATE's sizable family of organizations, sparked tremendous campus interest by instituting a soul-pie sale and erecting a blue, 'soul-box' kiosk." This sale of sweet potato pies, or "soul-pies," dovetails with Karagueuzian's description of the group as culturally and socially oriented.[102]

Coverage of the NSA in the *Golden Gater* during the group's second year indicates that the organization continued its sociocultural events and added more political activities. In 1964–1965, the NSA hosted a poetry show, a gospel concert, a lecture on relations between African nations, and a film called *Angola—Journey to a War*.[103] It co-sponsored campus activism in support of the civil rights movement, including a "Freedom Week" with various events, and a separate "Freedom Fast" where participants sacrificed a meal and donated to support the Student Nonviolent Coordinating Committee.[104] And it co-sponsored anti-Vietnam War protests, including an all-night vigil on campus.[105] Thus, by the spring of 1965, the NSA was openly supporting leftist politics, even if it remained principally a social group.

In 1966 the Negro Student Association changed its name to the Black Student Union, as the group reorganized itself as a political organization. This was both an outgrowth of earlier interests among the membership and a significant reorientation as the body fully embraced the Black Power movement. Several factors combined to motivate this transformation. One was the group's preexisting leftist orientation; another contributor was Black students' growing frustration at their declining population at SF State. Due to the 1961 incorporation of SF State into the California state college system and California's "Master Plan for Higher Education," San Francisco State went from serving the top 70 percent of high school graduates to only the top 33 percent. Subsequently, "African

American enrollment dropped from an estimated 11 percent in 1960 to 3.6 percent in 1968."[106] The falling enrollments of African Americans were also related to "the military draft into the war in Vietnam" and "a system of 'tracking' Black and poor students into schools for vocational education."[107] NSA members were primed for dissent as they observed declining Black enrollments due to institutionally racist policies.

Into this context stepped James Garrett, who was the other major factor in the evolution from NSA to BSU. By all accounts, Garrett provided a crucial stimulus for the group's expanding militancy. As stated in a report authored by William H. Orrick Jr., a San Francisco lawyer, for the National Commission on the Causes and Prevention of Violence, "In February of 1966, a black student transferred from East Los Angeles City College to San Francisco State College. His name was James Garrett, he was 24 years old, and was to become the single most important figure in creating the BSU that exists today [in 1969]."[108] Described by Karagueuzian as "short, skinny Jimmy Garrett," he was already a veteran activist by the time he arrived at SF State.[109]

Garrett was born in Dallas, Texas, in 1942. During his early childhood his family worked as migrant farm workers in Texas and Louisiana. Then later, during high school, Garrett and his family moved to South Los Angeles, and he became involved in the local chapter of CORE. In 1960, after high school, Garrett returned to Dallas and continued his activism.[110] As Garrett described it,

> I ended up joining a movement in Dallas, a kind of a renaissance of the Youth NAACP who demonstrated against segregation, this time, in department stores like S. H. Cress. And I was arrested seven times and I was hooked. The next year I was on the Freedom Rides, the late Freedom Rides in the August–September of '61 and I ended up spending twenty-two days in prison, in New Orleans Parrish Prison.[111]

From then on, throughout the early 1960s, he would continue to work with various protest groups, splitting time between Los Angeles and the South. He even helped organize a plane-load of celebrities to attend the 1963 March on Washington, including famed actor Sidney Poitier. Following the March on Washington, Garrett joined SNCC staff and worked in the Freedom Summer project and other efforts for about a year until he was brutally beaten by Mississippi state police. Garrett remembered, "I was stopped [for questioning] and I was hit with clubs. It ended up puncturing one of my kidneys." Garrett was subsequently jailed, and later, after received medical treatment, he was advised to leave Mississippi. He was warned that due to his injuries, he "couldn't take another beating like that," so he accepted a new role as chief of SNCC's chapter in Los Angeles.[112] While in that role, Garrett met Fred Thalheimer, a member of San Francisco's Friends of SNCC and professor of sociology at San Francisco State.[113] Coincidentally, the introduction to Thalheimer occurred during the same fateful road trip that featured the Garrett-Cobb wager, previously described. As a child, Thalheimer came to the United States when his French-Jewish family fled the Nazi invasion. He joined the SF State faculty in 1962 and was active in leftist politics throughout his life.[114] During their first conversation, Garrett mentioned his intentions to build a Black student movement and Thalheimer suggested he do so at San Francisco State.[115] Thus, with the help of Thalheimer and others, Garrett was a student at SF State by the early months of 1966.

On campus, Garrett's movement experience, intelligence, and force of personality quickly earned him a leadership position among Black students. He also arrived on campus with a strong Black nationalist orientation, which he would help to infuse into Black campus politics. His Black nationalism grew out of his previous civil rights involvement. As articulated by sociologist and Black Studies scholar Fabio Rojas, Garrett "believed that students needed black consciousness" and his previous experience in the South "persuaded him that an all-black political organization was necessary."[116] Garrett was not a Black separatist, but believed that a Black nationalist strategy was necessary for Black self-esteem and empowerment.[117] Garrett was convinced that Black activists should prioritize unity among themselves and alliances with local Black communities, and this became the centerpiece of the Black Student Union methodology. However, while no white members were allowed in the BSU, the organization was open to non-Black people of color. One such person was Pamela Egashira, a survivor of Japanese internment and BSU member at SF State by March 1967. As Garrett remembered, "[Egashira] was almost more Black nationalist than everybody because she had been born in one of those concentration camps, Tule Lake, I believe, during World War II."[118] Although it might seem counterintuitive given the name *Black* Student Union, the organization was not Black-only.

In February and March 1966, Garrett worked to draw together Black students at SF State through discussion groups and "strategy sessions" in various meeting places, including the campus library and Garrett's residence.[119] By the end of March, the group changed its name from Negro Student Association to Black Student Union, after weeks of debate.[120] Thus began the organization that would become "the most powerful pressure group" at SF State.[121] Within a year, the organization spread to "every state college in California."[122]

In addition to Garrett, who was elected the first chair of the BSU, another early leader was Jerry Varnado, who took the role of on-campus coordinator. Varnado was an Air Force veteran in his early twenties who was originally from Mississippi.[123] Prior to this, Varnado had been active in the NSA and Alpha Phi Alpha, a Black fraternity. Others who would take leadership roles in the group included financial coordinator Nesbitt Crutchfield, tutorial director Thomas Williams, education coordinator Jack Alexis, and Benny Stewart, who succeeded Garrett as chairman after one year.[124] This all-male leadership points to the presence of patriarchy in the foundation of the BSU, a characteristic that was endemic throughout various activist groups and society at large. The Orrick Report noted that a woman's auxiliary, the Black Sisters Union, was established at some point because the "Sisters" wanted leadership roles and "tried to figure a way to get out of their secretarial positions."[125] It's not clear what became of this Black Sisters Union, but the anecdote reflects the sex discrimination of civil rights and Black Power groups through the sixties. Yet female members were clearly present and made key contributions; in fact, the group's new name, *Black Student Union*, was first suggested by Patricia Ravarra.[126]

During the spring and into the summer of 1966, the BSU continued its consciousness-raising activities and began work on community service projects targeting inner-city Black neighborhoods.[127] As Jerry Varnado put it, "Having the name Black Student Union, we were not afraid to go to the ghetto. We were not afraid to go to Hunters Point," naming an impoverished neighborhood near San Francisco's once bustling World War II shipyards.[128] He continued, "We tried to recruit students to come to college. We wanted them to join the BSU also, but the primary reason was for them to get an education."[129] One BSU initiative was a tutorial program that taught reading and writing to mostly Black, low-income youth throughout San Francisco. Several years earlier, in 1964, this program began in the Fillmore neighborhood, "in a small Baptist Church on Divisadero Street," supported "with about $20 in Associated Students funds." In 1966 the BSU took leadership of the program and the tutoring soon "expanded to 22 centers involving more than 500 college students just before the [1968] student strike."[130]

The BSU brought a Black Power ethos to the program, stressing Black pride and insisting that the majority of the tutors be African American. Previously, the program's tutors were majority-white, which seemed to exacerbate self-esteem issues for the Black tutees. For example, as one concerned college student observed, "some of the kids were telling the [white] tutors they were more beautiful because they had long straight hair, and the tutors would reinforce this." Consequently, the BSU judged that having Black tutors would help dispel these notions of racial inferiority. Moreover, the BSU created Black Arts and Culture courses through SF State's Experimental College that encouraged white *and* Black tutors to abandon anti-Black biases.[131]

Demonstrating a remarkable commitment to public service and grassroots engagement, the Black Student Union launched a slate of programs, on and off campus, in addition to the tutoring. A BSU request for additional university funds in June 1967 outlined its range of initiatives: "black history and culture programs" in three local high schools; a BSU Theater Project that had "performed all over California in all communities"; and other on-campus programs "designed to educate and entertain the students of SFSC using black music, poetry, drama, and dance."[132] Off-campus, the BSU was a dues-paying member of the Western Addition Community Organization (WACO), a coalition group focused on resisting displacement of low-income Black residents by urban renewal policies and associated gentrification. The Reverend Hannibal Williams, a community organizer and member of WACO, praised the college students' local engagement. He said, "The BSU as an organization is operating on the principle that the college for the black student is not an ivory tower but a place where he gets some kind of preparation to come back to these ghetto communities" and address "the relevant needs of the people in those communities." Williams concluded, "These kids are beautiful and they are to be admired for this."[133]

Constituting the on-campus side of its activism, the Black Student Union created a slate of Black Studies courses between 1966 and 1968. As detailed in the BSU's spring 1968 Black Studies Program catalogue, "Black curriculum at San Francisco State College was first initiated in Spring, 1966. The class was taught under the auspices of the General Education Elective Program (GEEP), a program for new and innovative classes in education."[134] This inaugural course was titled Black Nationalism and taught by Aubrie LaBrie, a history grad student and BSU member.[135] Building from this initial course, BSU members created the Black Arts and Culture Series in the fall of 1966. As mentioned previously, this was executed within SF State's Experimental College, a program funded by the school that allowed students to create and offer classes of their own. The goal of the Black Arts and Culture Series was to "introduce, through a series of classes on Black culture and art, a positive focus on the life experiences of Black people in psychology, humanities, political science, and dance." Soon after, the BSU further expanded the course offerings and adopted the heading "Black Studies." By the fall of 1967 there were eleven courses, and this expanded to seventeen by the spring of 1968.[136]

The Black Studies catalogue from the spring of 1968 lists seventeen courses organized into nine subject areas: anthropology, dramatic arts, education, English, history, humanities, psychology, social science, and sociology. Indicating the rigor of the curriculum, two of the courses satisfied SF State general education requirements, including a composition course that satisfied an English requirement, taught by George Murray, a grad student and BSU member. The famed poet Sonia Sanchez also taught a creative writing course that semester. A representative sample of the other courses includes a Swahili language course, Ancient Black History, Introduction to Avant-Garde Jazz, and Sociology of Black Oppression. Another, somewhat surprising inclusion was "a survey of Far Eastern (China, Japan, Korea) history up to 1831," titled History of the Third World. This class reflected the BSU's multicultural solidarity and decolonial internationalism vis-à-vis the non-Western world.[137] The creation of this Black Studies program was a major innovation and a radical intervention in US higher education. Unlike the standard Eurocentric curriculum, Black Studies aimed to speak to the needs of urban Black residents. The word "relevant" was commonly used in the political vernacular of the time, and Black Studies was charged to be "relevant" to contemporaneous racial politics.

BSU members at SF State were part of a larger effort to expose Eurocentrism in US education, a school-based struggle within the Black Power movement. Historian Peniel Joseph dubbed it the "Black Studies movement":

> Building on the early-twentieth century "Negro History Movement" pioneered by historians Carter G. Woodson and J. A. Rogers, the modern Black Studies movement emerged from the hotbed of black radicalism produced during the 1960s. Black Studies provided a practical and political education for a variety of captive, and captivated, audiences during this era. The movement simultaneously promoted community building, black nationalist consciousness, class struggle, educational opportunity and restructuring, employment creation, and anticolonial struggles through think tanks and study groups [and curriculum].[138]

As described by historian Ibram X. Kendi, such educational content was not part of the standard course offerings at San Francisco State or anywhere else at the time. In Kendi's words, education up to the 1960s featured a "normalized mask of whiteness" where white supremacist ideas, perspectives, and scholarship were taken as the best and standard learning materials.[139] Kendi elaborated,

> Until black students called this into question, the paucity of courses and literature dealing with African Americans was *normalized* for higher education. Normalized as opposed to normal, since these lily-white curriculums were deliberately created and recreated over the years, ignoring black scholarship from W. E. B. Du Bois, Anna Julia Cooper, Zora Neale Hurston, J. A. Rogers, Chiek Anta Diop, and Alain Locke—to name a few. It was no coincidence or oversight.[140]

Therefore, the BSU created an innovative educational program that recognized and appreciated Black history and culture, valued Black learners and content creators, and responded to concurrent racial politics.

As they developed Black Studies, the students worked to have it implemented into the official college curriculum and established as a department, but were stymied by a convoluted bureaucracy and administrative foot-dragging. Joseph White, a dean at SF State and a Black administrator who worked closely with the BSU, described what happened:

> The students had to run from committee to committee. They have this very innovative thing, or what they consider is an innovative proposal, and no one to carry the ball for them. There was no one on the faculty who could cut through the tape. So, you have some students like Bennie Stewart who since they were sophomores have been going to committee after committee trying to articulate why black studies—only to wind up before the one they started with. It was frustrating, and gives you an idea of how the system runs you around.[141]

Due to mounting frustrations regarding Black Studies and related racial tensions on campus, the Black Student Union issued SF State president Robert Smith a list of ten demands on November 5, 1968. One of the other race-related controversies was the suspension of George Murray, a BSU member, Black Panther, grad student, and instructor in Black Studies. Earlier that spring, Murray attracted scrutiny from the college administration after he reportedly led a group of Black students in a confrontation and subsequent brawl with staff of the student newspaper, who at the time were unfriendly toward the BSU.[142] Murray subsequently caused further dismay that summer when he traveled to Fidel Castro's Cuba and made statements critical of US foreign policy. Among other statements, he said, "Every time a Vietnamese guerilla knocks out a US soldier, that means one less aggressor against those who fight for freedom in the US."[143] Leaders of California state government were appalled and pressured the educational authorities to respond. Consequently, Murray was suspended from his teaching role at SF State. When the BSU issued its ten demands in November 1968, one of the demands explicitly called for Murray's reinstatement. The other demands pushed for a range of reforms at the college, including greater resources and full departmental status for Black Studies, increased Black enrollment, improvements to the financial aid office, and amnesty for demonstrators.[144]

President Robert Smith refused to agree to all the demands and the student strike, initiated by the BSU, began on November 6; this strike would go on to become the longest student protest of the 1960s.[145] Soon after the strike's inception, the BSU was joined by the Third World Liberation Front (TWLF), an umbrella organization that included allied minority student groups: Philippine-American Collegiate Endeavor (PACE), the Latin American Student Organization (LASO), the Mexican-American Student Confederation (MASC), Intercollegiate Chinese for Social Action (ICSA), the Asian American Political Alliance (AAPA), and the Native American Student Organization (NASO).[146] Augmenting the BSU demands, the TWLF added calls for increased enrollment of students of color, and the creation of a College of Ethnic Studies that included Black Studies, Asian American studies, Native American studies, and Chicano/Latinos studies.[147]

On November 13 the faculty union joined the students' picket lines, motivated by long-simmering labor disputes over pay, benefits, and workload. Many faculty members also felt that the suspension of George Murray was a violation of academic freedom, free speech, and shared governance.[148] Hence, the strike, now led by the BSU and TWLF, garnered increasing support across campus. The strike caused major disruptions to campus life, and the heavy-handed response of the administration and local police encouraged further escalation and greater support for the strike.[149] Faced with a highly effective strike that paralyzed virtually all functions of the institution, campus officials relied on law enforcement to reestablish control. Between November 1968 and March 1969, from two hundred to six hundred police officers continually occupied the SF State campus, and at times used brutal tactics on demonstrators.[150] One particularly violent day was December 3; strike participant Margaret Leahy recounted what transpired:

> All those who participated in the Strike know Tuesday, December 3, as "Bloody Tuesday." Joining about 2,500 student and faculty demonstrators at a noon rally were leaders of the Black, Asian, and Latino communities, as well as religious leaders. By the end of the rally, one non-striker

estimated the crowd at approximately 5,000. The rally was attacked—no other word describes what occurred—by police coming from all sides. Fighting between police and demonstrators filled the central campus. The two sides were not evenly matched. While the demonstrators outnumbered the police, the police were armed with clubs and guns. Unarmed students lost all fear and jumped on the backs of police who were beating students, only to be pulled off and clubbed to the ground themselves. The afternoon WAS bloody![151]

During police riots like Bloody Tuesday, local community members and neutral bystanders were threatened and attacked by law enforcement, fueling more support for the strike. By one estimate, "over eighty students were injured by police in the process of their arrest, and hundreds more were beaten with police batons, dragged, punched, and slapped, but not arrested."[152] Providing a concurring account, Juanita Tamayo Lott, another strike participant, recounted that many strikers were repeatedly arrested, including "BSU/TWLF leaders Bridges Randall, Jerry Varnado, Roger Alvarado, and Hari Dillion and SDS leader Todd Gitlin" as well as "professors including Nathan Hare [Black Studies], Fred Thalheimer (Sociology), William Carpenter (International Relations) and Anatole Anton (Philosophy)."[153] Thus, the strike at San Francisco State was a period of intense danger and political struggle.

Some protesters also utilized violent methods: injuring thirty-two police officers, setting fires on campus, and causing vandalism.[154] Damaging school property was part of a strategy called the "war of the flea." This aimed to use numerous small acts of sabotage to force campus officials to negotiate. Ben Stewart of the BSU described this strategy:

We are the majority and the pigs cannot be everywhere, everyplace all the time. And where they are not, we are. And something happens. The philosophy of the flea. You just begin to wear them down. Toilets are stopped up. Pipes is out. Water in the bathroom is runnin' all over the place. Smoke is coming out the bathroom.[155]

With both sides refusing to give in, the strike became a war of attrition and the administration gradually strengthened its power, largely due to the maneuvering of college president S. I. Hayakawa, the successor to Robert Smith. Hayakawa undermined the strike with new policies permitting mass arrests and the expulsion of contentious students. Hayakawa acted with strong support from California governor Ronald Reagan and gained additional leverage by hiring new administrators who were willing to enforce the harsh policies. The student newspaper, which had become staffed by BSU/TWLF allies, was also suspended.[156] Off campus, the criminal justice system further hampered the strike as key demonstrators faced burdensome bail expenses, legal battles, and jail sentences.[157]

After five months the strike ended in compromise on March 21, 1969.[158] The BSU/TWLF won the establishment of the new academic departments that they wanted: "American Indian Studies, Asian American Studies, Black Studies, and La Raza Studies within a College of Ethnic Studies."[159] At the time of this writing, this remains the only such college in the nation.[160] Moreover, the strike led to greater enrollments of Black students and the allocation of additional financial aid.[161] The BSU/TWLF strike made a huge impact on SF State and inspired students all over the country to demand Black Studies and other minority studies programs.[162]

The Black Student Union at San Francisco State is an important organization for its impact on and off campus. Challenging dominant narratives that cast Black Power as central to the declension of the late 1960s, this organizational history displays how many African Americans within the Black Power movement were sincerely engaged in grassroots politics, genuinely open to multiracial alliances, and pushed for concrete and prosocial reforms. Moreover, the BSU at SF State is important for this study because, as detailed in the next chapter, it had a formative role in the creation of the Black Student Union in Seattle.

Highlighting the forerunners of the Black Student Union in the state of Washington, this chapter has discussed four historical threads that combined to create the foundation for the BSU. The first was the social, economic, and political struggles of Black Seattle from World War II to the 1950s. The second was Seattle's civil rights movement in the early 1960s. The third was the 1967 ascendance of Seattle's Black Power movement. Finally, the chapter outlined the Black Student Union at San Francisco State University. These trajectories of struggle indicate that the BSU in Seattle was heir to a number of activist legacies, which it utilized and enlarged during the late 1960s. These linkages to a broader landscape of Black protest and civic engagement help us understand the environment that facilitated the actions detailed in the coming chapters—how the BSU emerged, thrived, and carried forward the quest for racial justice.

2

"You Done *Really* Changed"

The BSU at the University of Washington, Fall 1967–Spring 1968

Between November 1967 and May 1968, Black students at the University of Washington in Seattle created their Black Student Union (BSU) and, in alliance with others, launched trailblazing protest campaigns at their university and beyond.[1] The BSU organization was conveyed to the Pacific Northwest by the Western Regional Black Youth Conference, held in Los Angeles during the Thanksgiving weekend of 1967.[2] Several dozen Black college students from Seattle traveled to Los Angeles by bus and attended the conference, where they learned about the Black Student Unions from students from San Francisco State University. Once they returned to Seattle, the young activists quickly implemented the political strategies learned at the conference.

This chapter recounts the origins of the BSU at the University of Washington (UW). In addition to the organization's subsequent on-campus impact, the BSU of UW is noteworthy because it ushered into the region what Ibram X. Kendi identified as the "Black campus movement." As Kendi put it,

> This struggle among black student nationalists at historically white and black institutions to reconstitute higher education from 1965 to 1972 has been termed the *Black Campus Movement*. . . . This late 1960's black power campus struggle represented a profound ideological, tactical, and spatial shift from early 1960s off-campus Civil Rights confrontations.[3]

The BSU at the University of Washington was a pivotal link between Black student activism in the state of Washington and throughout the rest of the nation, as the Seattle students responded to the local and national context. Thus, as we will see, the BSU group detailed in this chapter and the next was a movement lynchpin. To enrich understandings of the

BSU, this chapter begins with profiles of two BSU members, Verlaine Keith-Miller and Larry Gossett. From there, the remainder of the chapter will recount the initial campaigns of the organization, primarily during the early months of 1968. This was a crucial period when the Black collegians built a base of support on and off campus. Moreover, this chapter highlights how community organizing and public service were central elements of the BSU's effective outreach initiative.

Verlaine Keith-Miller and Larry Gossett

Verlaine Keith-Miller, born Verlaine Keith, grew up in Seattle and would have appeared to many as an unlikely militant. A petite and fashionable young Black woman who studied ballet throughout her childhood and adolescence, Keith-Miller generally avoided trouble. As Eddie Demmings recalled, Mrs. Keith, Verlaine's mother, was "very strict" and "very demanding," and guided several of her children to graduate from college. During Verlaine's childhood, the family was also "very poor" and lived in Holly Park, a low-income housing project.[4] As a Cleveland High School student, Keith-Miller earned a spot on the honor roll and was an officer in student government. She worked part-time as a member of the fashion board for a downtown department store, where her job was to participate in fashion shows, pose for publicity shoots, and assist with related activities. Moreover, in high school she had a white boyfriend who was captain of the football team. Therefore, many observers would have seen her as a success story of racial progress: academically successful, upwardly mobile, and racially integrated. Moreover, it is instructive to note here that the year she graduated from Cleveland High, 1966, was one year before the US Supreme Court struck down anti-miscegenation laws in *Loving v. Virginia*. This underscores the significance of Keith-Miller's interracial relationship.

Much of Keith-Miller's high school experience seemed primed for continued success in the American mainstream, and she was relatively apolitical. Yet Keith-Miller also had a headstrong and independent spirit, which fostered a simmering indignation at racial slights and double standards. One high school experience that encouraged this budding political consciousness was when a high school guidance counselor objected to her relationship with her white boyfriend. Remembering the experience, she described being called into the counselor's office, and intending to "just sit down and say nothing." But once the meeting began, "he and I proceeded to go at it" in a heated argument, she recalled. Apparently, the counselor and some other school officials felt that the relationship should end because of concerns for the boyfriend's future. In other words, school officials feared that the young man's future potential would be harmed if he continued to be associated with Keith-Miller. In response, Keith-Miller was furious, and was particularly piqued because *she*, not the boyfriend, was the honor roll student. She had just as much potential as anyone, so why weren't they concerned about her future, she thought to herself. So she told the counselor that her relationship was not his concern. Amused as she remembered the courage of her younger self in an interview over fifty years later, she said, "Yeah, I was kind of lippy even then."[5]

In hindsight, the racism of the school counselor is obvious, but the full significance of the encounter would not become clear to Keith-Miller until later. As it was for many young people of her generation and today, her political awareness would come in college. In the fall of 1966, Keith-Miller matriculated at the University of Washington. In her first two years at UW, two factors combined to spur her political consciousness of racism and its systemic nature: more incidents of bigotry and the influence of a friend, Larry Gossett. First, there were the racial insults she experienced as a college student. One involved a professor who refused to give her an A, despite her excellent work. As Keith-Miller described, "There weren't a lot of us [African Americans] there [at UW], but I remember some class where the teacher actually read my paper to the class [as a model paper], said I should think about having it published, and then gave me an A-. And I was just like, 'What's the minus for, I mean, I don't get it.'" Keith-Miller was sure that the professor was unwilling to give her a top grade because she was African American.[6] Another incident transpired at a department store near campus, when a sales clerk was especially rude:

I don't know if it was a J. C. Penney store [or a different store] at the U. I just felt treated so shabbily that I was like—. I mean, shabbily enough where I wanted to reach across and snatch her. And I [had] not been brought up to be violent. And that started me thinking a little bit more [about racism].[7]

Added to these incidents, Keith-Miller's growing political awareness was encouraged by a childhood friend and fellow UW student, Larry Gossett. As Keith-Miller later recalled, she would commonly carpool to campus with Gossett and her brother, Dan Keith. Often, the car ride conversations would turn to racial issues, with Gossett and Keith-Miller taking opposing viewpoints. For instance, Keith-Miller narrated one exchange when they debated the logic of urban rioting in impoverished Black communities:

> Yeah, he, and my brother, and I would go to the U. together. And that's when I was still, "I don't get why we do this. Why would you—? Blah blah blah." And Larry gave a nonjudgmental response. He said, "It's not like here. If you don't own anything in your neighborhood, there's no incentive to save it." And he just got me thinking about what it was like in other parts of the country.[8]

Gossett eventually persuaded Keith-Miller to think beyond individualistic explanations for rioting and poverty, and to consider historical and institutional factors. Over time, she found herself agreeing with Gossett more and more. By her sophomore year, when the BSU was established at UW, she quickly joined the organization along with Gossett, her brother, Dan, and others.[9] In fact, Dan Keith served as the first BSU president.

Like Keith-Miller, Larry Gossett would also seem like an unlikely activist by some, based on his high school days. His parents, Nelmon Bill Gossett and Johnnie Evelyn Carter, migrated to Seattle from east Texas in 1944, and Larry was born in the Emerald City the following year. Gossett was a good student, and he excelled as a high school athlete. In particular, he was known for his skill as a point guard on the Franklin High School basketball team. Although he was not especially tall at five feet eight, Gossett's abilities on the court reportedly led to "a Larry Gossett Fan Club" that "contained 33 devoted students" by his senior year.[10]

After graduating from high school in 1963, Gossett enrolled at the University of Washington and focused on his studies. At the time, he was an apolitical student intent on pursuing mainstream success. Gossett recalled, "To characterize myself at the time, I was a Negro student."[11] Here, Gossett used the term "Negro" to signify a subgroup of African Americans who pursued individualistic success, materialism, and integration, while eschewing political agitation and criticisms of US society. Using more scathing terms, Malcolm X invoked a similar notion of "Negro" in his *Autobiography* when he denounced Black community members who were "breaking their backs trying to imitate white people" while looking down on other African Americans whom they deemed "ghetto" or undignified.[12]

Gossett's life and political outlook took a dramatic turn during a stint in the Volunteers in Service to America (VISTA) program, a government initiative of domestic volunteerism modeled after the Peace Corps. He originally applied for VISTA to avoid being drafted into the Vietnam War; however, the eighteen months he spent in the program would set the trajectory for the rest of his life.[13] In VISTA, Gossett lived and worked in New York City's Harlem ghetto from the spring of 1966 to the summer of 1967. His assignment was to coordinate programs for Harlem youth, and this gave him a keen awareness of the poor living conditions of that community—much worse than anything he had witnessed prior. For example, the dire conditions were reflected in the high population density, with 9,211 people living on one city block. By comparison, only 150 lived on Gossett's block back in Seattle. Moreover, due to the poverty and hopelessness, many of the 1,366 youth in the neighborhood that Gossett was expected to serve were "getting high on glue and marijuana," including some who were only twelve years old or younger. Highlighting the institutional racism and segregation of New York City, Gossett remembered that many of the kids "had never seen Central Park even though they only [lived] seven blocks from it."[14] Seeing racial injustice impacting the children of Harlem began Gossett's political transformation.

Gossett's racial consciousness was also stimulated by cultural and intellectual resources he found in Harlem, such as the Apollo Theater, the famed performance venue, and the Black nationalist bookstore of Lewis H. Michaux. At the Apollo, he saw explosions of creativity, talent, and Black pride, the likes of which he had never before encountered. Added to this, the staff at Michaux's bookstore recommended texts on Black history, socialism, and communism. Gossett recalled, "I got exposed to books about Marcus Garvey and I was told that he had the biggest Black organization the country's ever seen, yet he had it from 1924 to '27. I never heard of no United Negro Improvement Association and the battles that went on trying to help improve the condition of Black people."[15] For Gossett, these new artistic and scholastic stimuli imbued a new sense of himself as a Black person and a passion to forward Black America's long struggle for justice. His observations and experiences in Harlem left him radicalized and transformed. In his words, by the time he left, "it was crystal clear to me that my country, the United States of America, needed a radical overhaul if Black people were to ever move out of the category of underclass, or a second-class, or super-exploited residents and citizens of this country of ours."[16]

Upon his return, Gossett was literally unrecognizable. He described a humorous incident when his mother and brother walked past him at the airport: "When I got off the plane to come home a year and a couple months afterwards, I had a dashiki, I had African beads, I had shades, and had a very big natural."[17] This attire both reflected his newfound political identity and was a marked contrast to his previous choices in clothing and hairstyle. So when Gossett's family saw him at the airport, they assumed he was someone else:

> I saw them coming. I thought they were going to greet me. They kept walking. They were looking for the little Larry Gossett they knew. But our voices don't change. I said, "Mama, this is me." And then she and [my brother] Patrick turned. The look in their eyes, they said, "Oh my lord." Mama said, "Boy, why you got all that hair? What's that mess you got on? Larry, what happened? You done *really* changed." And then, the first thing I said was, "Mama, my name ain't Larry." She said, "Oh my god! What's your name?" I said, "Aba Yoruba." "Uba what!? Oh, boy, wait until I get you home so your daddy can talk to you. And he gon' cut that hair too." I said, "No, mom, dad is not going to cut this hair."[18]

The name Aba Yoruba did not become Gossett's primary moniker, but the new political philosophy and dedication to the Black Power movement remained. After returning to Seattle, he was anxious to join a Black Power organization and soon became a member of the Seattle chapter of the Student Nonviolent Coordinating Committee. Later that year, with other like-minded Black students, he helped establish the Black Student Union at UW.

The Black Student Union Comes to Washington

As the 1967–1968 school year got underway, Black students at the University of Washington recognized the need to challenge the school's institutionally racist practices, which were epitomized by their small population. When he enrolled in 1966, BSU member Eddie Demmings found UW to be "overwhelmingly white." He added, "Overwhelming—I mean, that's the word. I felt overwhelmed. I literally felt overwhelmed, like I might as well [have] moved to Sweden or somewhere else, you know?"[19] By one estimate, "the University had only one African American professor, and of the 32,000 students enrolled, only 4 percent were students of color. Nonwhite staff were concentrated in the most unskilled jobs."[20] Another estimate stated that in 1968, "there were only 150 Black students on a campus of more than 30,000," equating to about .5 percent of the student body.[21] In addition, as Verlaine Keith-Miller's experience testified to, the one to two hundred African American students on campus experienced prejudice and discrimination at the university. BSU member Emile Pitre recalled this experience: "I was walking across campus one day and a student in braces said, 'Everywhere I go you damned niggers are here.'"[22] Pitre was a graduate student in chemistry who enrolled in 1967 after graduating from Southern University in Baton Rouge, Louisiana. Having been raised in the segregated South, Pitre was attracted to Seattle because of its liberal reputation, and was therefore keenly disappointed to find overt racism on campus. Pitre remembered, "I expected that in Seattle—. I'd heard that Seattle was very race-friendly and there were interracial interactions with no issues." Thus, being verbally assaulted with a racial slur was a shock. He added, "So that really caused me to become disillusioned and to not take it."[23] Beyond campus, a confluence of factors galvanized a subgroup of Black students toward activism: grassroots Black organizing in Seattle throughout the 1960s, national developments in the civil rights and Black Power movements, Stokely Carmichael's visit to Seattle in the spring of 1967, tensions over the Vietnam War, and a broader zeitgeist of youthful rebellion and resistance to convention.

When the 1967–1968 school year began, one Black student organization was active at UW: the Afro-American Student Society, established the previous year by Dan Keith and Onye Akwari, a student from Nigeria. The group's aim was to encourage dialogue and understanding between Black Americans and Black Africans.[24] In addition, a few Black students were also a part of the Seattle chapter of the Student Nonviolent Coordinating Committee, such as future BSU members Carl Miller, Aaron Dixon, and Larry Gossett. In the final months of 1967, SNCC members who were also students at UW and the Afro-American Student Society coalesced to establish the BSU.

While the Afro-American Student Society provided a bridge to earlier campus involvement, Seattle SNCC had a more profound impact on the BSU due to its political influence and its national network. In fact, Seattle SNCC was responsible for organizing the group from Seattle that attended the decisive Western Regional Black Youth Conference. After learning about the gathering from Los Angeles SNCC, the Seattle chapter recruited and sponsored a delegation from Seattle that consisted of approximately thirty to thirty-five individuals of college and high school age.[25] According to Larry Gossett, the Seattle chapter of the Communist Party also provided crucial funding for the trip:

> And we started organ[izing], putting money together for [the trip to Los Angeles]. I have to tell you, though. I don't know if this has ever been told. The organization [that] gave us the most money to be able to pay for a bus for thirty-one [*sic*] Black students to go to Los Angeles for four days was the Communist Party chapter in Seattle. I think they raised 80 or 90 percent of the money we needed to ride the bus. And two of their young dynamic activists, Valerie Rubisz and Linda Corr, two young Black girls in the Communist Party, they went with us. So it was a very, very progressive group. Everybody else was either in SNCC—remember this was before the BSU, before the Black Panther Party—or just wanted to be active in a movement. But SNCC, the Communist Party, [those were] the main groups I can remember.[26]

The relationship with Seattle communists does not appear to have extended much beyond this financial support, but this connection reflects the linkages of support that existed among leftist groups in Seattle at the time.

As Gossett recalled, the Seattle SNCC members who went to the Black youth conference included "Kathy Halley, we called her 'Nafasi,' Carl Miller, E. J. Brisker, Kathy Jones, Richard Brown, [and] Lee Leavy," and all members of the party were "between the ages of sixteen and twenty-four." The delegation also included at least one person from Oregon. Gossett recalled, "James Hill was with us. The head—. The activist from the University of Oregon in Eugene. But he was raised in Portland."[27]

Held in Los Angeles during the Thanksgiving weekend of 1967 and organized by Harry Edwards, professor at San Jose State University,[28] and others, the Western Regional Black Youth Conference featured two hundred participants from across the West Coast, representing various political philosophies within the Black Power movement: revolutionary nationalists, cultural nationalists, socialists, communists, and others.[29] As Gossett described it,

It was at that conference that we first got exposed to and met brothers from, and sisters from, the newly formed Black Power organization in Oakland, California, that was calling itself the Black Panther Party for Self-Defense. We had not heard of it before we went to that conference. It was at that conference that we met really strong, articulate Black men and women from San Francisco State University and UCLA who had begun forming Black Student Unions on their campuses, at both the college and high school level. It was at that youth conference that we met, met up with Stokely Carmichael and James Forman. . . . [Forman] ran workshops on building grassroots community organizations at this conference. It was at that conference that we met a group of very cultural nationalist oriented youth who called themselves Us, . . . and they were headed by Maulana Ron Karenga, who was the creator of the [holiday], Kwanza.[30]

Another historic feature of this event was a proposal, championed by Edwards, to boycott the 1968 Olympic Games in Mexico City. Prominent Black athletes like Kareem Abdul-Jabbar (then known as Lew Alcindor) attended the conference and their discussions eventually led to a slew of

Olympic protests, the most famous being when sprinters Tommie Smith and John Carlos gave the Black Power salute on an awards podium.[31]

This was truly a historic event overall, and specifically for the University of Washington students the conference prompted a new commitment and strategy for action. Conference attendees from San Francisco State and elsewhere presented the BSU concept in a workshop and encouraged those in the audience to establish their own BSUs. The Seattle students were deeply impressed and embraced the idea.[32]

> By the end of that conference we had made a commitment to go back to Oregon and Washington and organize Black Student Unions. . . . That was a very, very important conference and the thirty [*sic*] of us were very excited when we got back to Seattle and began to talk about what we were going to do to build a Black Power movement in our home community.[33]

As an organizing strategy, the Black Student Union program called for a particular set of goals and tactics. The central piece of this program was building relationships between on-campus activists and local Black communities, and then leveraging those relationships to press university and civic officials for reform within and beyond higher education. One goal was to improve the racial climate and accessibility of predominately white colleges and universities. A second goal was to utilize university resources to ameliorate the disadvantages of poor and working-class African Americans. James Garrett, member of BSU at San Francisco State University and a key architect of the BSU strategy, summarized the methodology. He recounted that the approach started with "building a base" of supportive allies by way of impactful community service. Garrett continued, "So first there was building of that base, because that's what you do in a project, you build your base. And you build community relationships with that base. So the object was to build a base, while at the same time connecting that to the community." As a veteran of the Student Nonviolent Coordinating Committee, Garrett adapted the community organizing strategies of SNCC to the college environment and envisioned BSUs as a means to support the self-determination of African Americans, on and off campus. In his view, on-campus politics was not meant to be the primary focus of BSU efforts; rather, the vision was to utilize colleges and universities as "a place for human capital development and supplies and support."[34] Therefore, the BSU chapters spearheaded community-based initiatives as they pursued university reforms like Black Studies and new retention initiatives.

One of the primary avenues for the BSU's community outreach in Seattle was a large and intensive program to empower and mentor Black adolescents. The college students built and expanded relational networks with local youths and encouraged them to organize auxiliary BSUs at their high schools and junior high schools. As Gossett described,

> We were specifically asked on the weekend of Thanksgiving 1967 at this conference if we would not just focus on college campuses, that we have to become rooted in the black community, so we had to organize Black students at the high school and junior high level. And we had a commitment to do that; [and we] began to do a blueprint on how to do it at this conference.[35]

For the BSU, serving Black adolescents was a savvy and effective tactic to advance its mission for Black empowerment and simultaneously win community allies. The outreach initiative boosted racial pride and political consciousness, and built invaluable rapport with the younger students' parents and other relatives. As to be expected, reaction among parental guardians was undoubtedly mixed. Some were concerned about their kids getting involved in the Black Power movement. Others were more receptive because their personal beliefs were compatible with Black Power, or they simply appreciated that the college students were encouraging the teens to pursue higher education. Regardless of the parents' particular perspectives, as detailed later in the chapter, what transpired is that the parents generally came to support the BSU, and this translated into valuable political capital for collegians.

Before the outreach campaign got started, the first action by the BSU at UW after they returned from the Los Angeles conference was an on-campus rally on December 6, 1967. As reported, it was "timed to coincide with similar rallies on campuses up and down the West Coast," which reflects the intercollegiate and interstate solidarity that existed between BSU chapters. As described by historian Craig Collison,

> About a week after the [Los Angeles] conference, flyers appeared around
> [UW] campus announcing a new student group. "Black is beautiful!!!"
> proclaimed the placard next to an illustration of a black panther. The
> Black Student Union, "formerly: Afro-American Student Society," would
> hold a rally "to inform people about the racist practices at San Francisco
> State."[36]

As the flyer stated, the rally marked the entrance of the BSU into campus politics at the University of Washington and urged support for BSU
members at San Francisco State University. "The [rally's] speeches asked
for support for the nine 'soul brothers' facing trial in San Francisco following expulsion from college for attacking the student editor [of the
campus newspaper] for what they called 'unfair, racist handling of black
material.'" The BSU members at the rally included Carl Miller, Ernestine
Rodgers, Eddie Walker, and Larry Gossett, whose official title was noted
as coordinator of Washington and Oregon Black Student Unions, sug-
gesting that campuses in Oregon remained part of the Seattle BSU's
sphere of influence. As reported in the *Seattle Post-Intelligencer*, the rally
drew a crowd of about one hundred mostly white students who "contributed to a 'defense fund' of bail money for the San Francisco students."[37]

After final exams and the winter break, the BSU resumed its outspokenness in January 1968. One of its first actions was lobbying campus
officials for a blackboard to be installed in the student union building
near an area where the Black students typically congregated. Eddie
Demmings remembered,

> We went to the administration of the HUB [Husky Union Building] and
> we said we want a blackboard put up in the area where we sit together
> so we can communicate with the other black students. And they did it,
> without any fuss or fight. And in a certain sense, as miniscule as that was,
> that was a very empowering act for us.[38]

Although trivial by some standards, the blackboard was a utilitarian victory that assisted communication and coordination within the group,
and it confirmed the belief that Black students could successfully petition for the university to address their concerns.

In February the Black Student Union was featured in the UW student newspaper, the *Daily*. The article, titled "New Black Image Emerging," described the new organization and quoted several BSU members discussing their philosophy and goals. Dan Keith, the inaugural BSU president, explained that the group changed its name from Afro-American Student Society "because of a new-found awareness of the common goals and problems of the non-white community." In specifics, the group aimed to increase the enrollment of Black students, along with other students of color, and push for a Black Studies department. E. J. Brisker, BSU vice president, added, "Today's black students are defining for themselves what their cultural values will be. . . . For this very reason we would like to see incorporated into the University a black curriculum of studies, a department planned, controlled, and influenced by the black community." Reflecting the BSU strategy, the report also noted, "The BSU hopes to form a power base from which to present certain demands to the university administration." The article outlined the BSU's vision for Black Studies as an interdisciplinary department and an undergraduate major that incorporated "black history, music, literature, and sociology." The students envisioned that the new Black Studies courses would serve all students regardless of race: "The classes would be open to white students, stressed Brisker."[39] This multiracial model of Black Studies contrasted with an intraracial model, which held that the new discipline should highly prioritize serving African Americans.

Sociologist Fabio Rojas elaborated on intraracial Black Studies using the term "community education," while analyzing Black Studies proposals at the University of Chicago and the University of Illinois at Chicago during the late 1960s and early 1970s. He wrote,

> At the two Chicago campuses, individuals proposed two versions of black studies, which I call "community education" and "academic black studies." Community education refers to black studies aimed at providing training for individuals who would teach or do social work in the African American community. Another goal for community education was educating African American and other urban minorities, rather than teaching whites about black history and culture.[40]

Interestingly, the BSU at UW did not pursue this intraracial or "community education" model of Black Studies, despite its commitment to community service and ongoing involvement in grassroots organizing. Likely, the Seattle students astutely judged that a model of Black Studies that served Black *and* white students would be the most palatable to university administrators, as was the case at the schools studied by Rojas.[41]

Two other distinctive characteristics of the BSU at UW were revealed in the "New Black Image Emerging" feature. The first was the BSU's multiracial membership. The piece indicated that the organization included "black students of American and African origin, as well as Indians [meaning Native American] and South Americans."[42] One of the indigenous BSU members was Marcie Hall-McMurtrie, a member of the Colville Confederated Tribes who grew up on the Colville Reservation in north-central Washington. Hall-McMurtrie entered UW in 1967 as part of the Upward Bound program, and became close friends with fellow Black students and staff in the program. These relationships led to her joining the BSU once it was established.[43] She described her BSU involvement as a component of her wider activism against the Vietnam War and related leftist struggles:

> We had a big thing about the ROTC [Reserve Officers Training Corps] being on campus. We were really bothered about that, and of course the Vietnam War, and so it was political upheaval, honestly. And there were all kinds of meetings. . . . I would go to the meetings at the University of Washington for the Black Student Union and we had this tiny little room that we went into. You could barely fit twelve people in the place.[44]

Although it was called the *Black* Student Union and always held central the betterment of Black Americans, the BSU supported other people of color and advocated for their betterment.

The second noteworthy characteristic mentioned in the article was the BSU's potential for militancy. The BSU stated its intention to work with university officials, but warned of disruptive actions if the administration was uncooperative. When asked by the reporter whether disruptive protests like what had happened at other schools were a possibility, several members answered in the affirmative. Encapsulating the sentiment, "Gossett declared, 'Our militancy is entirely dependent on the white reaction to the concrete proposals we make. It is the white communities' responsibility."[45]

One aspect of the BSU that the article did not reflect was the organization's female membership. During the BSU's first year there were about twenty core members, of which approximately 25 percent were female. In addition to Verlaine Keith-Miller and Marcie Hall-McMurtrie, described above, another Black woman in the group was Kathleen "Kathy" Halley, also known as Nafasi.[46] According to BSU member Emile Pitre, the most prominent leaders of the BSU included Verlaine Keith-Miller and Kathleen Halley, along with Brisker, Gossett, Demmings, and Carl Miller.[47] Another Native American young woman, Carmelita Laducer, was also an active BSU member.[48] Thus, women in the BSU played crucial roles in the formation and actions of the organization, even if they tended not to make public statements or newspaper appearances. For a range of reasons, they willingly accepted, or were assigned to, supportive roles in the group.[49] Speaking on this, Keith-Miller said, "Yeah, I think in terms of the roles women play, we're always subordinate, or seemed to be." Keith-Miller identified this patriarchal pattern in society at large and in the BSU, but also added that she personally was not upset about it at the time. Describing her BSU experience, she added, "I mean, they didn't exclude us, but I think [in the BSU] the people being interviewed, and on the news were the Black guys, which was just kind of okay with me because my parents were not champions of it anyway. And I never liked being on camera."[50] Performing behind-the-scenes work like answering phone calls, writing correspondence, setting up meetings, and taking notes, female members kept the group functioning from day to day.[51] Moreover, female members fully matched their male counterparts' courage, passion, and dedication. Later, by 1970, women in the group openly challenged patriarchal patterns and took more visible leadership positions.[52]

Following the "New Black Image Emerging" article, the next day's student paper included a statement written by the Black Student Union articulating its critique of the campus:

Who needs "whitey?" Who really needs "whitey?" . . . "Whitey" is a "stuffed-shirt" administration. "Whitey" is that professor who at mid-quarter tells you your class behavior is antithetic to anything he calls in-

terest, motivation, drive or intelligence, and this one really gets you, 'cause
he hardly knows your name. As a matter of fact, he never really knew you
at all! . . . You're the only black student in the class, and you are simply fed
up with this low-calorie bombardment so that your times away from the
University become cherished, for then you can be alone. For many black
students, even those who are afraid to admit it, this is a constant reality.
Now is the time for the black student to become an integral part of the
University scene.[53]

Written with the colloquialisms and rhetorical style of contemporaneous Black youth culture, this piece expressed the frustrations of Black
UW students. Here with its attack on "whitey," the BSU is joining
other Black Power adherents in utilizing intentionally confrontational
discourse. Doing so—namely, insisting on expressing oneself without
regard for white sensibilities—embodied an assertion of empowerment
and self-determination. Interestingly, this statement also indicates how
experiences of Black students at predominately white institutions in the
1960s have much in common with student experiences in our own time.

In addition to its statements in the student newspaper, the Black Student Union also directly addressed UW president Charles Odegaard in a
letter around the same time. The epistle called for a list of reforms: more
Black professors, counselors, and teaching assistants; classes in Afro-
American history, culture, and literature; African language courses; and
a university program to encourage Black students to graduate from college. In addition, the BSU letter demanded positive steps be taken to
eliminate racism in the athletic department, sorority and fraternity system, housing, and employment. In summary, it advocated for the university to be a leader within higher education in terms of initiatives to
serve African Americans. In its closing, the BSU boldly declared, "We
feel the University of a thousand years does not need another thousand
to determine action on these proposals. If you, Dr. Odegaard, do not act
promptly, we shall use any means that we deem necessary to ensure that
freedom and justice prevail on this campus."[54]

Building Relationships and Earning Allies, Spring 1968

To build its base of support, the Black Student Union launched two campaigns during the first months of 1968. One was an off-campus effort to foster auxiliary Black Student Unions at local secondary and postsecondary schools. The other was an on-campus campaign to raise awareness about the Eurocentric nature of the curriculum. Both projects successfully won support that the BSU would utilize to confront university leaders later in the school year.

In the off-campus recruitment and organizing drive, the BSU at UW worked with middle school and high school-aged youth to create auxiliary BSU chapters throughout Seattle. This type of outreach was a fundamental part of the BSU strategy, as it promoted linkages between the college students and local Black families. Often, the auxiliary BSUs began with personal connections; for instance, some BSU members had younger siblings in the K-12 schools. BSU member Aaron Dixon's younger brother, Elmer, was at Garfield High School; Larry Gossett had a brother, Richard, at Franklin High School, and a sister, Sharon, at Marshall Junior High.[55] These connections provided a starting point for organizing. Yet, not surprisingly given the official opposition to Stokely Carmichael's appearance at Garfield the previous spring, some school administrators tried to stymie the grade school BSUs. For instance, Elmer Dixon recalled that he and his comrades at Garfield were allowed to have a BSU only after a series of protests, often at school assemblies and pep rallies. "So we began to do disruptions at school, which resulted in me being kicked out of school five or six times. . . . The first thing that we did collectively—there were about six or seven of us—was that we refused to stand up for the Pledge of Allegiance [at school events]."[56] Dixon was conspicuous and a target for school discipline because he not only protested the Pledge of Allegiance, but also did so from his seat in the school band. These "disruptions" escalated over the coming weeks and culminated in a brief but effective boycott when students refused to enter their classrooms during a break between classes and amassed in the hallway. Dixon and his group had wide support from Black students and many white, Japanese, and Chinese students. Consequently, there were so many students in the hall that "it was impossible for even the principals to get out of their office." Seeing this show of force, the school officials finally approved the BSU's formation.[57] Sharon Gossett remembered similar challenges at Marshall Junior High.[58] Nevertheless, the high school and junior high BSUs were eventually established all over Seattle, particularly at schools with high enrollments of African American students.[59] Gossett described the successful outcomes of the recruitment effort:

> In January, by the end of January, we had organized BSU at Garfield, Franklin, Rainier Beach and Cleveland high schools. We had organized Black Student Unions at the junior high level at Washington, Meany, Asa Mercer, and Sharples. All, as you'll note, inner-city. However, because High Point [a low-income housing project] is out in West Seattle and a lot of Black students went to Chief Sealth, we had organized a Black Student Union at Chief Sealth High School too.[60]

Adding to these successes, the BSU at UW also organized sibling student unions at Immaculate High School, a Catholic all-girls institution, Seattle University, Seattle Central College, and Seattle Pacific University.[61] Having established BSUs all over the city, Gossett estimated that by March 1968 the combined membership of BSUs citywide totaled around nine hundred youths.[62] Moreover, all of these BSU chapters were joined together in the Seattle Alliance of Black Student Unions (SABSU). "Alliance members . . . met as frequently as once a week to discuss how to confront the problems facing Seattle's black students."[63] Each Sunday afternoon, throughout the spring of 1968, Gossett and other BSU members from UW met with representatives from the other student unions. This extensive outreach by Black UW students strengthened vital linkages with local youth. Furthermore, the UW students also conducted home visits where the collegians spoke directly to the parents of their adolescent recruits. During these visits, UW BSU members respectfully explained the purpose and goals of the BSU and requested the guardians' consent for their child's involvement. This gesture of deference toward the parents helped cement support for the BSU from adults in the Black community, some of whom were no doubt wary about their teenager getting involved in Black Power activism.[64] As described by Larry Gossett,

The majority of the Black kids in each of the BSUs that I've just spo-
ken to you about, us older cats—like Larry Gossett, Carl Miller, Aaron
Dixon—we went to their house. And I told their parents that "we'd like
for your kid to be involved in the BSU." But we told them that we're not
gonna let them be involved, or stay involved, if we don't talk to their parents and get their blessing. I'm telling you, Marc, that was one of the—I
didn't realize it until years later—smartest thing we could have done.[65]

Gossett estimated that he and the other "older cats" visited about sev-
enty to eighty homes as they organized the auxiliary BSUs, a significant
investment of time and energy, even if it did not constitute the majority
of the estimated nine hundred Black youth involved. Likely, the home
visits concentrated on a core group of BSU adherents at the various
schools. Gossett remembered that during these discussions with parents, some were initially skeptical of the BSU, but none said no to the
request for their child's involvement. And later, when BSU members
faced arrest and prosecution related to their activism, these meetings
"paid dividends" in terms of community support.[66]

In tandem with the community efforts, the BSU also mounted a si-
multaneous public awareness campaign on campus designed to dramatize the validity of its grievances. During the early months of 1968, the
BSU called attention to the white normativity and institutional racism
of the University of Washington, especially the curriculum. This project
was rooted in the members' personal experiences in UW courses, where
they found a near total omission of content on people of color. Whether
it was history, literature, psychology, or social work, the BSU faced entrenched Eurocentrism, an experience that also mirrored the standard
materials taught throughout the nation. Black students at UW and
elsewhere were fed up with faculty lectures and assigned readings that
marginalized and belittled the contributions of Black scholars, artists,
and intellectuals. For example, Eddie Walker, BSU member and resident
artist of the group, was outraged by an art professor who told him that
"there weren't any black artists of national merit." Walker knew this to be
patently false because he had collected "books listing African American
artists of international repute"; he was therefore quite frustrated about
the "miseducation" he was paying for at the university.[67]

To challenge this institutional and curricular racism, the BSU first conducted a survey to substantiate its allegation of a systemic bias in UW courses. The BSU found "that of the three thousand main course offerings in the Arts and Humanities, not only did no class deal with the Black experience but we couldn't find one professor or instructor that used a book written by or about African Americans, Asians, Native Americans, or Latinos."[68] The study confirmed what Eddie Walker and other Black students already knew, that the curriculum was dominated by covert and overt assumptions of white supremacy and normativity.

Emboldened by its findings, the BSU next started interrupting college courses with impromptu teach-ins to dramatize the issues and highlight the need for Black Studies. The Black student activists prepared for these interventions by conducting research beforehand and then used the information gathered to confront faculty and students. Arriving unexpectedly in the targeted class, BSU members would walk in and start talking, saying, for example, "This is an institutionally racist campus and the curriculum is racist." Then, if it was a colonial American history class, members would say something like "Y'all in here learning about old George Washington and Thomas Jefferson and calling them your forefathers. They might be your forefathers, but they were much more likely to be our daddies, our slave owning daddies."[69] Statements like these were intentionally provocative, but also raised valid information. Here, they highlighted the tragic history of rape and sexual exploitation of enslaved Black women by slave-owning white men, which often produced offspring, as in the well-documented case of Thomas Jefferson and Sally Hemings. This is what the BSU members were referencing when they said that Jefferson and Washington were likely their "slave owning daddies."

The BSU continued, "They cannot be our forefathers and you need to ask these kinds of questions about whether or not they're yours if their humanity did not include anything but white folks with property." The Black militants then described African Americans of the American Revolutionary period whom they viewed as more deserving of veneration, such as Crispus Attucks, Peter Salem, Salem Poor, and Richard Allen.[70]

Teach-ins like this raised awareness on campus for the need for curricular reform, and showcased the validity of the BSU's assessments. While confrontational, these classroom demonstrations indicated that

BSU members had a level of intelligence that matched their boldness, and that their criticisms were valid and well researched. All of this was part of a deliberate strategy to win support from white faculty and students. Similarly, according to Eddie Demmings, the BSU also held weekly seminars for a time, wherein white students attended voluntarily and learned about the organization's actions and goals. Elaborating on their strategic outreach, Demmings said,

> As far as the white students—I mean, we weren't dumb. We recognized that getting the support of white students was a key part of what we needed to do. We campaigned hard on campus to get the white students to support what we were doing. . . . Many white students supported the BSU, but it didn't happen by accident. We actively sought out their support.[71]

Concurring with Demmings, Larry Gossett remembered that these consciousness-raising efforts established a certain level of legitimacy for the BSU and "helped the white students not be real hostile toward us by the time we had the sit-in [in May]."[72] Of course, many white students and faculty remained opposed to the BSU, but overall this public relations effort was effective in garnering political capital for the coming direct-action protests.

The BSU Further Radicalized, March–April 1968

In March and April 1968, a cascade of historic events added new urgency to the Black Student Union's mission at the University of Washington; these included a local high school protest, the assassination of Martin Luther King Jr., and the funeral of Black Panther Bobby Hutton. The first episode centered on Franklin High School, where on March 29 an estimated one hundred Black students took over principal Loren Ralph's office and forced the school into early dismissal.[73] The civil disobedience was led by the Franklin BSU and its leaders, Trolice Flavors and Charles Oliver, along with Aaron Dixon, Larry Gossett, Eddie Demmings, and Carl Miller of the BSU at UW. Sources differ on the direct cause of the confrontation. According to Larry Gossett, the protest was ignited when school officials expelled two Black female students for wearing the "natural" or "Afro" hairstyle.[74] "Gossett recalled Ralph told the young women that they can return to school when they learned to look more 'ladylike,'" thereby insulting natural Black hair as uncomely and unfeminine.[75] Contemporary newspaper accounts, by contrast, hold that the protest followed the suspension of Charles Oliver and Trolice Flavors after a hallway scuffle on March 28, a day before the protest.[76] Reportedly, many of Franklin's African American students were outraged that only Oliver and Flavors were punished for the fight, while the white student or students involved were not reprimanded.[77] Undoubtedly, both occurrences could have contributed to the conflict, along with other racial grievances at Franklin High. In a *Seattle Post-Intelligencer* article that ran in June of that year, Edward P. Morgan, a national racism critic, identified Franklin as a "sick school.[78] Thus, evidence suggests that school officials had a pattern of prejudicial policies, and this context almost certainly helped spark the March 29 protest.[79]

After learning of his punishment for the hallway fight, Trolice Flavors made a special appeal to Principal Ralph for reconsideration because he was given an especially harsh penalty. Both Oliver and Flavors were suspended, but Flavors was also accused of "making a physical threat to Franklin Vice-Principal Charles F. Shearer and was suspended immediately and indefinitely."[80] Since Flavors was a senior, this basically amounted to an expulsion that threatened his ability to graduate. When direct appeals to Ralph failed to remedy the situation, Flavors contacted Carl Miller of the BSU at UW. Miller then contacted Dr. Eugene Elliot, assistant to UW president Odegaard, and asked him to try and arrange a meeting with Ralph the next day. Miller and the other BSU members hoped that with the help of the UW officials, Ralph could be persuaded to reduce the punishments.[81] Yet, by the following day, Ralph had refused all mediation, leaving Flavors and the other Franklin students few options.

Consequently, on a rainy Seattle Friday, Miller, Gossett, Demmings, and Dixon went to the school to help the teenagers coordinate a protest, knowing that the Franklin situation was growing tense. Once there, they found that the high schoolers literally wanted to "burn the school down" as an act of political vandalism, but the college students persuaded them to take a different approach during an impromptu planning meeting at the Beanery, an eatery across the street from the school. There, the

UW and high school students formed a plan that would allow the teens to express their objections without destroying school property. At approximately 12:45 p.m., one hundred students marched in to Ralph's office chanting "Ungawa, Black Power!"[82] This crowd likely included Black students from other Seattle high and junior high schools, especially Garfield High. Led by Gossett and Miller, the students "marched two abreast" from the eatery to the school to demand that Flavors be reinstated and other concessions. The group "proceeded into the administrative office, drowning out the pleas of the little white secretary," who tried in vain to get them to leave.[83] Not only did the demonstrators at Franklin call for leniency for Trolice Flavors and Charles Oliver, they also pushed for more Black and other teachers of color to serve non-white Franklin students. In addition, the group challenged the exclusion of Black people in the curriculum and visual culture of the school, calling for the creation of an African American history class, and for the posting of images of Black heroes on school walls alongside other historical figures already featured.[84] Using the moment to call for greater reform highlights the astuteness of the high school and college BSU members.

Ralph and other school officials were surprised and unprepared for the protest. At about 1:45 p.m., after trying unsuccessfully to disperse the demonstration, Ralph cancelled all school activities for the rest of the day and evacuated the building.[85] Seattle police arrived on the scene around this time, sealed off the building, and surrounded it with officers.[86] Demonstrating the great alarm the protest caused among school and civic authorities, the local police also amassed nearby, apparently preparing to storm the Franklin school building. According to Gossett,

Seattle responded by sending 65 percent of the police . . . to surround Franklin High School. They didn't know how to deal with it. Can you imagine—a sit-in in Seattle? They said that stuff happens down South, not up here. So they said something must be wrong, some virus or something has infected our Negro youth. So they sent most of the police. And at that time, Lowes [hardware store] . . . in Rainier Valley, that used to be Sicks Stadium, it was a baseball stadium in Seattle right below Franklin. So they mobilized the entire police force in the parking lot of Sicks Stadium. Can you imagine? It's a baseball stadium so it had a big parking lot. So, while

we were sitting-in, some of our people went down there and they got a
message back to us that "it looked like the whole force was at Sicks Stadium ready to attack Franklin if you'all don't leave." And we said, "We're
not going to leave."[87]

Despite the ominous police presence at the stadium about half a mile
from the school, the protesters insisted on continuing their sit-in
until their demands were addressed. Fortunately, a police action was
prevented by the arrival of community leaders from the Central Area
Motivating Program (CAMP) and staff of the Seattle Schools' Intergroup
Relations Office. They persuaded the sit-in participants to accept a compromise, which stipulated a meeting the following Monday to discuss
their demands and racial issues at Franklin High. At 3:45 p.m., the students accepted the offer and left the building.

That following Monday, April 1, the agreed-upon meeting occurred,
hosted by the local Human Rights Commission. The students were allowed to express their concerns and the suspensions of Flavors and Oliver were reversed due to "discrepancies in the testimony concerning
the . . . suspensions."[88] Overall, the meeting was a qualified victory for
the BSU. However, at the meeting, Seattle schools superintendent Forbes
Bottomly hinted at possible legal action against the protesters, saying,
"We want to be sure that the loitering ordinance is upheld and that the
schools are protected from outsiders coming in and disrupting our
schools."[89] Apparently, Bottomly and other school officials were intent
on responding to the protest as if it was a product of outside agitators
and lawbreakers, rather than the result of the school's discriminatory
policies. Consequently, on April 4, three days after the meeting, Aaron
Dixon, Carl Miller, Trolice Flavors, Larry Gossett, and his younger
brother Richard were all arrested by Seattle police and charged with unlawful assembly. Clearly in a coordinated effort, most of the arrests occurred between 8:30 a.m. and 9:30 a.m.[90]

The students' arrests and detention in King County Jail also occurred on the same day that Martin Luther King Jr. was assassinated,
a tragic event that set off Black outrage nationwide. Although most in
the Black Power movement questioned King's philosophies of nonviolence and moral suasion, his death was still marked with sadness and
consternation. The murder of Dr. King, precisely in spite of his steadfast

advocacy of nonviolence, convinced many in the Black movement that intransigent white Americans would repress and even kill anyone who challenged the prevailing racial hierarchy, no matter how benign that challenge might be.[91] As Aaron Dixon recalled, King's death

> began a series of riots and rebellions all across the country. And there were rebellions in Seattle that night as well. And the fact that Martin Luther King had been assassinated I think for me and for many, many other, not only Black people across the country but other young people across the country, it was a signal to us that it was—that no longer did we feel that peaceful demonstrations were going to work. That we were now going to look toward other methods of demonstrating and getting our point across.[92]

King's assassination marked a turning point for Black activists nationwide, as many agreed with Dixon's sentiments. Walt Crowley, a Seattle-based writer and local historian, documented that on the night of King's murder, "Central Area youths pelted buses and cars with rocks and torched four local businesses."[93]

It might seem reasonable to speculate that the arrests of the BSU members from Franklin and UW were in part motivated by King's assassination and the resulting unrest. If the students were already viewed as troublemakers, local authorities might have concluded that having the BSU members in jail would help thwart large-scale protests in Seattle. Yet the timing suggests that this was not the case, given that most of the arrests happened in the morning and King's murder occurred at approximately three o'clock in the afternoon, Pacific Standard Time.

For the young men arrested in Seattle following the Franklin sit-in, King's murder had an added significance because of their experience in jail. While in the King County Jail, the BSU members and other inmates learned of King's death. Initially, some of the Black inmates wanted to vent their anger at King's loss by attacking their fellow white inmates. However, as they did during the Franklin sit-in, the BSU members de-escalated the situation by leading all the inmates, Black and white, in a discussion of the day's significance. "Dixon, Gossett, and Miller counseled against any violence, persuading the inmates that taking out their anger in a violent fashion would not honor King's legacy. The BSU leaders decided to gather all the inmates and encourage them to talk about their personal problems and current world affairs."[94] Thus, what could have become a prison riot was redirected into dialogue. One might imagine that the jail authorities would have appreciated this calming influence of the young activists. But, to the contrary, once officials learned of these jailhouse conversations, they expedited the arraignment and release of the BSU leaders:

> Later that night, the word got out [that] we were having discussions throughout the whole jail and by that morning the director of the King County Jail was demanding that the three of us [Gossett, Miller, and Dixon] get put out of jail. That had never happened, where the jail commander says, "Get these people out of this jail. They're actually having prisoners talk and work with one another." That was an outrageous thing to them, that prisoners would be talking about their own self-interests and what they could do collectively to exercise that.[95]

On April 5, Gossett, Dixon, and Miller were brought into court with Judge James J. Dore presiding. Several hundred people attended the hearing in support of the defendants, who were brought in with handcuffs and chains around their wrists, waists, and ankles. Describing the scene, Gossett recalled, "They had the guards holding the chains, about four feet in back of us, as they brought the three of us in the court, you know, like we were the coldest murderers that ever hit Seattle, not some people that had been busted for a misdemeanor [unlawful assembly]."[96] The purpose of the hearing was to determine whether the defendants should continue to be held in jail on $1,500 bail until their trial. After hearing statements "from an array of friends, relatives, UW faculty" and the defendants themselves, testifying that the students were respectable in character and would show up for the trial, Judge Dore released the students on personal recognizance and no bail requirement. In response, "the group of 400 people that sat in the courtroom cheered."[97] This controversial court case would continue in the summer with eventual convictions that were later overturned, but at this point the legal proceeding receded into the background for the BSU.[98]

Within days after their release from custody, the radicalizing experiences continued when BSU members traveled to the San Francisco

Bay Area of California and attended a second Black empowerment conference, held at San Francisco State University.[99] On April 6, around the start of the conference, local police clashed with the Black Panther Party in nearby Oakland. Hostility between the police and the Panthers stemmed from the latter's outspoken advocacy of Black Power, harsh criticism of police brutality, and armed surveillance of police actions.[100] In the ensuing April 6 shootout, police gunfire killed Black Panther Bobby Hutton and wounded Eldridge Cleaver, another Panther, leaving the organization stricken with grief and anger.[101]

This controversy surrounding the shooting affected African Americans throughout the Oakland-San Francisco area and dominated the conference. The chairman of the Black Panther Party, Bobby Seale, delivered the convention's keynote address and conference participants attended Bobby Hutton's funeral. As Gossett described, the Seattle activists were profoundly moved by the Panthers:

[We] were immensely impressed with the discipline and the solidarity and the youthfulness of the Black Panther Party on that visit because we went to Oakland, to his funeral, and we saw about a thousand Black men and women in leather coats and black berets and shades, and very disciplined as revolutionaries, talking about they would continue to work for Black Power, they would continue to work for revolutionary change.[102]

Following the funeral, Bobby Seale gave a speech that was a rousing call to action. Remembering it years later, Dixon said it was "one of the most inspiring speeches that I have ever heard, even up until this point. And you could tell that he was in a lot of pain, but even though he was in a lot of pain he was still very defiant in terms of what he was talking about."[103] That Bay Area trip had a deep impact on the conference attendees from UW, and the Seattle chapter of the Black Panther Party was established shortly thereafter, the first chapter outside California.[104] On April 14, 1968, Seale traveled to Seattle to guide the formation of the Seattle Black Panthers. Dixon remembered, "Then a week later [after the conference], he [Seale] came to Seattle and stayed at my parents' house. We met with him with about twenty other people from the community, and we sat down for a couple of days talking about the Black Panther Party and Huey P. Newton [who co-founded the party with Seale]." After these meetings, Seale approved the new chapter and appointed Aaron Dixon as captain.[105] The fact that the Black Student Union in Seattle was the precursor to the city's Black Panther Party is significant, as it reflects the far-reaching reverberations of BSU activities. The Seattle Panthers pursued several years of activism that stretched into the mid-1970s and included free breakfast programs, a medical clinic, and other social services. Moreover, the fact that the BSU facilitated the Seattle Panthers' establishment contradicts and complicates the account in *Black against Empire: The History and Politics of the Black Panther Party*, by Joshua Bloom and Waldo E. Martin Jr. There, Bloom and Martin mischaracterize all Black Student Unions as an offshoot of the Black Panther Party.[106] This clearly was not the case in Seattle, and not the case in Oakland/ San Francisco, where the first BSU was established approximately seven months before Huey Newton and Bobby Seale formed the Panthers; the BSU at San Francisco State was established in March 1966, as detailed in the previous chapter, and the Black Panthers started later that year, in October. Thus, while there was considerable overlap between the BSU and Panthers in Oakland, Seattle, and elsewhere, the research here shows that the BSU deserves to be recognized as a co-equal branch of the Black Power movement, rather than merely an extension of the Black Panther Party.

This succession of radicalizing experiences in March and April 1968 galvanized the BSU at UW to take stronger action, as described in the next chapter. The cascading effects of the Franklin protest and arrests, Martin Luther King Jr.'s assassination, and exposure to the Bay Area Black Panthers was a collective catalyst to further radicalism of the BSU, and confirmed the organization's conviction that it was a part of a larger historical moment with truly revolutionary potential. In May the BSU's passion for justice was refocused back onto the UW campus and, come what may, the students were determined to achieve concrete progress on their demands before the school year's end.

This chapter began with vignettes of two notable BSU members, Verlaine Keith-Miller and Larry Gossett. It also chronicled the formation of the Black Student Union at the University of Washington and its early activities between November 1967 and May 1968. The preceding pages examined the group's origin and early organizing efforts, which are impressive for their hard work, sophistication, and success. The

BSU's campaign to raise awareness about the need to challenge Euro-centrism and white normativity in the university's curriculum, and its efforts to organize and mentor auxiliary BSU groups in Seattle schools make clear that the Black Student Union was mounting effective out-reach campaigns on and off campus. This contradicts the conventional narrative of Black Power, which casts it as entirely counterproductive, antisocial, and disconnected from the grassroots. This chapter also re-counted how a series of politically charged developments in March and April further radicalized the BSU, so that by May the group was primed for a major show of political force. In the next chapter, we will see how the BSU's determination soon materialized into a direct-action protest that transformed the University of Washington.

3

"We Tired of Y'all's Half-Stepping"

The BSU's May 1968 Sit-In and Its Aftermath

It is hard to overstate the tumult of 1968. From the Tet Offensive in February, which shook Americans' confidence that their government was winning the Vietnam War, to the April assassination of Martin Luther King Jr., to the June assassination of Robert Kennedy, to the August street battles in Chicago between police and protesters outside the Democratic National Convention, and more, 1968 was an especially turbulent year in US history. In addition, on the global scale, leftist and youth-oriented protests were happening around the world. As ethnic studies scholar Carlos Muñoz Jr. described the foment of 1968 and the surrounding years,

> We had youth emerging as protagonists in the human drama of revolu-
> tionary struggle. It was a historical moment that was very unique, not
> only in the history of our country, the USA, but also the world. Because
> there was not only a youth rebellion here, in this country, in this part of
> the world, but it was all over the world. [It was] in Africa, Latin America,
> Europe, Asia—you name it, it was happening.[1]

With this national and international wave of confrontations with established power, it should not surprise us that Seattle too was a site of struggle. Indeed, as noted by local journalist and historian Walt Crowley, the Emerald City had its share of discontent. Consider the month of April as a representative example. On April 5, the day after King's murder, Black youth in the Central District vented their frustrations by throwing rocks at "buses and cars" and setting fires to "four local businesses."[2] Two days later, "nine thousand mourners filled Memorial Stadium" for Seattle's tribute to King.[3] Later that month, on April 27, an estimated two thousand Seattleites marched from the King

County Court House to the Seattle Center to express their opposition to the Vietnam War.[4] Despite Seattle's relative geographical distance from urban centers like New York City and Chicago, the reverberations of national events were deeply felt in the city.

Given the spirit of youthful rebellion that marked the 1960s, and especially the late 1960s, college campuses were active battlegrounds for social, political, and ideological struggles. For instance, the student strike at San Francisco State University began in November 1968 and continued into the following spring.[5] Similarly, a major protest occurred at the University of Washington at Seattle (UW) when the BSU launched a takeover of the university president's office. This event would prove to be a crucial turning point for race relations at the institution, and a number of groundbreaking reforms materialized thereafter. The BSU compelled UW to expand access and opportunities for African Americans and other people of color, establishing greater equity at the school.

Aaron Dixon and E. J. Brisker

Aaron Dixon and E. J. Brisker are two BSU members who played key roles in this period of the BSU. Their backgrounds provide additional context to this history. For those familiar with the life of Aaron Dixon, he is most known for serving as the founding "captain," or leader, of the Seattle chapter of the Black Panther Party. He held that position from 1968 to 1972, after which he moved to Oakland to work for the Panthers' Central Committee.[6] Dixon's time as the Panther captain brought a high degree of local media attention and earned him ardent admirers and harsh critics. Yet, as we saw in the previous chapter, the Black Student Union predated the Black Panthers in Seattle. Before Dixon was a Panther, he was active in the Black Student Union at the University of Washington.

At the age of eight, in 1957, Dixon moved to Seattle from Chicago with his family and soon settled into a racially "mixed neighborhood called Madrona Hill in Seattle's Central District."[7] A generation earlier, Dixon's parents had migrated as children from the South to Chicago. His mother, Frances Emma Sledge, was born in Mississippi, and his father, Elmer Dixon Jr., was from Kentucky; both moved to Chicago during the 1920s.[8] In high school, Aaron Dixon's budding political consciousness was stimulated by Stokely Carmichael. As mentioned in chapter 1, Carmichael visited Seattle on April 19, 1967, and his evening lecture was delivered in the auditorium of Dixon's Garfield High School.[9] Sitting in the front row of the packed gymnasium, young Aaron was inspired by Carmichael's message of Black pride and political empowerment. Soon after, he joined the Seattle chapter of the Student Nonviolent Coordinating Committee and became increasingly involved in the Black Power movement. After high school, he enrolled at UW in the fall of 1967 and subsequently helped establish the Black Student Union there.[10]

Based on his memoir and public persona, Aaron Dixon was something of a tough guy. As an adolescent, he hung with a "tough crowd" and got into numerous fistfights.[11] Later, his cool bravado was on full display in an iconic 1968 cover of *Seattle Magazine* where Dixon defiantly sits in a police car. He confidently leans out of the front window and stares straight at the viewer. The photograph expresses a bold challenge to established authority and is a fitting representation of Dixon's swashbuckling image.[12] Yet BSU member Verlaine Keith-Miller recalled that Dixon was not always so serious. She described a story where the two, as "a lark," playfully "stole a watermelon from some little store" and ate it while studying. Keith-Miller continued, "So we would have our books and our snacks for the munchies. And just, you know, study. Actually, those were fun times."[13] This lighthearted recollection hints at Dixon's playful side, and reflects the fact that BSU members were still fun-loving college students, despite their serious political activities.

E. J. Brisker was another prominent BSU member. Emanuel James Brisker was born in St. Louis, Missouri. By the fifth grade, he had lived in Oakland, California, and the Louisiana towns of Rayville and Monroe, before returning to St. Louis, where he remained until he finished high school. In 1960 he graduated near the top of his class from the city's prestigious, and previously all-white, William Beaumont High School. Unfortunately, Brisker's academic success did not spare him from bias and discrimination at the school. Characterizing his experience, Brisker wrote that he was part of a small group of Black students who "survived the racist teachers, administration, and student body" at the elite institution.[14] Undoubtably, Brisker's high intellectual abilities and his experiences at Beaumont helped inspire his ensuing political activism.

After high school, Brisker enrolled at Morehouse College, where he was the editorial editor for the student newspaper, *Maroon Tiger*. At Morehouse, he joined the local civil rights movement, beginning with Atlanta's sit-in protests in 1960 and 1961. In 1964 Brisker left Morehouse to be a full-time organizer for the Student Nonviolent Coordinating Committee in Mississippi. That same year, he was part of Freedom Summer, which famously brought mostly white college students to Mississippi to help seasoned organizers create Freedom Schools and register Black voters. Brisker coordinated three Freedom Schools in Canton, Mississippi. By 1967, Brisker had relocated to Seattle, but remained a part of SNCC, serving that year as chairman of Seattle SNCC's Internal Education Committee. As BSU member Emile Pitre remembered it, Brisker was specifically sent to Seattle by the national SNCC office after a request from Carl Miller for someone to help Seattle SNCC increase its impact.[15]

In the fall of 1967, Brisker was part of the delegation from Seattle that attended the Western Regional Black Youth Conference, and returned determined to organize a Black Student Union at the University of Washington. Brisker officially enrolled as a UW student in January 1968, and later helped Dixon and others establish the Black Panther Party of Seattle.[16] In the BSU, Brisker's official title was vice president, but within the first months of 1968 he emerged as the de facto leader of the group, as the BSU president, Dan Keith, faded into the background. Pitre recalled,

> E. J. Brisker was the vice president at the time. And the more the group [BSU] became militant, if you will, the more Danny Keith and some people from his group started to stop attending. So I really thought of it as, pretty much as a coup. E. J. Brisker pretty much just really took over the leadership; he started to become the spokesman. But he was the most knowledgeable politically. He had the deepest political consciousness. He was very bright.[17]

When BSU veterans recall Brisker and his impact on the organization, they commonly used words like "brilliant" or "very bright." In nearly every interview, respondents mentioned Brisker's outstanding intellect, as did Pitre in the previous quote. Just as James Garrett, a BSU member from San Francisco State, said, "Now, E. J. Brisker was a brilliant—I mean, E. J. Brisker, an encyclopedic memory, brilliant guy. I need to say that. He was a brilliant, brilliant guy."[18] Similarly, BSU veteran Larry Gossett mentioned Brisker's outstanding intelligence when describing how both of them led Seattle Black Panther study groups: "I remember the study groups. The Black Panther Party was one; they were serious about study. Because E. J. Brisker and I did a lot of the study groups. E. J. did more than any of us, though. That was a brilliant cat."[19] Elaborating, Pitre added a brief description of Brisker's reading prowess: "And [he] could read, you know, just turning the page, he was reading. He was a speed reader."[20] These descriptions, generally given with no particular prompting from the interviewer, clearly indicate that Brisker's mental abilities were widely recognized and respected within the BSU. Therefore, it is not surprising that he quickly emerged as the de facto leader of the organization, given his intelligence and experience in the southern civil rights movement.

Yet Brisker was no mere bookworm. Given that he became the most prominent member of a strident Black Power group, the Black Student Union, it should not surprise us that Brisker was also described as the "most bold" member of the group, and as a leading "risk-taker." Brisker's 1970 résumé gives a glimpse of his boldness, along with a spirited irreverence that might also be read as comedic. For example, near the top of the résumé, it says, "Key Distinguishing Feature: Beautifully Black." Similarly, he introduced the education section that listed schools attended with the following statement: "Before you read this section, it is important that you understand that in spite of these institutions I have somehow not gone insane, and have developed a sense of self."[21] Hence, his résumé corroborates Brisker's reputation as a person unafraid to challenge authority and upset conventions. These vignettes of Aaron Dixon and E. J. Brisker help us humanize the members of the BSU and provide a window in the paths that brought them to activism.

The BSU at UW in April and May 1968

As detailed in the previous chapter, the Black Student Union at the University of Washington launched its initial push for social change in the early months of 1968. These efforts included making statements to the campus newspaper, meeting with university officials, and holding impromptu teach-ins in college classes. Additionally, the BSU bolstered its on-campus activism with off-campus outreach efforts, especially a campaign to develop auxiliary BSUs at secondary and postsecondary schools around Seattle. This activity on campus and off campus created the groundwork for further BSU protests in April and May 1968.

By late April, the Black Student Union was meeting regularly with UW president Charles Odegaard and other officials to discuss the BSU's demands for increased minority recruitment, Black Studies, and other reforms. In general, President Odegaard was open to the Black students' recommendations and concerns. This contrasts with the attitudes and actions of university presidents at other schools, some of whom adopted a hardline stance on demonstrators and resisted institutional change. Explaining Odegaard's perspective and approach to the BSU, James Garrett gave an illuminating interpretation. After he helped create the BSU at San Francisco State University, Garrett became intimately familiar and involved with the BSU at UW in 1968. Consequently, he became well acquainted with key figures at UW. Garrett compared Odegaard to John Summerskill, president of San Francisco State from 1966 to 1968.[22] Drawing a parallel between Odegaard and Summerskill, Garrett observed that both could take conciliatory approaches to BSU protests because of their ideology and social class, or "Brahmin" status, as Garrett termed it:

> I mean, it's part of the kind of liberal Brahmin, the kind of upper-crust, well-educated people who see education as a safety valve for everybody in the country, a kind of a liberal coalition type person. A Cold War liberal, like Odegaard and Summerskill, they wanted to have these kinds of conflicts. They weren't against conflict and struggle as long as people didn't get hurt. And so Odegaard, who was, who I met a couple times informally, he was like Summerskill who I—. I mean, Summerskill and me, at San Francisco State, we would confer daily, almost daily. . . . They want relationships; they were not afraid to have relationships with people of color.[23]

Here, Garrett is drawing attention to several interconnected factors that help to explain Odegaard's and Summerskill's relative openness to calls for racial reform. One factor was their elevated socioeconomic class, which insulated them from feeling threatened by the prospect of Black upward mobility. Unlike white Americans in the middle class or working class, Garrett is saying, these "Brahmins" felt secure in their social and economic privilege and were thereby relatively open to change. Another related factor was Cold War liberalism, grounded in the view of America as leader of "the free world," global champion of human rights, and a beacon of democracy. Such Cold War thinking led some, like these college presidents, to support the expansion of economic and educational opportunities for African Americans, either because it was ethical or because it served the nation's public image, or both. Thus, to understand Odegaard's openness to the BSU, we should combine this Cold War imperative, "upper-crust" positionality, and what was likely a genuine sympathy for marginalized groups.

Furthermore, it is also worthy to note that as president Odegaard had established a clear record of advocating for racial reforms. This began on February 3, 1959, when his administration issued "University Memorandum No. 22," which committed the school to "equal opportunity, without regard to race, creed, or color."[24] Later, in 1963, Odegaard created an advisory group to address low Black enrollment, and in 1965 this body was expanded into a Committee on Special Educational Programs. Other initiatives at UW that supported racial equity materialized under Odegaard's presidency, such as an Upward Bound program that began in 1966 and supported low-income and first-generation high school students. Consequently, Odegaard deserves credit for promoting efforts to create greater racial and ethnic inclusion even before the activism of the BSU.[25]

Despite these shared principles, the BSU and Odegaard were at odds during much of the spring, as the president insisted on institutional protocols and bureaucratic steps that slowed the pace of change on campus. From the perspective of the Black student activists, the racial situation around the country and at UW was at a crisis point and swift action was required. Consequently, the BSU soon grew frustrated by the seemingly endless string of meetings, and what it judged to be the administration's inaction. Describing an April 30 meeting, E. J. Brisker said, "Dr. Odegaard didn't respond in exactly the way we wanted him to respond. . . . I thought he was being wishy-washy." BSU member Carl Miller added that Odegaard "talked around the point" and that "everyone left the meeting with a headache."[26] Clearly, patience was already wearing thin by this point in the school year.

In May the BSU shifted its tactics and increased the pressure. No longer content with boardroom meetings, the Black Student Union sent a pointed list of demands to Odegaard on May 6. This letter was initially kept secret "because of a 'gentlemen's agreement' between the BSU and Dr. Odegaard," reflecting the working relationship between the students and administrators. Yet the demands strongly asserted the group's goals and "threatened further action if [Odegaard] fails to 'reply or take positive action.'"[27] The following is an extended excerpt from the BSU's May 6 letter that details their demands and objectives:

(1) All decisions, plans, and programs affecting the lives of black students, must be made in consultation with the Black Student Union. This demand reflects our feeling that whites for too long have controlled the lives of non-whites. We reject this control, instead we will define what our best interests are, and act accordingly.

(2) The Black Student Union should be given the financial resources and aids necessary to recruit and tutor non-white students. Specifically, the Black Student Union wants to recruit: 300 Afro-American, 200 American Indian, and 100 Mexican students in September. Quality education is possible through an interaction of diverse groups, classes, and races. Out of a student population of 30,000, there are about 200 Afro-Americans, 20 or so American Indians, and 10 or so Mexican-Americans. The present admissions policies are slanted toward white, middle-class, Western ideals, and the Black Student Union feel that the University should take these other ideals into consideration in their admissions procedures.

(3) We demand that a Black Studies Planning Committee be set up under the direction and control of the Black Student Union. The function of this Committee would be to develop a Black Studies Curriculum that objectively studies the culture and life-style of non-white Americans. We make this demand because we feel that a white, middle-class education cannot and have [sic] not met the needs of non-white students. At this point, an American Indian interested in studying the lives of great Indians like Sitting Bull or Crazy-Horse has to go outside the school structure

to get an objective view. Afro-American members of the Black Student Union have had to go outside the school structure to learn about black heroes like Frederick Douglass, W. E. B. Du Bois, and Malcolm X. One effect of going outside the normal educational channels at the University has been to place an extra strain on black students interested in learning more about their culture. We feel that it is up to the University to re-examine its curriculum and provide courses that meet the needs of non-white students.

(4) We want to work closely with the administration and faculty to recruit black teachers and administrators. One positive effect from recruiting black teachers and administrators is that we will have role models to imitate, and learn from.

(5) We want black representatives on the music faculty. Specifically, we would like to see Joe Brazil and Byron Polk [Pope] hired. The black man has made significant contributions to music (i.e. jazz and spirituals), yet there are no black teachers on the music faculty.[28]

Key characteristics of the BSU are spotlighted in this excerpt. It shows that the BSU continued to pursue a specific, well-defined set of goals throughout its inaugural campaign: greater minority enrollment, Black Studies, increased Black students, faculty, and staff. In addition, the BSU's multicultural ethic is also visible. For instance, the recruitment of Mexican Americans and American Indians is explicitly outlined in demand number two, and references to Sitting Bull and Crazy Horse are made in demand number three.[29] Furthermore, demand number three suggests that the Black Studies curriculum that the BSU envisioned included content on Native Americans and other people of color. Here we see that the BSU called for some of the multicultural educational policies that have now become mainstays in US higher education.

In the last paragraph, regarding the music department, the BSU recommended the appointment of Joe Brazil and Byron Pope to the music department because both were strong candidates and accomplished local musicians. Pope was a saxophonist and sextet leader.[30] Brazil played the saxophone and flute, was a combo leader, and was already employed at UW as an assistant in the Applied Physics Laboratory. Thus, it was reasonable for the BSU to suggest these specific individuals in its demands for minority hiring.[31] Taken as a whole, the BSU put forth a well-articulated, reasonable set of demands that reflected the group's convictions and vision for a more inclusive university.

On May 9 President Odegaard responded in a letter that expressed his support for the BSU's ideas; however, the president pointed to communication problems as the reason why reforms were stalled. To improve communication, Odegaard requested that the BSU identify "a designated, named group of individuals with whom some continuity of relationship can be established and who can readily be contacted when advice is needed." Additionally, Odegaard responded to each of the BSU's demands and stated that some were already being addressed by existing programs, but that he would continue to support new initiatives.[32] In closing, he wrote,

> I repeat here, as I did in our meeting, my desire to see the University make a greater contribution to the lives of all men and especially to those of black men. For years I have been actively seeking to find positive and inventive ways of bringing this about. Your help in constructive solutions to our problems will be much appreciated.[33]

The following Monday, May 13, another meeting of the BSU, Odegaard, and other administrators took place and continued for two and a half hours. At the conclusion, the BSU announced that it was "somewhat encouraged" by Odegaard's verbal commitments to its demands. Carl Miller explained, "Odegaard gave preliminary agreement to our suggestions for implementation of our demands. However, stress should be placed on the word preliminary because there are many details to be ironed out."[34] In particular, what needed to be "ironed out" was the availability of university funds to support the BSU's recruitment goals and other proposals. The BSU wanted some of its members to be hired by UW to recruit new students of color. Yet, as the negotiations unfolded, Odegaard insisted that procuring the necessary funds would take significant time.[35]

Another indication that the BSU was gradually winning over campus officials was an announcement for a planning meeting the following week "to discuss the development of more effective recruiting of minority students with representatives of the BSU and other student groups interested in the program." This initiative, which also resulted from the

May 13 meeting, was to be headed by Dr. Eugene Elliot, special assistant to Odegaard. At this time, UW already had programs to recruit African American students, including a recruitment committee within the Associated Students of the University of Washington (student government), but both the BSU and the administration agreed that these efforts needed to be expanded.[36]

Progress on a new Black Studies program also materialized soon after the May 13 meeting. As the student newspaper article stated,

> Another positive action was the decision to set up a series of meetings to discuss curriculum changes in the College of Arts and Science. Black student representatives will meet soon with representatives of the departments of English, music, psychology, history, sociology, anthropology and art after Dean Phillip Cartwright works out the details. Black student representatives also are expected to meet with the dean and members of two college committees—Curriculum and General Studies.[37]

Hence, in the days following the May 13 meeting, there was already significant movement on the BSU demands. In effect, the BSU had largely won the ideological battle over the validity of its grievances. Yet these positive steps on BSU priorities still left the issue of funding unresolved, and the Black students feared that the actual implementation of reforms would be hampered by a lack of financial resources. These concerns were piqued when the BSU requested that James Garrett and Professor Nathan Hare, both from San Francisco State, be hired as paid consultants to help create Black Studies at UW. Explaining this, Miller said, "These two men have set up very effective programs in the Bay Area and we feel their expertise will heighten and aid our program." While agreeing on principle, Odegaard resisted the immediate allocation of funds.[38] Consequently, the BSU felt that its campaign was far from over, despite the administration's acceptance of its ideas.

The popular support won by the BSU was on full display during the May 13 meeting, as three hundred BSU sympathizers gathered outside the administration building, now called Gerberding Hall, to show their support. After the meeting ended, a rally was held where many white students voiced their support for the BSU demands, especially Black Studies. Robbie Stern, a white law school student and local leader of the

Students for a Democratic Society (SDS, a predominately white protest group), said,

> It is terribly important that we be here. It is also important to understand that these demands are in our own best interest as white students because they involve the kind of education we are getting here. . . . The education that we get here is white and middle-class. It is clear at this point that what is happening in the world requires us to have an understanding of non-white America and a non-white world.[39]

Concurring, Kathy Halluran of the Black and White Concern Organization declared, "There are 23 million black people in America today and we need to know about them. We are the ones being hurt by the lack of courses on black culture."[40]

This student demonstration indicates that the Black Student Union's teach-ins and other efforts to critique the standard Eurocentric curriculum were working. Their message was getting through and many white members of the campus community had accepted the BSU as a thoughtful group worthy of backing. Yet, instead of relaxing, the Black activists pushed on. Possibly sensing that they had the momentum and that they needed to strike while the proverbial iron was hot, the students turned to even bolder actions.

Another motivating factor was the recognition that the school year was ending soon, and the BSU undoubtedly recognized that this level of political pressure would be difficult to maintain throughout the summer and into the next school year. As Larry Gossett recalled, the BSU felt that dramatic action was necessary "because time is running out, school will be out at the end of May. And man, we don't want to go all summer and not have our demands met, that's crazy. Plus, we told these cats [people] that we wanted this to be done by the end of this school year."[41] Seeing the school year end without significant, tangible reforms was unacceptable to the BSU, so on Thursday, May 16, it sent another set of demands to Odegaard—by letter and by phone. Keying in on the funding issue that remained a sticking point in the deliberations, the BSU demanded that Odegaard allocate $50,000 for BSU initiatives and deposit the funds into the BSU account by June 1.[42] Threatening future action, the letter stated,

If you fail to meet these just and final demands of the Black Student Union, its membership will be forced to take new action to implement the Black Studies Program and expose resolutely, the intransigent racism which exists at the University of Washington. Remember, "There shall be political consequences for political mistakes."[43]

E. J. Brisker telephoned Odegaard's office to reiterate the message. He said, "Dr. Odegaard, we tired of y'all's half-stepping. And we want $50,000 put into the BSU account."[44] Brisker gave the deadline of noon the next day, Friday, for the pledge of money. If there was no pledge of money, the BSU warned, there would be "political consequences." Despite this, Odegaard allowed the Friday deadline to pass without any statement.[45]

On Friday, to further dramatize its grievances, the BSU decided to take its demands to Dan Evans, governor of the state of Washington, who happened to be at UW reviewing ROTC troops in Husky Stadium. Through negotiations with UW vice president Ernest Conrad, assistant attorney general Gary Little, and other officials, "Brisker and [Aaron] Dixon were allowed to hand over a 'position paper' to Evans. It contained a demand for money and a list of grievances against Odegaard and University administrators." After doing this, Brisker and Dixon left the stadium; Evans "appeared unperturbed and said nothing."[46]

That weekend, with its deadline ignored, the BSU prepared to launch an unprecedented protest at UW. Eddie Demmings recalled, "Our thinking was words are not enough, it's just that simple. We gave them the words and now we're going to give them the action. We're going to shut this thing down to let them know that we are serious and we expect our demands to be met."[47] The action plan, proposed and discussed throughout the weekend, was a sit-in and occupation of a meeting between President Odegaard and Governor Evans. Once begun, the sit-in would aim to keep both officials in Odegaard's office until the BSU's demands were met.[48] Contemplating this bold and likely dangerous idea, the BSU considered the risks involved, such as possible expulsion from school, arrest, police violence, and even death. This was a heavy decision. Some were not sure that it was the right choice, and advocated postponing the sit-in and giving Odegaard more time. However, this question was put to rest after an inspiring statement by one BSU member, Gordon Dewitty, a blind member of the group, who pointed out a compelling irony. As Larry Gossett remembered, Dewitty said,

> "Man, I've been listening to y'all. This is crazy. I'm blind and I can see better than any of you that we have no choice. We told the guy [our deadline], and if none of y'all are going I'mma take my behind over there to the president's office at the time we're talking about." Then he sat down. There was no more discussion about not doing it [after that].[49]

Pointing out the irony that he could "see" better than some others, and expressing his determination in spite of his disability, Dewitty's short speech settled the discussion about whether to carry out the protest or not.

Another line of internal debate was about whether the sit-in plan imprudently focused too much energy on campus issues. Advocating this perspective, James Garrett tried unsuccessfully to steer the BSU in a different direction. Describing his position, Garrett said, "I didn't feel it was useful to occupy buildings or, you know, those kinds of things." He continued, "I never wanted the campus to be the center of activity. I wanted people to be trained on the campus and take them to the community. But that's not how it worked out."[50] The basis of this view was the contention that the BSU's top priority should be serving in local Black communities, and that it should treat campus reform as secondary. In this conception, campus activism was merely a means to garnering resources for the grassroots, and the sit-in was too disconnected from that strategy. Despite the merits of the point, the group decided to proceed with the sit-in plan anyway, probably concluding that campus reforms could also benefit off-campus populations. Yet, in a partial win for Garrett's view, the BSU altered its plan. Instead of holding the president's office indefinitely, members now intended to hold the space for a brief period, perhaps a few hours, and then leave. This would allow them to dramatize their grievances, garner media attention, and increase the pressure on school officials without being bogged down in an extended building occupation.

The Sit-In

On the following Monday, May 20, the BSU took action. Accounts differ on the precise time the protest began. Newspaper descriptions said that the confrontation began at approximately 5:15 p.m., when a large group of BSU members and supporters burst into Odegaard's office suite.[51] Giving a slightly different start time for the protest, the official meeting minutes state, "At 4:50 p.m., several unidentified persons, thought to be representatives of the Black Student Union, opened the door to the Regents' Room and walked through the room and then back into the outer reception room in the President's Offices."[52] This discrepancy in the reported start time speaks to the surprise and chaos of the event.

The BSU intended to find Odegaard and Governor Evans there, but instead interrupted a meeting of Odegaard and the Executive Committee of the Faculty Senate, and Evans was not present.[53] Several protesters entered the meeting room and sat on the floor while others secured the doors. The previous topic being discussed was immediately tabled, with heated negotiations between the demonstrators and administrators.[54] As detailed in the meeting minutes, Odegaard stated that if the protesters insisted on disrupting the "normal procedures of the University," they would first be asked to leave, then removed by police if necessary. Interjecting a more conciliatory tone, Professor Charles Evans, president of the Faculty Senate, suggested that the meeting turn to the BSU demands, which were already included in the meeting's agenda. E. J. Brisker then spoke on behalf of the demonstrators: "We feel the action that we are taking is right and so we won't move. We have told the brothers and sisters present not to touch you and not to hurt you. We are going to stay here. We don't want to move until we get what we want." Brisker then reiterated the BSU's demand for $50,000.[55]

While expressing support for the BSU's goals, Odegaard reiterated that policy changes needed to be approved through the proper institutional channels, that progress on the BSU's goals was already being made, and that he fully intended to continue working with the BSU in this direction. When this failed to convince the demonstrators to leave, the discussion then shifted and Brisker was asked to clarify the BSU's $50,000 demand. Pressed to give a budget explaining how the funds would be used, Brisker said,

We want to recruit 300 black students, 200 Indians and 100 Mexican Americans next summer. We want to set up tutoring and help them find their weaknesses. We want to come up with curricular changes— interdepartmental black studies programs. We want black studies. We want representation on the music faculty. In terms of how the money will be allocated, we think we need $5,000 to $7,000 to do the intensive recruiting that we need. We figure in terms of consultants that [James] Garrett should be hired for $12,000 to $18,000 a year as a full time consultant for black studies. The recruiters' salaries say $100 to $110 a week plus expenses. State cars could be made available for travel. Then $100 to (?) to three students to consult. Stanford would pay $25,000 for Garrett, but we are very close friends so he would come here instead, but he won't do it for free.[56]

Also responding to the administrators' questioning, Brisker then outlined the specific students the BSU wanted to serve on the university's Black Studies committee, as recruiters, and as liaisons between the BSU and the administration.

ODEGAARD: A week ago we asked you the names of your liaison committee. We have never heard.
GIRL STUDENT [UNNAMED]: Oh, we sent you a letter.
ODEGAARD: No letter has ever been received. Can you name your committee members now?
BRISKER: The Black Studies Planning Committee is: Larry Gossett, Carl Miller, and E. J. Brisker. The Recruiting Committee is: Marcy Hall, Carmelita Laducer, Jesse Crowder, Gary [sic] Owens and Dan Keith. The Liaison Committee is: Verlaine Keith, Lee Levy, Marshall Buford, Darrell Williams, and one as yet unnamed member from the freshman class.

After further deliberations failed to end the confrontation, the meeting was officially adjourned at 6:30 p.m. At this point, Odegaard and most of the other administrators withdrew into a side office within the suite of adjoining rooms, and were subsequently barricaded in by the demonstrators.[57] This left the protesters in the outer office, the Regents' Room, where the meeting had taken place; a few faculty members from the Executive Committee chose to stay with the BSU and continue the negotiations. As described by the meeting minutes,

> Upon official adjournment of the meeting, the following members of the Executive Committee retired to the President's Suite adjoining the Regents' Room: Chairman [Charles] Evans, President [Charles] Odegaard, Professors [Douglas G.] Chapman, [Morton M.] David, [Vernon B.] Hammer, [Robert] Petersdorf [,] and [Constantine G.] Christofides. Others present at the meeting who accompanied the aforementioned members of the Executive Committee to the adjoining offices included: Vice Presidents [F. P.] Thieme, [Robert G.] Waldo, and [Donald K.] Anderson, Chief [Ed] Kanz, and Secretary [of the Faculty, Oliver W.] Nelson.
>
> The following members of the Executive Committee remained in the Regents' Room in continued discussion with the BSU delegation: Professors [Julius] Roller, [Charles] Sleicher, [Patricia] Keller, [Edward T.] Chambers, [Arval] Morris, [Melvin M.] Rader, and [Julian] Ansell. Professor [Robert A.] Aldrich also lingered for a time and later joined Chairman Evans and the group assembled in the President's secretarial offices.[58]

Of the faculty that stayed with the students, Professor Arval Morris was one of the most effective mediators, helping the BSU achieve its goals while also de-escalating the conflict. In a series of phone calls between the demonstrators and officials, Morris acted as an intermediary.[59]

By 7:00 p.m., the sit-in had grown to approximately 150 demonstrators, mostly young African Americans but including several non-Black members of the Black Student Union such as Marcie Hall (later Hall-McMurtrie) and Carmelita Laducer, both Native American, and Jesse (Jesús) Crowder, who was Latino.[60] All three were named by Brisker to the Recruitment Committee because they would help to recruit Native and Latino students, an explicit goal of the Black Student Union. The sit-in also received support and participation from grade school BSU members, Black Panthers, community activists, and white students like Robbie Stern. Estimating the white sit-in participants, Professor Julius Roller gave a separate account of the sit-in that said that the white demonstrators numbered "less than twenty," which one can surmise equates to about fifteen to nineteen.[61] As the sit-in was happening a group of supporters also gathered outside, in front of the building. Jesse Crowder said, "I vividly recall the takeover of the administration building, and I recall that on one side of the building, you could look out over the campus and as word got out over the campus of what was going on at the administration building, that lawn out there started to fill up with students."[62] Describing the wide spectrum of support, Eddie Walker added, "We had a nice crowd, a multiethnic crowd of Latinos, and Indian students, and white students, and Asian students. So, it was a multiethnic takeover and just led by the Black Student Union."[63] This multicultural aspect of the sit-in is important to consider because it again highlights the cross-racial solidarity of the BSU and the Black Power movement.

As the sit-in stretched later into the evening, campus law enforcement took steps to assert control over the situation. The university police attempted to cordon off the building and prevent protesters from entering or exiting. But in spite of police efforts, groceries and a record player were lifted up to a third-floor window and at least two individuals, Eddie Walker and Bobby Morgan (a member of the Seattle SNCC), circumvented the barricade by rope-climbing up the side of the building.[64] By 7:30 p.m. the Seattle police arrived on the scene and assisted the UW police in sealing off the building.

At 8:15 p.m. vice president Donald K. Anderson and UW police chief Ed Kanz tried to deliver an ultimatum that either the protesters leave on their own by 8:30 p.m. or they would be removed by force. Reportedly, this exchange was hampered by the difficulty for protesters and the officials to communicate through the heavy office doors, but BSU members were aware of a possible police raid. Carl Miller recalled, "We were worried every other minute that the police or the National Guard was going to come in and you know arrest us all and take us away."[65] Eddie Walker echoed these concerns: "While we were inside, we were worried that state troopers and all that stuff, who were I think in one of the other halls that had a connecting underground tunnel to [the administration building], were going to come up into the building and just whoop, beat us out of there."[66] Fortunately, the sit-in ended soon after, with neither violence nor arrests. Before the building was sealed, civil liberties lawyer Michael Rosen arrived on the scene and joined the mediators.[67] Before long, with the help of Morris, Rosen and others, Brisker and the BSU finalized a document for Odegaard to sign. The document was delivered to Odegaard by Morris and, after some final revisions, Odegaard signed it at 8:45 p.m., bringing the demonstration to an end. The document basically reiterated that Odegaard and UW leadership supported the BSU's ideas. No new concessions or policies were explicitly outlined in the document; thus, in hindsight, the agreement appears to be a symbolic gesture that allowed both sides to de-escalate the confrontation without appearing to capitulate. Despite these limitations, the Black Student Union embraced the agreement as a major political victory and immediately ended the sit-in. The statement said,

> We, the below listed members of the Executive Committee of the Senate, acting individually, heard the demands of the Black Student Union wherein members of the Black Student Union request the University to find ways to fund an expanded recruitment of minority-group students with the aid of minority-group students, and an expanded Black Studies program in the University Curriculum, but did not demand authority and control of the programs. We believe that the Senate of the University of Washington, and President Charles E. Odegaard should pledge themselves at the next Senate meeting to continue to take the steps necessary to secure funds from private and public sources and to implement the above demands, recognizing throughout that the responsibility of the University is to maintain its authority and control over its programs, and that it must operate through its existing, or its newly created, channels.[68]

The agreement further stated, "We are signing this statement because it is a restatement of the position which has already been taken and indicated in previous printed communications."[69] Odegaard and the Executive Committee all signed.

The Black Student Union saw the signed statement as an unmitigated victory. In part, the mere fact that the students and their allies had taken this bold step, held the president's office for several hours, and left on their own terms was itself a cause for elation. No one was harmed, no one was arrested, and the BSU emerged with a bolstered reputation for boldness and militancy. Clearly the entire affair could have ended much worse for the activists. Remembering their feelings of jubilation, Eddie Demmings said, "We left the university administration in triumph."[70] As

BSU members walked out, they chanted, "Beep-beep, bang-bang, Ungawa, Black Power!"[71]

As we consider why and how the BSU sit-in ended in peaceful negotiations, rather than police tear gas and billy clubs, we must turn our attention once again to President Charles Odegaard. As UW professor Charles Evans explained, Odegaard was a major reason why the police did not raid the sit-in. "There was one alarming factor [of the sit-in] and that was that we [administrators] heard that law enforcement was planning to come to the campus. And as I recall it, we understood that Dr. Odegaard was stalling [the police]. He didn't feel that this was necessary."[72] At other schools, police were called in to crush student protests, which often further inflamed campus unrest. Odegaard sought to avoid such an episode at UW. Moreover, not only did he forestall police intervention, but he also made sure that no disciplinary action would befall any of the sit-in participants in the days and months that followed. Demmings shared insightful analysis on this point:

> The administration of President Charles Odegaard could have reacted quite differently than the way that they did. There were then and there are now tools of repression. There could have been arrest warrants. There could have been expulsions. There could have been any [number of punishments] or student disciplinary hearings of some sort. There could have been a lot of things that we would have been confronted with and perhaps if those things had occurred, the struggle would have been different. But Charles Odegaard didn't do those things and he wasn't of that type.[73]

Unquestionably, the leadership of Odegaard was an important factor in the characteristics and outcomes of the sit-in. Yet the students of the BSU deserve the bulk of the credit due to their successful community organizing and the network of support the organization established on and off campus. These crucial political maneuvers created a context that fostered the cooperation of Odegaard and other officials. Moreover, this is a key insight that future activists can learn from this history. Building a base of political support was an essential tool for the success of the Black Student Union, and it can be a useful strategy in the future.

What emerged after the sit-in was even greater cooperation between the Black Student Union and campus officials. The sit-in was a crucial turning point in the history of race relations at UW. Building on the momentum of the agreement signed by Odegaard and the Executive Committee, Brisker addressed a full Faculty Senate meeting on Thursday, May 23, and won its endorsement for BSU reforms. In the address, which at that point was the second speech ever delivered by a student to the Faculty Senate, Brisker said,

> We (the BSU) would like the support of the Faculty Senate in three key areas. One, in the area of recruitment of non-white students. Two, the development of programs, i.e. remedial and tutorial, that will aid newly recruited students in making the difficult transition to university life. Three, the development of a Black Studies Curriculum which will enable both non-white and white students to learn about the culture and life style [sic] of such groups as Afro-Americans, Mexican Americans and Indian-American peoples.[74]

The speech to the senate, and the senate's endorsement of the BSU plan, effectively clinched the victory, and new reforms soon materialized. Despite any lingering concerns from Odegaard and others about proper approvals and procedures, UW implemented the BSU demands with new urgency and effectiveness. The subsequent weeks and months saw dramatic results, including an unprecedented increase in the enrollment of students of color. As they had wanted, BSU members were hired that summer as recruiters, targeting Black students from the Seattle metro area, as well as Mexican American students from the Yakima Valley and Native American students from the Makah Reservation and elsewhere.[75]

Approximately eight student recruiters were hired, including BSU members and non-members, and they were supervised by a staff member, Bill Hilliard.[76] Marcie Hall-McMurtrie was one of the recruiters and remembered weeklong recruiting trips. She recalled that they would arrive in a community and visit local establishments like restaurants, where "we'd subtly look around and then we would approach people." Once they found a prospective candidate willing to talk to them, Hall-McMurtrie and the others tried to convince the person to believe that a college degree was a possibility for them. She recalled, "We loved our job. We really did. You know, we tried to inspire all these people. We'd get them way interested in the university. 'Yes, come to the university. Yes, we'll be there for you.'"[77] Eddie Demmings, another recruiter, remembered visiting a migrant labor camp in the Yakima Valley where the laborers lived in "tin huts" and endured other deplorable conditions.[78] Due to these efforts, hundreds of new students of color entered UW in the fall of 1968. Comparing fall 1967 to fall 1968, one researcher estimated that Black enrollment increased from 150 to 465, Chicano from 25 to 100, and Native from 10 to 90.[79] The successful outreach to Latino and Native students signifies that the BSU followed through on its interracial ideals and "Third World consciousness," a contemporaneous term for interracial and interethnic solidarity.

Once on campus, the new recruits soon found programs to help them succeed. One was called the Special Education Program (SEP), led by Professor Charles Evans. Its purpose was to promote the retention and graduation of historically underrepresented students.[80] The program included recruitment, tutoring, and advising services. The tutoring was especially important because many SEP students had not received the necessary preparation for college-level work; thus tutoring was established in a variety of subjects along with remedial English and math courses.[81]

Other BSU goals were met as well: the number of Black faculty and staff increased, and Black Studies was established. According to research at the time, African American staff at UW increased from 327 in January 1968 to 493 in October 1968; Black faculty rose from seven to the all-time high of fifteen by 1969, with new professors in urban planning, medicine, dentistry, and engineering.[82] As we have seen, proposals for Black Studies received increasing faculty support before and after the sit-in.[83] Consequently, several new Black Studies courses were offered in the fall of 1968: Social Biology of the American Negro, Afro-American History and Culture, and a language class in Swahili.[84]

Cementing the reforms, Dr. Samuel E. Kelly was appointed as UW's inaugural vice president of minority affairs in 1970. Under his leadership, the Office of Minority Affairs (OMA) was established and took responsibility for the continuation of SEP and related programs. Around this time, SEP was renamed the Educational Opportunity Program (EOP), and it continued to provide recruitment and retention support for underrepresented students, including Asian/Pacific Islanders and poor white students.[85] The tutoring services were also brought under the supervision of OMA in 1970, and in 1976 an expanded tutorial facility, the Instructional Center (IC), was opened.[86] In 1982 BSU member Emile Pitre returned to UW to work in the IC, and subsequently served as director from 1989 to 2002, before being further promoted to associate vice president of OMA.[87] Honoring the IC's outstanding service to students, UW bestowed two prestigious awards on the program in 2001: the Brotman Award for Instructional Excellence and the Brotman Award for Diversity.[88] Two additional facilities, the Ethnic Cultural Center, a sociocultural space, and the Ethnic Cultural Theater, an artistic space, were added to OMA's portfolio in the early 1970s. All of these entities, the Educational Opportunity Program, the Instructional Center, the Ethnic Cultural Center and Theater, and the Office of Minority Affairs, are part of the legacy of the BSU and continue to benefit students as of this publication.[89] In fact, over twenty-four thousand OMA students graduated from UW between 1970 and 2007.[90] Moreover, Black Studies continues as a part of the department of American ethnic studies (AES). The successful creation of Black Studies led to Chicano and Asian American studies, and in 1985 these programs were combined to create AES, which continues its pathbreaking work at UW.[91] Each of these institutional reforms and innumerable corollaries are indisputable evidence of the Black Student Union's indelible impact on the University of Washington.

Activity Following the Sit-In

The Black Student Union's May 1968 sit-in at the University of Washington president's office was a pivotal moment in the history of the institution, whose reverberations are still being felt over fifty years later. Had the BSU faded from the public stage immediately after this campaign, its legacy as a pioneering student protest group would have already been cemented at UW. But, to the group's credit, it remained highly active throughout the following years. What follows is a brief account of some of the BSU's political involvement between 1968 and 1970.

The first series of events transpired during the summer of 1968 and related to the trial of the BSU members arrested for their role in the Franklin High School demonstration the previous April. On April 4, as detailed in the previous chapter, Carl Miller, Aaron Dixon, and Larry

Gossett were targeted as ringleaders of the protest and charged with unlawful assembly. Larry's younger brother Richard Gossett and Trolice Flavors, members of the Franklin BSU, were also arrested and charged, but their charges were later dropped due to their being minors and other mitigating circumstances.[92] On June 10, the trial of Dixon, Gossett, and Miller began.[93] American Civil Liberties Union lawyers Michael Rosen and Mrs. Kenneth Young represented Gossett and Dixon, respectively; Miller was represented by local lawyer Andrew Young.[94]

Each day of the trial, numerous supporters sat in the courtroom with signs such as, "'Call off your Pigs,' 'Black Control for the Black Community,' 'Free Aaron Dixon,' and 'Support the Panthers, Not the Pigs.'" As reflected in many of the signs, much of the media and community attention was focused on Aaron Dixon, who was by this time widely known as the leader of the Seattle chapter of the Black Panther Party.[95] The trial included four days of legal motions and testimony. Charles Odegaard, UW president, and his assistant Dr. Eugene Elliot both testified for the defense, while Franklin principal Loren Ralph testified for the prosecution. Ultimately, on June 13, after ninety minutes of deliberation, Dixon, Gossett, and Miller were found guilty of unlawful assembly by an all-white jury.[96] On July 1 they were given the maximum sentence for this misdemeanor offense, six months in jail.[97] This harsh sentence outraged many in Seattle's Black community and sparked a small riot in the city.[98]

The riot took place in the Central District in the direct vicinity of Garfield High School. It began around 8:30 p.m. on the day of the sentencing. The disturbances lasted several hours, included 175 to 200 participants, and led to twelve arrests. Mostly, the rioting consisted of rocks and bricks being thrown at cars and local businesses. According to the *Seattle Times*, "A number of persons, including police officers, suffered minor injuries. Police cars and other vehicles were pelted with rocks. Windows of businesses were broken and some firms were entered." The report added that "windows were broken in Assistant Police Chief M. E. Cook's car as he drove past with Mayor [James "Dorm"] Braman as a passenger." Additional reports held that several pedestrians were attacked by the rioters and treated for "bumps, cuts and bruises"—one victim also had eight dollars stolen from his pocket.[99] "A total of 125 police officers were involved in quelling the disturbances," which also allegedly included attempts to use firebombs.[100]

Besides the riot, the conviction of the BSU members inspired other actions by sympathetic individuals and organizations. Plans immediately materialized to appeal the convictions and a legal defense fund was established. Five hundred dollars was raised for each of the defendants and they were granted bail pending their appeals. Therefore, Dixon, Gossett, and Miller were released from jail around 3:00 p.m. following their sentencing. Donors included the Ecumenical Metropolitan Ministry, the Law Student Civil Rights Research Council at UW, and the local NAACP.[101] What followed was years of litigation and appeals that finally concluded in January 1971, when the Washington Supreme Court ordered a retrial and the prosecution declined to proceed.[102]

Meanwhile, another headline-grabbing controversy erupted in the spring of 1969, when the BSU at UW and its allies at Seattle Central Community College led a challenge of the Seattle Community College system.[103] The Seattle Community College system had different campuses throughout the city. Because of the segregated nature of Seattle's neighborhoods, different racial-ethnic populations tended to enroll at one college or another depending on which was closest to their homes. Seattle Central Community College was popular among Seattle's residents of color because of its proximity to the Central District and adjacent Chinatown, also known as the International District. In May 1969 some students at Seattle Central, including Frank Williams, a member of the BSU there, learned of a plan by the Seattle Community College Board of Trustees to shift most of its academic programs to the North Seattle facility and concentrate vocational programs at Seattle Central. This proposal reeked of institutional racism to Williams and his allies because North Seattle's student body was mostly white, and because of long-standing educational discrimination in Seattle and across the country. Seeing this plan as unjust and racially biased, the BSU objected and demanded that at least one of the five all-white trustees resign in favor of a BSU appointee.[104]

While the BSU rejection of this policy as institutionally racist may seem rash to some, the reasonableness of the charge is supported when viewed within long-standing patterns of educational discrimination in America. For instance, the legal battles that culminated in the 1954 *Brown v. Board* Supreme Court decision, and the 1950s and 1960s integration struggles that followed, were in part due to racially biased assumptions that non-whites were unsuited for academic or intellectual pursuits. In addition, throughout the 1960s and beyond, schools and school districts across the country used policies like "tracking" to funnel Black and brown students away from college preparatory courses and toward working-class professions. Moreover, the late 1960s also saw major protests against inequitable education like the student walkouts of six Los Angeles high schools in March 1968, demonstrating that this was not just a problem of the South.[105] Thus, the controversy at the Seattle Community College system is best understood within this wider context.

After fruitless negotiations, the UW and Seattle Community College BSUs jointly called for a student strike on May 8, 1969. The relative ineffectiveness of this initial protest spawned a much larger protest on May 22. On that day, a few hundred members of the BSU and the Students for a Democratic Society (SDS) stormed the Edison Technical School Building (a Seattle Community College facility) and occupied it until the Seattle police's tactical squad, or SWAT team, forced them to leave. The next day there were additional protests and confrontations with police, culminating with brick throwing and tear gas. After reaching this high point, the violence subsided and the controversy came to an end on July 24 when trustee Carl Dakan resigned and was replaced by Marvin Glass, and the plan to move the academic programs was reviewed.[106]

In 1970 the Black Student Union became involved in another major conflict, this time concerning the University of Washington's Husky athletic program. This controversy centered on a campaign by the BSU to force the UW Huskies to cut all athletic and institutional ties with Brigham Young University (BYU). The reasoning here was that BYU's parent institution, the Church of Latter-Day Saints, or Mormons, discriminated against African Americans.[107] In addition, this confrontation with the athletic program grew out of past conflicts between Black players and the football coach Jim Owens, who suspended four Black players the previous October under questionable circumstances.[108] Thus, the conflict over the UW-BYU relationship was connected to larger complaints of prejudice in UW athletics.

By the beginning of 1970, the BYU controversy was the BSU's most prominent campaign. Specifically, the BSU objected to the Mormon Church's priesthood system, which had a de facto ban on Black males.

The Mormon priesthood was not a professional order, but was a necessary status for certain religious privileges like being married in the temple, holding important leadership positions, and entering the highest level of heaven. Generally, all males entered this priesthood at the age of twelve, but Black males of any age were denied admittance. This policy, along with other anecdotal evidence of anti-Black tendencies in the Mormon culture, convinced the BSU that both the Mormon Church and its school, BYU, were racist. Hence, the Black students concluded that the University of Washington was endorsing racism by engaging with BYU.[109] Notably, the BSU at UW was not alone in this view. By this time, there had been several protests against BYU, including a highly publicized case involving football players at the University of Wyoming, and an announcement by Stanford University that it would schedule no new athletic events with BYU.[110] Following these and other events, the BSU at UW began a direct-action campaign in January 1970, sabotaging a gymnastics meet between BYU and the Huskies. Just as the contest was set to begin, about twenty Black protesters entered UW's Hec Edmundson Pavilion and threw garbage, raw eggs, catsup, and oil on the gym mats and knocked over tables and chairs. When a UW coach yelled at them to leave, water was thrown in his face.[111]

In addition to the protest, a student petition also expressed opposition to BYU. A Black member of the UW gymnastics team, Lynn Hall, began circulating the petition requesting that the school cancel all remaining athletic events with BYU. In early February the petition was delivered to Joe Kearney, UW director of sports, with over 1,500 signatures. In response to the protest and petition, Kearney began a series of meetings with stakeholders: Black athletes, Mormon students, alumni, and community leaders. Believing that this investigation was merely a stalling tactic, or "bullshit committee meetings," the BSU demanded that the administration make a clear policy announcement by March 5 or "it would 'act accordingly' against the University's silence." On March 4, the day before the BSU deadline, Kearney finished his investigation and sent his report to executive vice president John Hogness, who was the acting president as Odegaard traveled in Europe. That same day Hogness announced that the administration needed more time to make a decision and would make a final announcement no later than April 1.[112]

Unsatisfied, the Black Student Union launched a new round of large-scale protests on Thursday, March 5, in cooperation with the Seattle Liberation Front (SLF, a predominately white radical group similar to SDS). That day, nearly a thousand people rallied on campus at noon, ten representatives of the BSU met with Hogness, and a group of protesters occupied Thompson Hall until 3:30 p.m. The next day, an even larger group gathered and marched around campus and employed "hit and run" tactics to disrupt the campus. This method was to enter a building, tell the students and faculty to leave, occupy the building for ten minutes, then leave and repeat the process in a different building. In response, the administration called in Seattle police, and the protesters dispersed before the police arrived.

In response to the escalating civil disobedience, Hogness obtained a temporary restraining order on behalf of the university, which barred "employing force or violence, or the threat of force or violence, against persons or property on the plaintiff's premises."[113] In spite of the court order, the demonstrations continued the following week, with up to 3,500 participants. On Wednesday, March 11, the protests reached their most disruptive phase as 700 protesters occupied eight buildings on campus. In a few classrooms, students trying to attend class angrily challenged the protesters and refused to leave, which led to violence. In at least one case, protesters burst into a history class, threw garbage, shouted obscenities, and beat members of the class.[114] Again, the police were called and the protesters dispersed. After Wednesday's actions, Hogness called in the Seattle police department's SWAT team, taking a more hardline approach to the demonstrations. On Thursday, police and King County sheriffs patrolled campus all day and made sure there were no more disruptions.[115] Speaking at a BSU rally that same day, Carl Miller noted the danger of police violence and cautioned against continued demonstrations:

> Anybody here, who believes that those policemen that they got out there will not kill you, is in for a rude awakening. We do not intend to commit suicide. We do not intend to place our bodies in front of his guns and billy-clubs. The effect of that we've seen over and over again[:] people get hurt, and nothing changes.[116]

This rally marked the end of the campaign. Despite the widespread support of the BSU's criticism of Mormon policies, this effort did not achieve its stated objective as the UW administration continued its institutional relationship with Brigham Young University. As explained by assistant attorney general James B. Wilson, "The University cannot declare a policy of refusal to engage in activities with BYU solely because of a creed of its religious sponsor, regardless of how strongly we may disagree with that religious creed." To do so, the administration claimed, would be in violation of constitutional protections for religious freedom. In addition, the officials noted, BYU had been investigated by the Office for Civil Rights and found to be in compliance with the Civil Rights Act of 1964.[117] Therefore, the administration maintained, it was unable to agree to the BSU demand. The most it could do was offer a compromise:

> After consulting with the Board of Regents, Hogness developed an official University policy on BYU. The University would honor all current contracts with BYU, but make no plans to enter into any further contracts. Hogness also emphasized that "no student is required to participate in any event with any institution if he objects to participation as a matter of conscience."[118]

Needless to say, this policy was far less than the BSU's demand for a complete disassociation with Brigham Young University and it found this compromise unsatisfactory. However, as the rest of the year unfolded, most student activists left the BYU issue and turned to other controversies, especially the national outcry following the escalation of the Vietnam War and the Kent State University shootings in late April and early May. Two final notes came later: in 1971 the university renewed its contract with BYU, and in 1978 the Mormons opened up their priesthood to Black members.[119]

Taken together, the prosecution of BSU members in the summer of 1968, the confrontation with the Seattle Community Colleges in 1969, and the campaign to sever athletic ties with Brigham Young University in 1970 show that the Black Student Union of UW continued to be a leading force in student activism following the group's 1968 sit-in.

As detailed in this chapter and the preceding one, the actions of the Black Student Union make it deserving of a special place in the history of the University of Washington, and the history of the Black Power movement. The record of its first year is nothing less than remarkable, as it was the first organization at the University of Washington to advocate so successfully for people of color. Within one year, the BSU pushed UW to address institutional racism, Eurocentrism, and inequitable educational opportunities. Like the Black Student Union at San Francisco State and elsewhere, the BSU at UW was a powerful pressure group that commanded attention and won significant institutional reforms. This chapter began with a discussion of two prominent Black Student Union members, Aaron Dixon and E. J. Brisker. From there, it described the BSU actions in May 1968, including the sit-in and occupation of the university president's office on May 20. Next, the chapter described the transformational new policies instituted at UW in the months and years following the BSU sit-in, and it ended with a brief overview of some of the post–sit-in political involvement of the BSU from 1968 to 1970.

Part of the national Black campus movement, this BSU chapter was a leader in the region and set the tone for other Black student protests in the Pacific Northwest. Its role as a lynchpin and catalyst for youth organizing and activism cannot be overstated. Throughout the city of Seattle and beyond, the group was a direct influence on scores of Black youth. In addition, this BSU chapter embodied themes that characterized much of the Black Power movement. It championed Black empowerment while also advocating for similarly aggrieved racial and ethnic groups, namely, Native and Latinx peoples. Admittedly, Asian Americans and Pacific Islanders were not a major part of this initial coalition, likely because racism against Asian/Pacific Islanders was not initially as salient to the BSU as the injustice faced by others. However, by 1970, Filipinos and other Asian/Pacific Islanders from economically disadvantaged backgrounds were served by the Office of Minority Affairs, as were white students with similar challenges, and the BSU supported these expansions.[120] The BSU's record of grassroots engagement is also outstanding, as it built a strong web of community support through its youth outreach and mentorship. Without question, the BSU's multiculturalism, community organizing, and achievement of reforms at UW created new opportunities for future generations. In the next chapter, the story of the BSU continues at another higher education institution, Washington State University.

4

"Never Just a Tea Party"

The BSU and Black Power at Washington State University, 1967–1968

On May 14, 1968, Black students at Washington State University (WSU) boldly confronted racial prejudice on their campus. They wrote, "We are writing this letter to say that we want an explanation as to why some students here at WSU, our wonderful school, had to act like indecent pigs?" This impassioned statement, combining outrage with sarcasm like the comment "our wonderful school," called attention to a recent episode of racial discrimination targeting a group of visiting African American high schoolers. Continuing, the Black WSU students wrote,

> When a group of black students from Garfield High School in Seattle come to visit our college campus, is it too much to ask or demand that our students act human? Are you still living in a day where you think blacks are low, uncouth people? Well, people, "IT IS A NEW DAY!" BLACKS ARE NOT TAKING IT ANY MORE![1]

This statement and the surrounding incident are emblematic of the intrepid activism of African Americans at Washington State University in the late 1960s. At WSU, Black college students took up the charge to reform their institution, just like their counterparts nationwide. White normativity and anti-Black prejudice were firmly ensconced in the campus culture at WSU, not unlike many other predominately white colleges and universities at this time.

As scholars Brian Purnell and Jeanne Theoharis wrote in their co-authored introduction to *The Strange Careers of the Jim Crow North: Segregation and Struggle outside the South* (2019), Americans have been taught the erroneous notion that the Jim Crow system, legally and socially sanctioned white supremacy, was only a feature of the South.[2]

Moreover, the North is commonly conceptualized as relatively free of racial conflict. In truth, the North had its own long-standing, entrenched systems of racial subordination, and this "Jim Crow North" encompassed a range of manifestations: from racial slurs and physical violence to more subtle choices of policy and other institutional actions.[3] The history of the BSU at WSU is an instructive window into the Jim Crow North, both on campus and within the larger region of eastern Washington. The Black Power activism that emerged therein encountered more explosive racial conflicts than what occurred elsewhere, distinguishing this episode of struggle from what occurred at the University of Washington, detailed in the preceding chapters. Taken as a whole, the story of the Black Student Union at WSU provides unique insights into the Jim Crow North and Black Power activism in a rural setting.

In the late 1960s, when Black Power student activism reached its zenith, the organizational home for most politically involved Black students throughout the West Coast was the Black Student Union, and this was also true at Washington State University. There, African American students founded the BSU in the spring of 1968, responding to both on-campus issues and political developments off campus. The BSU chapter at WSU served as a vital connection point among BSUs throughout the state and the region, emerging as an influential part of the Black campus movement across the Pacific Northwest.

One illustration of the prominence of the BSU at WSU vis-à-vis other campuses in the region was a conference entitled "Black Studies in the Pacific Northwest," held December 1–2, 1969, at WSU. The attendees represented approximately twenty colleges and universities across the region, including sixteen schools in the state of Washington, two in Idaho, one in Oregon, and one in Montana.[4] The gathering promoted the budding discipline of Black Studies and enabled supporters of the field to share strategies and collaborate; also, the event's intercollegiate representation reflected that WSU was a key site for Black Power in the inland, tri-state area. The BSU at WSU was a consequential organization that merits the close analysis of *Washington State Rising*. This chapter establishes the context of this history, first elaborating on the demographic and geographic characteristics of Washington State University and the surrounding area. Then, the chapter introduces Dr. Johnnetta B. Cole, a leading Black activist at WSU. Finally, the chapter describes Black student activism during the 1967–1968 school year, which included the founding of the Black Student Union.

Pullman, Washington

Unlike West Coast urban centers like Seattle and San Francisco that saw large migrations of African Americans around World War II, the small town of Pullman, Washington, remained overwhelmingly white into the 1960s. The same was true for the surrounding Whitman County. The town and the county were rural, agricultural, politically conservative, and part of a larger area called the Palouse, which includes communities in eastern Washington and northern Idaho. In fact, Pullman itself was less than ten miles from its neighbor to the east, Moscow, Idaho. Indicating the minuscule Black population, census data from 1970 showed that Whitman County had a total population of 37,900; Pullman was its largest city, and only 2.5 percent of Pullman residents were African American.[5] Moreover, this 2.5 percent was undoubtably an all-time high resulting from many newcomers who arrived in the late 1960s.

Throughout the Palouse and Whitman County, the term "monoculture" was a fitting descriptor for both the farm products and the population. Its distinguishing topography was rolling hills, with miles of wheat fields and similar crops of dry cultivation. Green and lush in the spring, the famous wheat fields of the Palouse were a golden-brown for most of the year. Likewise, the population also featured an overwhelmingly white homogeneity. The dominant sociopolitical point of view was decidedly to the right of the political spectrum and largely at odds with the leftist social movements of the era. For instance, Whitman County was one of only three Washington counties to vote a majority for Barry Goldwater, the arch-conservative Republican, in the 1964 presidential election. Washington State University in Pullman, previously known as Washington Agricultural College, largely mirrored the demographics and culture of the region, characterized by farming and small-town life. Writing in 1967, a reporter for the student newspaper aptly summarized the school as "quiet, conservative WSU."[6]

For the Black students who enrolled at Washington State University in the 1960s, most of whom came from predominately Black neighborhoods like Seattle's Central District, the campus and its surroundings were a foreign and isolating environment. Prior to the 1970s, the university did not keep official records of student enrollment based on race.[7] However, oral history accounts provide estimates of the Black student body. According to Felicia Gaskins, who enrolled in 1961 as one of the few African American students, the total Black enrollment that year was about twenty-four.[8] For comparison, the total student enrollment at WSU in 1961 was 7,828.[9] Thus, the Black student population constituted about three out of every thousand students, or 0.3 percent. Black enrollment remained low throughout the decade, although Gaskins estimated that the total grew to about fifty Black students by 1966.[10] Providing a similar estimate, Robert Cole, a white economics professor, recalled that when he arrived in 1963, "there were about a half dozen graduate students and about a dozen football players," along with "a few" Black women students.[11] Separately, the campus newspaper corroborated these approximations, reporting that during the 1967–1968 school year WSU's Black enrollment reached an all-time high of sixty students, and that population expanded to a new record of eighty students during the subsequent school year.[12] The eighty Black students of the 1968–1969 school year still constituted less than 1 percent of the total student body, and the number of Black faculty was similarly minuscule. Rutledge Dennis, a BSU member and Black graduate student in sociology, arrived in 1967 and later described the campus setting: "You're talking about a very small, predominately white community in the wheat lands that had never seen many Blacks."[13] Therefore, Black WSU students had to navigate a racial minefield as they integrated classrooms, dormitories, athletic teams, social events, and other settings.[14] Not surprisingly, then, African Americans created a support network for each other, out of which Black student activism soon materialized.[15]

Johnnetta B. Cole and the Afro-American Alliance

One unique aspect of the Black Student Union at Washington State University was the involvement and leadership of Dr. Johnnetta Betsch Cole. Officially, her role was faculty advisor to the BSU, yet she operated more like a co-chair of the organization. In contrast to the typical faculty advisor, who largely remains on the sidelines of student activities, Cole was directly involved in the exploits of the group during her tenure as a WSU professor: planning strategy, leading protests, serving as a spokesperson, and more. Thus, as a woman, a professional, a mother, and someone who was in her thirties and therefore older than the prototypical Black Power advocate, Cole provides a noteworthy example of how the Black Power movement appealed to a range of demographics.

Cole was born in Jacksonville, Florida, in 1936, and her activism was undoubtably shaped by her childhood, including the economic self-sufficiency and educational attainment of her family. Her maternal great-grandfather, Abraham Lincoln Lewis, co-founded the Afro-American Life Insurance Company, and the success of the business provided a comfortable lifestyle for successive generations of the family. Mary Frances (Lewis) Betsch, Johnnetta's mother, attended Wilberforce University in Ohio. Later, Mary Frances taught English courses and served as the registrar at Edward Waters College, before eventually working for the family's insurance business. Johnnetta's father, John Betsch Sr., also worked in insurance, first at Atlanta Life Insurance Company and later at Afro-American Life.[16] Therefore, Cole grew up in an environment that was a living rejection of white supremacy and Black racial inferiority. Despite the family's relative prosperity, however, Johnnetta still faced southern racism.[17]

At fifteen years of age, Cole attended Fisk University for a year, then transferred to Oberlin College. After graduating from Oberlin, she earned graduate degrees from Northwestern University, a master's in 1959 and a doctorate in 1967. In the intervening years, she married Robert Cole in 1960, a white son of Iowa dairy farmers. The couple lived in Liberia, West Africa, from 1960 to 1962, after which Robert was hired as an assistant professor of economics at Washington State University, and the couple moved to Pullman with their newborn son. Johnnetta Cole began teaching at WSU in the anthropology department soon after their arrival, first as a lecturer and later as an assistant professor. She subsequently won Outstanding Faculty Member of the Year in 1965, and her second son was born in 1966.[18]

Johnnetta and Robert Cole became two of the most prominent members of a small but vocal group of progressive, activist faculty. In a report marking the couple's departure from campus in 1970, the student newspaper dubbed them the "Eldridge and Kathleen Cleaver" of WSU. Among other political involvement, Robert was advisor of the WSU chapter of the Students for a Democratic Society (SDS), a mostly white, anti-war student group. Johnnetta, meanwhile, concentrated her energies on Black students and race relations on campus.[19] Cole's conspicuous leadership in the BSU challenges reductive assessments of Black Power as fundamentally sexist and patriarchal. As Ashley Farmer argued in *Remaking Black Power: How Black Women Transformed an Era* (2017), African American women within various Black Power organizations pushed their respective groups to embrace more flexible and inclusive gender ideologies.[20] Johnnetta Cole's activism is another illustration of this dynamic. In addition, it is also notable that after her time at WSU, Cole went on to hold a number of illustrious posts, including president of two women's colleges—Spelman in Atlanta, Georgia, and Bennett in Greensboro, North Carolina—and director of the Smithsonian's National Museum of African Art.

The first Black political organization at Washington State University was the Afro-American Alliance (AAA); it was founded in 1966 and preceded the BSU by two years. Capturing the essence of the Afro-American Alliance with a humorous flair, Johnnetta Cole said, "It was never just a tea party to sit around and admire each other's naturals."[21] Here, Cole was making the point that the AAA was a serious political organization, along with its activities to celebrate the "natural" or "Afro" hairstyle (and by extension pro-Black aesthetics). Black students at WSU were attuned to and motivated by the ongoing developments in the national civil rights and Black Power movements. They may have been geographically isolated, but they remained informed via news media reports, and information grapevines fostered by connections with family and friends off campus. Many of WSU's Black students were from the Seattle area; they traveled home periodically and heard the latest news firsthand.[22] Some were also politically active prior to enrolling at WSU, so their campus involvement was a continuation of their prior activities. For instance, Ernest Thomas, a BSU member from Austin, Texas, was part of an NAACP voter registration campaign while in high school.[23] Likewise, before coming to Pullman, BSU member David Covin was a co-chair of the Congress of Racial Equality while earning his master's degree at the University of Colorado.[24]

Elaborating on the interconnectedness between WSU's Black student mobilizing and national protests of the 1960s, Covin recalled,

Everybody, wherever they came from, had that kind of background in which they were aware of all the stuff that had been going on, in both the civil rights and the Black Power movements. And a lot of them wanted to be involved in doing what people were doing in those movements, so those were big motivating factors [at WSU].[25]

By the early months of 1968, the Afro-American Alliance was an outspoken advocate for, and a part of, the Black Power movement. For instance, on February 21 the AAA hosted a memorial for Malcolm X, titled "Malcolm X Made It Plain—A Presentation of Black Definition."[26] Malcolm X, who championed Black pride and empowerment since the 1950s, gained an even greater following after his 1965 assassination. Around the country, many African Americans increasingly identified with Malcolm's militancy and defiance as the turmoil of the latter sixties unfolded. The historian William L. Van Deburg outlined Malcolm's influence on the younger generation:

Before his assassination, Malcolm constantly urged this constituency to question the validity of their schoolbook- and media-inspired faith in an integrated American Dream. Many responded. Following his death, Malcolm's influence expanded in dramatic, almost logarithmic, fashion. He came to be far more than a martyr for the militant, separatist faith. He became a Black Power paradigm—the archetype, reference point, and spiritual advisor in absentia for a generation of Afro-American activists.[27]

The Afro-American Alliance's decision to memorialize Malcolm underscores the group's identification with Black Power. As one unnamed AAA member told the campus newspaper, Malcolm X was "a true Afro-American cultural hero" and his life "epitomized the most fruitful direction for blacks in this country to follow." Quoted in the same report, Johnnetta Cole added, "Malcolm X felt that blacks will rise up and revolt, and that 'no one rises up non-violently.' He visioned [sic] that Black American revolt emerging into a world-wide Black revolt. He felt that Blacks needed, wanted, and will strive to achieve power—and that they must conceive of getting it by any means necessary."[28] During the weeks and months following the Malcolm X memorial, Afro-American Alliance members continued their outspokenness on campus; Johnnetta

Cole, for example, made public statements defending and explaining Black Power.[29] Thus, even before the establishment of the Black Student Union, the Afro-American Alliance constituted a beachhead of Black Power in eastern Washington.

Between March and April 1968, the Afro-American Alliance renamed itself the Black Student Union and elected Barbara Williams its first chairperson.[30] As Johnnetta Cole remembered, "The name was changed to be more consistent with other black college groups in Washington."[31] This was most likely a reference to the influence of the Black Student Union at the University of Washington (UW) in Seattle. During this same time, the spring of 1968, the BSU at UW was engaged in an extensive recruiting drive to foster sibling BSUs at secondary and postsecondary schools across Seattle and throughout the state. Larry Gossett, a prominent member of the BSU at UW and key organizer of this outreach effort, recalled visiting Pullman during this period. He recounted, "I think it was April or something, we went over to Washington State and got a lot of their football players as well as the few other Blacks that were there to meet with us and organize a BSU."[32] Thus, the BSU at UW fostered the BSU in Pullman, building off the preexisting political consciousness and earlier Black activism at WSU. Following this, the two BSUs would maintain a strong relationship during the rest of the sixties.

Another major event of this time that spurred the BSU at WSU was the April 4 assassination of Dr. Martin Luther King Jr. This tragic killing, and the outpouring of grief and anger that followed, galvanized African Americans in Pullman. David Covin recalled,

One of the things that really kind of jumpstarted the organization that already existed, but that gave it a huge momentum shift, was when Dr. King was assassinated. So a lot of the students who hadn't been active in the BSU before that, who hadn't even been interested before that, when he was assassinated, really wanted to get involved, so they joined the organization and were very enthusiastic and wanted to get things done. [They were] so upset that they wanted to do something. . . . They knew about Black Student Unions and then when this happened, and since there was already one on campus, that gave them an opportunity to do something and they all felt compelled, that they had a responsibility to do something to try to improve conditions for Black people.[33]

The period between March and April was an important pivot point for the Black Student Union at Washington State University. The outspokenness of the Afro-American Alliance, encouragement from their Seattle counterparts, and dismay at Martin Luther King's death combined to bring the Black Student Union to life in Pullman. Also around this time, the racist episode involving visiting high school students would compel the BSU to denounce racism at WSU like never before.

The Black Student Union and the Project 408 Incident

In May a local controversy at Washington State University highlighted bigotry on campus and drew the ire of the Black Student Union. On Thursday, May 9, African American high school students visited WSU as part of a statewide tour of colleges and universities. The group included fifty-four Black juniors and seniors from two Seattle high schools, Garfield High and Franklin High. The trip was organized as part of Project 408, an initiative of the 1965 National Higher Education Act that sought to increase the college enrollment of academically capable students from economically challenged backgrounds.[34] Around 6:00 p.m., the teenagers arrived at WSU and the prejudicial treatment soon began as they checked into their assigned dormitories. At one dorm, Stephenson Hall, a portion of the Black youths were told by the staff that they had to provide their names and addresses because of recent thefts at the dorm, insinuating that the visitors were untrustworthy. A campus investigation later found that collecting names and addresses of overnight guests was standard procedure, but the Project 408 youths were not informed of this. Instead, they received the impression that they were being singled out as suspected criminals.[35]

Later, after getting their rooms, eating dinner, and attending a BSU-sponsored social event, they experienced additional insults from dorm staff. At around 11:00 p.m., the group returned to Stephenson Hall for what they had been told would be a dance in their honor. However, when they arrived, they were rudely turned away. Harold Mattraw, program coordinator of the Stephenson Residence Center, told the students that there would be no dance and that the students needed to leave the premises, except for those who had been assigned to sleep there. The other adolescents, who were assigned to rooms in other dormitories, were instructed to leave. In spite of Mattraw's statements, the high schoolers could apparently see that Stephenson's Residence Center appeared to be set up for a dance, with lights dimmed, furniture pushed aside, and music playing from the jukebox. Thus, the youths and their chaperones suspected that the dance had been abruptly cancelled when they arrived, due once again to racial bias. Upset and disappointed, the group initially refused to leave, but after about forty-five minutes they were persuaded by their chaperones to return to their respective rooms.[36]

The group split up as the youths went to their separate residence halls, and some of the boys were subjected to further harassment as they walked to their rooms in Orton Hall. They were reportedly talking loudly and using "vulgar language" as they approached the building, and white students proceeded to yell insults at them from their dorm windows. The white students used the slur "nigger" to insult the youths, and threw pebbles, paper trash, and cigarette butts on the Black students' heads. They also threw a glass bottle that hit the ground near the adolescents.[37] Melvin Minnis, a Black WSU student and Garfield High graduate, told the *Daily Evergreen* that he heard the commotion outside Orton Hall that night and went to the high schoolers to ask them what was happening. While he was doing so, he said, debris was falling on all their heads from the dormitory windows above. Minnis was quoted as saying, "Basically I saw two guys from Orton. . . . It was a small group of troublemakers."[38] The Black high schoolers got away from the confrontation and went to their rooms, but the insulting treatment continued later when Orton staff refused their request for extra blankets. Disgusted by the series of slights, the teens in Orton soon reconvened with the rest of the group and the entire party decided to cut short the visit to WSU. The students promptly left that night, Friday, May 10, at 2:30 a.m.[39] The experience of the Project 408 students and their sudden departure set off a chain of reactions, which eventually marked a turning point in race relations at Washington State University. Both the Black Student Union and the campus administration were compelled to take action.

The magnitude of the controversy was heightened by significant media coverage across the state. Not only was the incident front-page news in the campus newspaper, the *Daily Evergreen*, but the story was also covered in major outlets such as the *Seattle Times, Seattle Post-Intelligencer, Spokane Daily Chronicle*, and *Spokesman-Review*.[40] In the wake of Martin Luther King Jr.'s assassination and other national developments in race relations, the incident attracted significant attention.

In addition, Black students of WSU organized and mobilized to ensure that the Project 408 incident was publicized and addressed. In one effort, Black football players at WSU spoke out. The WSU Cougars football team was scheduled to play its annual spring game the day after the high schoolers left the campus, on Saturday, May 11. But, appalled by what happened to the teens, a group of Black players boycotted the game. The protesting student athletes, led by running back Mark Williams, approached their newly hired head coach, James Sweeney, and requested to be excused from the spring scrimmage. Moreover, the players insisted that they would not play until the university issued a public apology. Sweeney was reportedly sympathetic to the players' point of view and granted their request to be excused. After sitting out the spring game, the players called off their boycott the following Monday due to a flurry of developments that included the apology they had demanded.[41]

This player boycott, although brief, suggests a notable level of solidarity between Black athletes and non-athletes at WSU. Despite the prevalence of Black campus organizing during this period, such cooperation between activists and athletes did not always materialize. This was due to the unique pressures and vulnerabilities that come with involvement in collegiate athletics. Unlike the typical student experience, the athletes' regimented schedules of games and practices fostered close surveillance of players by coaches and administrators. In the charged atmosphere of the late 1960s, team members who publicly advocated leftist politics, such as anti-Vietnam War or pro-Black Power positions, jeopardized valuable playing time and athletic scholarships. Consequently, athletes sometimes shunned activism, causing tension between them and other students. For instance, in April 1970 the Black Student Union at the University of Washington publicly ridiculed two Oregon State University sprinters, Willie Turner and Willie Smith, for not joining several other Black athletes who had left OSU amid racial conflicts.[42] Given all this, the boycott by the WSU football players is a notable instance of Black Power politics within college athletics and suggests strong bonds between Black athletes and non-athletes at WSU.

Separately, as the football boycott unfolded, the Black Student Union launched its own letter-writing campaign in response to the Project 408 incident, targeting officials and soliciting support. One letter was sent to Dan Evans, governor of the state of Washington. It urged him to find those responsible for offending the teens, institute measures to prevent similar offenses in the future, and issue a formal statement denouncing racism in Pullman. A similar letter was sent to WSU president Glenn Terrell. The Black Student Union also sent letters to other BSUs on the West Coast, requesting that they send their own missives to Terrell expressing their condemnation.[43] Lastly, the BSU wrote an open letter to the WSU community that was published in the student newspaper. It recounted the ill-treatment of the youths and rebuked the university community for its behavior, as quoted at the beginning of this chapter.[44]

If the incident is conceptualized as an isolated event, one may wonder why Black WSU students reacted so strongly and mobilized in response to the Project 408 incident. Here, it is instructive to recognize that the BSU viewed the insults to the 408 adolescents as part of a larger pattern. For the BSU, the suspicion and hostility experienced by the youth reflected the quotidian white racism of the campus and community. Many African Americans could point to personal experiences of injustice. As a case in point, Johnnetta Cole recounted a representative story: "Here's a classic example of harassment. I have a black professor friend who liked to jog in the morning. She is constantly being stopped by the cops and asked what she's doing. How many times do the cops stop a white professor just because he is jogging in the morning?"[45] These ubiquitous personal insults, along with institutional racism evidenced by the low Black enrollment and Eurocentric curriculum, convinced African Americans that WSU needed racial reform just like other institutions across the country. The Project 408 episode was the catalyst that brought these preexisting grievances into focus.

Along with the letter writing, BSU members also met directly with Glenn Terrell, WSU president, for forty-five minutes the day after the visitors departed. As the meeting was taking place, rumors circulated on campus that a group of Black students had taken over the French Administration Building, and that "two negroes" had kidnapped President Terrell. In reality, the meeting was "cooperative and cordial," and Terrell was receptive to the students' concerns.[46] Shortly afterwards, Terrell issued a public statement expressing his concern about the treatment of the high schoolers, and his sympathies for racial injustice. Terrell said,

I don't know all the facts concerning what happened last night, and won't for a little while. . . . However, I do want to say that WSU is proud, and justifiably so, of the multiracial character of its student body and faculty. Members of all races have always worked and lived together in harmony and with mutual respect.[47]

Terrell is no doubt guilty of some boosterism here, as he extolls the "multicultural character" and "harmony" of WSU, but the statement reflected his genuine openness to the grievances of African Americans. As a next step, Terrell quickly established a fact-finding committee to investigate the Project 408 incident, and included two BSU members on the committee: Johnnetta Cole and Barbara J. Williams, BSU president. Also appointed to the committee were Professor Richard Ott (veterinary medicine), Coach James Sweeny, ASWSU president Steve Kikuchi, and Professor Robert A. Johnson (psychology) as committee chairperson.[48] The creation of this committee and its membership of campus leaders further make clear the importance of the controversy. The committee met several times over the weekend, interviewing students and staff and reading staff reports; this culminated in a report completed by the end of the weekend.[49] The report concluded that the Black teenage visitors were subjected to derogatory name calling and insulting treatment, yet there was no evidence that WSU staff violated any antidiscrimination laws. Furthermore, the committee found that a lack of communication between Project 408 coordinators, the WSU Admissions Office, and dormitory staff was partly to blame for the visit's poor outcomes. For instance, it was noted that the visitors' schedule was changed multiple times by Project 408 staff, both before and after they arrived on campus, and this contributed to communication problems.[50] After receiving the fact-finding committee's report, Terrell issued a public apology on Monday, May 13. In the apology, Terrell stated, "It appears that a few WSU students insulted our visitors on that evening and for that we are extremely sorry. I am certain that virtually all of us at this institution agree that there is no excuse for this behavior. Anyone, however, who knows the excellent character of WSU's student body knows that this kind of offensive behavior was far from typical."[51] After Terrell's apology, the crisis died down, but the currents of change released by the incident led to new initiatives during the following months.

Spring and Summer 1968

Following the Project 408 incident, the Black Student Union and the university administration launched new racial reforms at Washington State University. This new effort began two days after Terrell's May 13 apology, when the president announced the creation of a Social Responsibility Committee (SRC) charged with addressing bigotry and racism on and off campus.[52] The new committee was instructed to focus on "the underlying dynamics of racial inequality and the ways WSU can contribute to the educational, occupational, and social equality of all the races and ethnic groups in America."[53] BSU members Johnnetta Cole and Barbara J. Williams were again appointed to the Social Responsibility Committee. The SRC also included faculty and staff members Arnold M. Gallegos, Harlan E. Jones, Leonard B. Kirshner, Susan Rutherford, James F. Short, and Louis D. McNew as chair. The SRC had three specific tasks: (1) review existing university programs and initiatives, (2) recommend new measures to better meet social needs, and (3) recommend priorities for these measures.[54]

Much like Charles Odegaard, president of the University of Washington discussed in previous chapters, President Glenn Terrell by all accounts was genuinely willing to support Black students, faculty, and staff. As BSU member Rutledge Dennis described, "I met so many times with President Terrell, and he was a very gentle man, and I think he was behind the effort to do the right thing."[55] Providing a less sanguine assessment, Rudy Martin, BSU member and American studies PhD student, remembered Terrell as initially hesitant to support the BSU's proposals. "My general sense was that Terrell didn't want to move too fast. He was not convinced right off that this [the BSU demands] is the way the university should go despite all the activity around the country." However, due to ongoing agitation, Terrell became more supportive, Martin added. "Glenn Terrell wasn't anxious to move in our direction, but under pressure, and frankly under a certain amount of moral suasion, he came around."[56] Generally, as these anecdotes from Dennis and Martin reflect, Terrell was seen by the BSU as congenial, even if tepid in his support for reform.

Terrell's hesitation to fully endorse sweeping changes in the social order of the university was likely related to his newness at WSU. In the spring of 1968, when the Project 408 incident occurred, he had served as president for less than a year.[57] Previously, he was a dean at the University of Illinois–Chicago and therefore did not have much time to build a strong base of support at WSU. This may have constrained his ability to embrace the BSU's calls for change. However, to his credit, Terrell had publicly supported more just policies related to race and ethnicity throughout his time in office. When announcing the Social Responsibility Committee, he reminded the campus of this, writing, "In a number of public statements, including my inaugural address, I have taken the position that universities have the responsibility of devoting more of their resources to the search for solutions to the pressing problems of society."[58] Thus, Terrell's leadership was an important factor in the success of racial justice politics at WSU, as he permitted avenues of protest for the BSU that likely would not have existed with a more hostile campus leader.

With support from Terrell, the BSU and the Social Responsibility Committee began working; their initial focus was recruiting more Black students to attend their school. Specifically, they created a new program, first called the Experimental Admissions Program and later renamed the Experimental Education Program (EEP). The strategy of the EEP was to admit Black students and other students of color who would not otherwise have met the regular admissions criteria, and support them with student services. Many institutions created such programs during the late 1960s in response to protests against institutional racism by Black activists and their allies.[59] Like their counterparts elsewhere, BSU members at WSU were eager to increase educational access for minority students. As the EEP program took shape, recruits were admitted despite real or perceived academic deficiencies, and were paired with academic assistance once on campus.[60]

The initial proposal, penned by SRC chairman Louis McNew, described the outreach effort: "We urge that, even though it is late in the year, we should, through the Admissions Office, augmented by interested faculty and students, attempt to get in touch with prospective students." In addition to the outreach, the SRC-BSU worked to secure financial aid and other assistance for the approximately twenty students they planned to recruit.[61] Describing the retention efforts, McNew wrote, "We . . . are confident that we can develop . . . a program which would make it possible within one year for these students to acquire the ability to compete successfully in a university program. We are now discussing teaching, orientation programs, and housing as they relate to an experimental group."[62]

To find prospective students, members of the Social Responsibility Committee and the Black Student Union served as college recruiters. Typically, a WSU faculty or staff person and a BSU member would visit high schools and community settings to explain the program. For example, Rutledge Dennis remembered being hired to go on recruiting trips with an Admissions Office staff member: "We traveled throughout the state trying to recruit Black students to the campus. And I was paid, of course, to do that."[63] The BSU was integral to this initiative, as indicated in a July memo from the SRC to President Terrell that praised the BSU and suggested that they be allocated office space. "The Black Student Union has volunteered 100% support for the university's educational experiment; they do request, however, they be able to maintain a headquarters and meeting place not directly tied to the offices of those responsible for that program."[64] The strong partnership between the SRC and the BSU continued throughout the summer. This highlights that Washington State University has a history of anti-racist, white allyship that it can and should be proud of.

This summer effort successfully reached its goal of enrolling approximately twenty new Black students by the following autumn semester.[65] Further success was shown by the tutoring services established or expanded to support the EEP students. As explained by Rutledge Dennis,

> The Experimental Education Program was designed to bring in students and to give them assistance by creating tutoring programs. . . . There were tutoring programs in English. There were tutoring programs in math. And I think there was, already was in existence, a reading and writing center or program, but I think that was even intensified as they were gearing up with the recruitment program, and with the Experimental Education Program, to bring in more students. So the reading and writing center, of course, was already there for the white students who were there who also had some handicaps to some extent, but the programs were intensified.[66]

Although the overall number of new EEP students was fairly small at twenty, the number of programs of support that were coordinated in a matter of months was commendable.

This chapter has detailed the inaugural activism of the Black Student Union at Washington State University, and related activism at WSU during the 1967–1968 school year. As described above, the Afro-American Alliance was the direct predecessor of the BSU at WSU, and it first established the Black Power presence on campus. Between March and May, a series of local and national controversies, especially the assassination of Martin Luther King Jr. and the Project 408 incident, sparked the emergence of the Black Student Union as a reinvigorated vehicle for anti-racist struggle. Due to the BSU's organizing efforts and a productive partnership between the Black students and campus officials, a summer recruitment drive marked a new chapter in the history of the institution. This unprecedented effort to address educational disparities and promote greater access produced what was then the largest population of Black students at WSU. Never before had the university been compelled to take such affirmative measures to diversify its student body. The new cohort of twenty students was a clear victory for the BSU, but paradoxically represented only a modest change in the racial demographics of the university. The total Black student population still amounted to less than 1 percent of the student body. Other grievances also remained for the BSU, thereby setting the stage for continued agitation during the following school year, chronicled in the next chapter.

5

"Well, Glenn-Baby, What's Up Now?"

The BSU and Black Studies at Washington State University,
1968–1970

In its second year at Washington State University, the Black Student Union continued its trailblazing campus activism, which put the group on a collision course with reactionary forces at the university and in the surrounding area. At the most harrowing point of the 1968–1969 school year, the BSU faced off with local law enforcement at the Whitman County Jail. There, approximately sixty BSU members and their allies took the bold action of intentionally blocking the building's entrance. Their objective was to use civil disobedience to thwart the incarceration of five of their brethren, BSU members who had recently been convicted of assaulting white fraternity men. In the eyes of the Black activists and their allies, the conflict with the fraternity and the prosecution of the five Black students were tainted by racism. Consequently, the demonstrators banded together to stop the jailing, sparking a weekend-long confrontation. This episode of direct-action protest was the crescendo of a school year full of dramatic and unprecedented actions by the BSU at WSU.

As detailed in the preceding chapter, the Black Student Union at WSU was founded in the spring of 1968 following a confluence of local and national racial controversies. In particular, outrage at the murder of Martin Luther King Jr. and the discrimination against visiting Black high schoolers prompted the BSU to take more assertive steps toward change. As a reflection of their increased stridency, the students changed the name of their campus organization from Afro-American Alliance to Black Student Union.

This chapter details how the BSU continued its efforts during the organization's second year. As we shall see, Black activists at WSU operated in a context that was often hostile to their presence and their vision for change. The college town of Pullman, located in eastern Washington, was far removed from both a sizable Black community and a network of allied community groups. Yet the BSU nevertheless persisted in its demands for racial justice. Along the way, Black students faced threats and repression that surpassed what was experienced by their counterparts at the University of Washington in Seattle, which was the other leading BSU in the state. Thus, in addition to highlighting a noteworthy instance of Black Power student organizing, the story of the BSU at WSU offers a window into the racial politics of rural areas of the Pacific Northwest. Contesting popular notions of Jim Crow racism that locate it in the South, scholars have documented how such racial inequality was endemic throughout the United States, North *and* South. As historian Matthew J. Countryman wrote, "Racism was never just a southern problem. Nor were civil rights activists solely concerned with southern variants of racial segregation and inequality."[1] Adding new evidence to the analysis of Countryman and others, the BSU at WSU illuminates the presence of "Up South" or "Jim Crow North" sociopolitical dynamics in the Evergreen State.[2]

To tell this story, the chapter describes two leading members of the BSU, whose experiences provide insight into the racial climate of WSU at the time and the characteristics of the BSU. Following that, the chapter chronicles the BSU's struggles on and off campus and its successful campaign for Black Studies.

Ernest Thomas and David Covin

One of the leading members of the Black Student Union was an undergraduate named Ernest Thomas, then commonly known by his nicknames Ernie and "Stone." After growing up in segregated East Austin, Texas, Thomas enrolled at WSU to pursue a career in physical therapy. As he described, he deliberately left Texas to escape racial injustice:

> At the time, in 1965–66, when I was starting my undergrad career, in the state of Texas, because of racism, they were not admitting a lot of brothers and sisters [Black people] to schools of physical therapy. Matter of fact, the school of physical therapy that I looked at, in Corpus

Christi, they had never admitted an African in America [Black person]
into the school.[3]

Consequently, Thomas searched for out-of-state schools and eventually
chose WSU, expecting that a school far away from Texas would provide
an escape from racial discrimination and prejudice. When he arrived,
he quickly discovered that Pullman was indeed quite different from East
Austin, but not in the ways he had hoped. After a plane ride from Texas to
Seattle and a long bus ride to Pullman, he arrived at the local bus station.
Hungry and unsure where to go, he asked one of the workers to point him
toward "the Black part of town." Surprised, the clerk burst into laughter.
After a hearty laugh, she gave the question some thought and said she
knew of "one Black resident" in town. Telling the story over forty years
later, Thomas remembered, "Based on her laughter, I knew I was in trouble." The clerk helped him find a meal, but of course, Thomas never found
"the Black part of town" because none existed in Pullman. And with this
began Thomas's experience in what felt like a totally foreign environment.[4]

Undeterred, Thomas persisted with his studies, matriculating in the
spring semester of 1966. Later, by the fall of 1968, he was a leading member of the Black Student Union. His college activism was a continuation
of his previous participation in Austin's civil rights movement, and it was
a reaction to the racial bias he encountered at WSU. In Texas, Thomas
was part of an effort by the National Association for the Advancement
of Colored People (NAACP) to promote voter registration, where he
helped adults prepare for the required literacy test. As he described it, he
also participated in "a couple of little sit-ins and all that kind of stuff." At
Washington State University, he was frustrated to find that racial bigotry
was not just a southern phenomenon:

> See, you often hear in the South, they call you a nigger to your face and
> don't think nothing of it. In the state of Washington, they just treat you
> like a nigger. And at that particular point, that's the way it was. They
> weren't as bold as southerners, in terms of their vernacular, but the be-
> havior was pretty much the same.[5]

One example of the disrespect that Thomas encountered was a professor who questioned his intelligence in front of the entire class, a deeply

humiliating experience. Thomas remembered the professor saying, "You're not going to make it in this program [physical therapy] because you ain't got enough science in your background. Plus, I looked at your ACT scores, and it doesn't look like you really should be in college." Not only was this a harsh assessment that would undercut the confidence of any undergraduate, but it was especially belittling because the professor expressed this view in front of all the other students in the class. Separately, another incident occurred while Thomas was a part of the WSU football team, on which he played linebacker and defensive end. One coach had a penchant for referring to Thomas and the other Black players as monkeys. This coach also directed particular scorn at Thomas for his Afro hairstyle. Eventually, Thomas spoke up for himself:

> Coach, now, this is part of my heritage. I have nappy hair. And when it grows long, it's going to come out in a 'fro. And that's the way I want it. Now you ain't saying nothing about this shaggy-haired, straggly-haired white boy with long hair. Why are you coming and talking crazy to me?[6]

Thomas kept his Afro, but the racial animus on the team continued. Experiences like those with the professor and the coach left Thomas with a firm belief that racial injustice was endemic at WSU. Therefore, like other Black students, he decided to channel his dissatisfaction into activism in the Black Student Union.

Another BSU member was David Covin, who arrived in Pullman in 1967 as a PhD student in political science. He came to WSU from Bakersfield College in Southern California, where he taught college courses. Prior to that, he earned a master's degree at the University of Colorado, and a bachelor's at the University of Illinois. Like Thomas, Covin arrived in Pullman with a background in the civil rights movement. As a graduate student in Colorado, Covin served as the co-chair of the local chapter of the Congress of Racial Equality. In that role, he helped raise funds to support the southern movement for Black rights. Later, he shifted his thinking and embraced Black nationalism, a change that resulted from his study of political science, national developments in Black politics, and radicalizing personal experiences. One such galvanizing personal moment occurred during the 1965 Watts Riot. Covin was not in Watts during the riot, but happened to be driving to Bakersfield and heard a jarring announcement on the car radio. Responding to the disturbance in Watts, the mayor of Bakersfield quoted Winston Churchill: "We will fight on the streets, we will fight on the beaches, we will never surrender." This historically laden phrase effectively equated the Black Watts residents to invading Nazis, and declared war on the rioters. This, for Covin, highlighted white America's demonization of Black protest, and a related refusal to recognize the valid grievances of Black Americans. This was a moment that confirmed his budding disillusionment with the strategy of racial integration.[7]

Covin recalled being startled by two things when he arrived in Pullman: the lack of trees and the lack of Black people. The untimbered landscape was a feature of the wheat-growing monoculture that dominated the Pullman area, and the absence of African Americans was indicative of the region's white majority. To Covin, a paucity of African Americans at white-dominated colleges and universities was typical, as his previous institutions had similar demographics. However, Covin was dismayed to find no sizable Black community in the surrounding area. As a WSU student, Covin recalled, many of his interactions with white students and employees were positive. Yet racial bias was also part of his student experience. One illustrative example was a supportive white faculty member who consented to sponsor Covin's independent research project on Black politics. However, while agreeing, the professor worried out loud that the research might be unworkable because of the lack of published work by Black authors. As Covin recalled, the professor said, in all sincerity, "I don't believe a Black person has ever written a book." Covin was stunned by the ignorance of the statement, which was apparently said without any intention to offend. And knowing it was patently incorrect, Covin proceeded with his research plans. Later, by the fall of 1968, he too joined the Black Student Union after being attracted to its campaign for Black Studies, an initiative that addressed the Eurocentrism expressed by his professor and connected to his own research interests.[8]

During the 1968–1969 academic year, Covin and Thomas worked together as BSU members, along with other students such as Barbara Williams, Bill Ross, Eddie Leon, Rutledge Dennis, Jack Craig, Mark Williams, and Rudolph "Rudy" Martin. Their style of activism was thoughtful and strategic, but also brash and confrontational, mirroring larger characteristics of the Black Power movement. For example, Covin described how Thomas, or "Stone," would often use flippant language when addressing the university president, Glenn Terrell. He recalled, "I remember Stone used to start our meetings often saying, 'Well, Glenn-Baby, what's up now?'"[9] This colloquial greeting was partly youthful rebellion, but was also a rhetorical maneuver to interrupt conventional hierarchies of race, class, and social status. Referring to the president in such an informal manner was a transgressive political statement and implicitly asserted that Black undergraduates deserved the same respect as a university president. This disruption of conventional norms of race and power was central to the BSU's mission.

Black Studies

David Covin's well-meaning but misguided professor, who doubted the existence of any Black writers, underscores the impetus for Black Studies at WSU. This was a curricular reform that countered the exclusion and denigration of knowledge by and about Black people. The BSU's effort to correct this erasure became a yearlong campaign. In September, right as the new school year began, the BSU announced its primary goal for the year, the establishment of a Black Studies department. The group asserted that WSU had failed "to properly prepare its white students to live in a pluralistic society." Moreover, the Black activists specifically outlined "that areas of the social sciences and the humanities and music should include courses that emphasize Black contributions to studies in those areas." Likewise, the existing curriculum on African Americans, most notably the sociology department's Race Relations course, was "inadequate in explaining the institutionalization of prejudice and discrimination in American society." Speaking on the group's behalf, Rutledge Dennis said, "We're trying to awaken the black student to be himself and to awaken the white population to the plight of the Blackman."[10]

As was apparent in Dennis's statement, the model of Black Studies endorsed by the BSU at WSU aimed to educate Black *and* white students. In fact, the student activists proposed that "one course in Black history or culture be required by the University for all students."[11] This interracial model of Black Studies differed from a intraracial model that intended the new discipline to primarily focus on serving Black people, on and off campus.[12] Those who advocated the intraracial model were ambivalent or hostile to the involvement of white Americans, expressing the Black nationalist sentiment that white participation would undermine Black empowerment. The BSU at WSU did not pursue this intraracial vision of Black Studies, nor did its counterpart at the University of Washington in Seattle. Black activists at both Pacific Northwest schools apparently decided that it was strategically better to advocate interracial or "academic black studies," as sociologist Fabio Rojas termed it.[13] Also, the demographic circumstances of Pullman undoubtably contributed to this decision of the BSU at WSU, given the absence of any significant African American population.

At WSU, African American calls for Black Studies first emerged during the previous academic year, following the assassination of Martin Luther King Jr. Channeling their outrage into policy proposals, politicized Black students put forth Black Studies as a means to address racism. Black Studies was judged to have several merits: undermining anti-Black prejudice among white students, celebrating Black achievements, promoting Black pride, and creating a pipeline of future Black faculty. By the fall of 1968, the BSU has already won some support for Black Studies at Washington State University. President Glenn Terrell publicly endorsed the idea by this point,[14] as did the university's Social Responsibility Committee (SRC), a body of reform-minded faculty and BSU members.[15] The student government also backed the creation of "problem-oriented courses (preferably of a seminar nature) in areas of poverty, urbanization, Negro history, and others relating to the problems of racial inequality."[16] Adding to the student voice, a fall editorial in the *Daily Evergreen*, the campus newspaper, said, "Places of higher education have traditionally been charged with the responsibility of preparing the leaders that should solve some of society's problems. Yet, the most pressing problem of them all, the nation's race problem, isn't really being confronted on this campus."[17] Thus, the editorial continued, "one solution to ending this lack of involvement with black America would be the addition of a Black Studies curriculum."[18] Yet, even with this support, it still necessitated a yearlong struggle of pressure and organizing to bring Black Studies into being.

As the BSU continued its agitation, many white members of the campus community grew increasingly uncomfortable with the Black Power activists. Compared to the previous fall, African American enrollment at WSU had increased by about 33 percent, from sixty to eighty students, constituting the largest Black student population in the history of the school.[19] This helped to unearth racial tensions on campus, which could more easily remain in the background when the Black student population was easier to ignore. One instructive controversy was sparked by two *Daily Evergreen* editorials, which contrasted with the student newspaper's support for Black Studies mentioned previously. The first ridiculed the Black Student Union and Black student activism in general. It scolded, "If the Black Student Union ever gets over its paranoiac fear of 'white power' it might be able to accomplish some of its goals around here." The editorial proceeded to lecture the BSU to temper its demands for change and avoid "any type of black extremism" in order to retain white liberals' support, presumably including the author of the editorial.[20] The overarching message of the piece was that Black people and their grievances merited consideration only if presented in ways that were palatable to white liberals. It thereby expressed a latent hostility to Black empowerment, and particularly to the Black Power movement, which was premised on the notion that African Americans could and should express themselves in ways they found affirming and productive. Black Power advocates insisted that white sensibilities would no longer be taken as the central concern of strategic and rhetorical choices.

The second editorial was titled "No Harmony in the Barnyard" and expressed a similar paternalism, but in the form of an allegory about a "Black Sheep Union." In the thinly veiled critique of the BSU, the Black *Sheep* Union terrorizes the other animals of the barnyard, demanding "more food, even more stalls, special hay privileges and more than their share of space in the Barnyard Times, the animals' newspaper."[21] At the end of the story, the "black sheep" have selfishly commandeered all the resources they can, and the opportunistic leader of the group leaves to cause havoc elsewhere. Both these editorials were published in the same issue of the *Daily Evergreen* and therefore sent a clear message. Many white students shared the mainstream view of the Black Power movement as counterproductive or worse, and saw the BSU as suspect. In response to the editorials, the Black Student Union picketed the newspaper's office and won a half-hearted apology from *Daily Evergreen* staff.[22] Thus, as the school year began, the climate was primed for political struggle. Helping to explain this situation, Rutledge Dennis pointed out how integration was almost certainly a new experience for Black and white WSU students:

> Many of these [white] students did not go to integrated schools. They went to segregated schools just as Black students went to segregated schools, so that the integration that was being experimented with at WSU was very new—new for Black students as well as for white students. . . . So you can understand that under these circumstances and under these conditions there were areas of misunderstanding.[23]

Amidst this environment, the Black Student Union advanced its campaign for Black Studies as the fall semester progressed. One outgrowth of its efforts was a Colloquium on Afro-American History and Culture, led by Professor Alfred Crosby (history), with Professors Johnnetta Cole (anthropology) and Robert Cole (economics) as "discussion members." Crosby and the Coles were well known for their leftist activism, and Johnnetta Cole was the BSU's intrepid faculty advisor. This colloquium, a weekly non-credit course, began in October and was jointly sponsored by the local Young Men's Christian Association (YMCA) and Young Women's Christian Association (YWCA).[24] Separately, that same month, Crosby also received approval for a new, credit-bearing Black history course for the following spring semester, and was reportedly planning the class in consultation with the BSU.[25]

Adding to the momentum for Black Studies, E. J. Brisker, a leading member of the Black Student Union at the University of Washington, gave a keynote address at Washington State University sponsored by the sociology department.[26] On October 17 Brisker emphasized the value of Black Studies, saying that the curriculum was "vital to the survival of the Black race," and he advocated comprehensive Black Studies departments that included "chemistry and physics as well as history and sociology."[27] Brisker's record of activism was impressive and included involvement in the Student Nonviolent Coordinating Committee, the BSU, and the Black Panther Party; moreover, his appearance at WSU speaks to the political linkages that remained between African Americans in Pullman and Seattle.[28] Also, the sociology department's support for Brisker's appearance indicates a cooperative relationship between the BSU and at least some members of the department. In fact, sociology at WSU was nationally recognized for its graduate program's success with Black doctoral students. In a national study of sociology programs between 1955 and 1964, WSU's sociology department was found to have awarded 27.8 percent, or five out of eighteen, of its doctorate degrees to African Americans, the highest rate in the nation.[29]

In November and December the BSU continued its campaign for official approval of Black Studies through additional talks with the student government and the university administration. The WSU student government, or Associated Students of Washington State University, was led by its Board of Control (BOC). Rutledge Dennis, Jack Craig, and Eddie Leon of the BSU met with the BOC and presented a slate of Black Studies proposals. Reiterating the need for the insurgent discipline, one unnamed BSU spokesperson said, "Whites are ignorant about Blacks. This ignorance results from the lack of exposure to information about Blacks in the educational system. This ignorance also plays a major part in the relationships developed between Blacks and whites when they confront each other at WSU." The BSU proposals were largely directed at the university as a whole, but were submitted to the student government for its endorsement. Most notably, the BSU put forward that Black students needed to be included in any university-level Black Studies committees or planning efforts.[30]

About two weeks of meetings and debate ensued. Jim Rowland, the graduate representative on the BOC, questioned the insistence on Black instructors for Black Studies courses, pointing out the scarcity of Black PhDs.[31] Dave Cardwell, ASWSU vice president, expressed disapproval of the term "Black Studies" and instead suggested "ethnic studies." A significant focus was BOC members' concern about whether the BSU was a Black-only or separatist organization, but the BSU explained that anyone could join the BSU if they "attended a certain percentage of meetings" and met other criteria. Eventually, after the BSU addressed all of its concerns, the BOC voted to approve the BSU's proposal and recommended that BSU members Bill Ross, Eddie Leon, Rutledge Dennis, and Jack Craig be included in the university administration's efforts to create Black Studies.[32] This collaboration between the BSU and campus leaders materialized by December, a resumption of a partnership from the previous summer, described in chapter 4. As Christmas vacation approached, Ernest Thomas spoke on behalf of the BSU and gave a positive assessment of the organization's progress: "Eventually we hope there will be a Bachelors of Arts offered in Black Studies to prepare people to work with Blacks in social agencies and other areas. There is much to go through with the administration before we reach this point. I am pleasantly cautious about the progress."[33]

The Conflict with Alpha Gamma Rho

Following the winter break, in the early weeks of 1969, the Black Student Union continued its campaign for Black Studies, working in consultation with supportive campus officials. Meanwhile, a new racial controversy came to the forefront. Beginning as a fistfight between a BSU member and some white fraternity brothers, the conflict grew over the following two months to become a campus-wide and region-wide firestorm. The initial clash occurred during an intramural basketball game between Alpha Gamma Rho (AGR), an all-white fraternity, and Goldsworthy Hall, a campus dormitory. The game occurred on Thursday, January 9, and Ron Henderson, a member of the BSU, was on the Goldsworthy team.[34] Sources differ on exactly what happened. According to a contemporaneous newspaper report, one of the AGR players called Henderson a "black bastard," and this led to a brief scuffle between Henderson and multiple AGR members.[35] Giving a different description, Ernest Thomas recalled that the AGR players were playing excessively rough basketball against Henderson and delivered numerous hard fouls. When Henderson finally retaliated, a fight broke out and "three Alpha Gamma Rho dudes, I think it was three, more than one, jumped on the brother and messed him up. His face was *messed up*."[36] After the game the conflict died down, but was reignited the following week when the BSU received a menacing phone call. Reportedly, the caller said that the AGR members "were ready to talk to a group of Blacks and they were also prepared for any other kind of action." The BSU interpreted this, especially the phrase "any other kind of action," as a provocation and threat of further violence.[37]

After discussing the phone call at the next BSU meeting, a group of Black students decided to confront the AGRs at their fraternity house that very night. On January 15 at around 11:00 p.m., ten to twenty African American students approached the AGR residence, went inside, and demanded that the student who had "jumped on [beaten up] Ron" identify himself. Moments later, a brawl occurred.[38] In its account, the Alpha Gamma Rho stated, "The house president came out from the kitchen, saw a negro standing on a table and asked him to get off. The house president was then physically assaulted along with other AGRs who were in the area."[39] Thomas, who was one of the BSU members involved, remembered it differently. As he described it, after the BSU members entered the house, they engaged in a heated argument with the fraternity members. Then the AGR president escalated the confrontation. "And then the dude—I guess he was a president or something—he got real indignant and told us, 'Niggas, get out of here. This is where we live. We don't want you here anymore.'"[40] That remark, according to Thomas, sparked the melee, which "was like one of those saloon fights you see on TV or in the movies," with everyone hitting someone.[41] Adding to the chaos, at least one firearm was discharged during the altercation. The fraternity said that "shots were fired by the Negroes both inside the house and from outside the house."[42] Separately, an eyewitness reported, "One of the retreating [Black] men turned and fired two shots at the [outside of the] house." The police arrived soon after and found two shotgun bullet patterns near the front door. Miraculously, in spite of the weapons involved, only minor injuries were reported by five AGR members: Harold Boyd, Bob Mattingly, Ernie Schwartz, Marty Warner, and Eric Thorn, AGR president.[43]

News of the clash sent a shockwave of fear through much of Pullman and the surrounding white community. A news report from Spokane stated, "Campus officials were deluged with phone calls Wednesday night from parents of youngsters on the campus."[44] The *Lewiston Morning Tribune* encouraged and reflected the alarm with an incendiary headline: "Shots Fired as Blacks Invade WSU Fraternity House."[45] Likewise, the *Daily Evergreen* noted that on campus "tensions are high," due, in part, to "extreme and unfounded rumors."[46] The local police also reacted with great alarm. Once on scene, Pullman police, WSU police, and other agencies worked together to guard the AGR house and patrol the neighborhood.[47] One officer who was guarding the AGR house told the student newspaper that "in the rush at the Pullman Police Station after the report of the incident was turned in, he had forgotten his gloves and his hands were cold because he could not put them in his pockets and still hold his shotgun."[48] This officer was apparently unwilling to put down his shotgun regardless of the cold winter night, signifying the level of fear among officers. Police officers also took special precautions to protect white women in the area, as "women in sororities were instructed [by police] to remain in their houses for the rest of the night."[49] African American men have long faced unfounded accusations of sexual aggression toward white women, and it seems that that stereotype was also on the minds of Pullman law enforcement.[50]

Unpacking an element of the panic among law enforcement and other white residents, David Covin recalled a revealing announcement on local television that night. Uninvolved in the confrontation at the AGR house, Covin first learned that something had happened while watching TV:

> The first thing I heard about it was, my wife and I were watching television and the broadcast was interrupted with an announcement that the Black Panthers were on their way to Pullman. And everybody should make sure, if they had a gun it was ready and that they could defend their houses. The Black Panthers had been identified descending on Pullman.[51]

Suspecting correctly that this outlandish report was false, Covin soon contacted other Black students and learned about the fight. Yet this report likely terrified white viewers and contributed to the anxiety of the moment. Interestingly, there is evidence to suggest that alarmist reports of marauding "Black Panthers" was not unique to Pullman. In the 1976 epilogue to his book *Black Like Me*, the acclaimed writer John Howard Griffin wrote about this occurring in various cities. In the epilogue, titled "What's Happened Since *Black Like Me*," Griffin wrote that similar reports were made in numerous locations such as Cedar Rapids, Iowa, Ardmore, Oklahoma, Fort Worth, Texas, Roanoke, Virginia, and Reno, Nevada. All such cases were erroneous reports of imminent attacks from "carloads of armed blacks"; often the reports set off emergency measures from local officials and calls for armed resistance among white townsfolk.[52] Given the foregoing, it seems that Pullman's reaction to the AGR-BSU altercation fit a larger pattern and spotlights white anxieties about Black people and the Black Power movement.

On Friday, January 17, two days after the incident, both President Terrell and the local prosecutor responded. At WSU, Terrell issued a statement that he was working with university and city officials to gather all the necessary information.[53] Separately, Whitman County prosecuting attorney Phillip H. Faris filed charges against three Black students in connection with the AGR incident. These three, initially charged with second-degree assault, were Ron Henderson, Richard Lee Smith, and Ernest Thomas.[54] This was the beginning of a swift investigation and trial that won convictions by the end of February.

On January 21 the Black Student Union issued a statement, asserting that racial prejudice was at play in the AGR-BSU incident and its aftermath:

> We fully and unconditionally support our brothers in the current struggle. We deplore the divided attention towards our black brothers and demand equal time be directed towards the AGR fraternity. Only the brothers are charged with felinous [*sic*] assault. Only the brothers are attacked by rumor and invidious slander. Only the brothers are assumed guilty. We will explore all avenues to assure that the brothers receive justice. *Bila shaka ni lazima tushinde*. We shall conquer without a doubt.[55]

As the investigation progressed, the BSU's accusation of racial bias was further substantiated by racial profiling by law enforcement. As described in a statement issued later, the BSU complained of "the issuance of subpoenas to a majority of black, male WSU students" ordering them to appear in the courthouse.[56] Elaborating on this, Covin recalled that the Black students who appeared were subjected to an informal police lineup. The Black students "really raged at this lineup thing when they had to go up the stairs and the fraternity guys were pointing at people as they went up the stairs and so on." He continued, "I think every Black male in Pullman got a subpoena" and the Black community on campus was "just furious."[57] This mass roundup of Black students as suspects outraged the BSU and escalated tensions.

Meanwhile, during the following days, as the litigation unfolded, the university was conducting its own disciplinary investigation. Addressing this, Terrell promised that the university's investigation would be "fair to both sides."[58] Yet here, too, the BSU believed that the process was prejudicial; Johnnetta Cole resigned from WSU's Disciplinary Committee on or around January 23. Cole explained her decision by saying that she was displeased with the committee's handling of the AGR incident and that "there was an 'unconscious assumption of guilt about Blacks by Committee members.'" In addition, Cole asserted that university discipline amounted to "double jeopardy" and a violation of the Fifth Amendment of the US Constitution, since "no one should be forced to face the same charges twice."[59]

The first court hearing for Ron Henderson, Richard Lee Smith, and Ernest Thomas was held in Pullman Justice Court on Monday, January 27, with Judge D. L. McMannis presiding.[60] During the hearing, Tyrone J. Daisy and Kenneth Walker, both Black students, came forward and admitted in court that they had fired the guns.[61] Consequently, the court charged Daisy and Walker with second-degree assault, and the charges against Henderson, Thomas, and Smith were reduced from second- to third-degree assault. All were ordered to appear in Superior Court in February.[62]

Back on campus, as the next court date approached, the matter was hotly debated. A few individuals and groups expressed support for the BSU and the "brothers" facing charges. The Pullman chapter of the American Civil Liberties Union helped raise legal funds for the Black defendants, and a supportive editorial was penned by Dave Mathiason, a *Daily Evergreen* reporter.[63] The local chapter of the Students for a Democratic Society (SDS) also expressed support, condemning the racial prejudice in evidence throughout much of the campus:

> If one judges on the basis of letters to the *Evergreen* and conversations going on all over the campus the inescapable conclusion is that the WSU community has focused exclusively on the actions of the black students on [January] 15 and that the campus is rather united in its resentment of the Black Student Union and its constituency.[64]

Confirming SDS's assessment, several letters published in the *Daily Evergreen* condemned the Blacks involved in the fight and expressed hostility toward the BSU. One letter stated that, by defending the Blacks involved in the AGR incident, the BSU "have identified themselves as a reactionary group that is not out to better the race relations between the blacks, and the whites, but to continue the ever growing insurrection that is so prevalent in our American society." In conclusion, the letter stated, "The Black Student Union has no place upon the Washington State University campus if it is no better than a Black Panther Organization at an intellectual level."[65] This was one of several letters claiming that the Blacks involved in the fight deserved no sympathy and that the BSU had destroyed its credibility by supporting them.[66] This suggests that the majority view was decidedly against the BSU.

On Thursday, February 27, the trial was held, following the charging of a sixth Black student, Ron Taplin, with second-degree assault.[67] Ron Henderson, Richard Lee Smith, and Ernie Thomas were represented by a white Pullman lawyer, Wallis Friel. Tyrone Daisy, Kenneth Walker, and Ron Taplin were represented by Carl Maxey of Spokane. Maxey was a Black, trailblazing civil rights lawyer known for taking race-related legal cases throughout the state of Washington.[68] Appearing before Judge John A. Denoo, all of the defendants pled guilty and were sentenced the same day, except Taplin, whose charges were later dropped after further investigation. Henderson, Smith, and Thomas pleaded guilty to third-degree assault and were sentenced to thirty days in Whitman County jail and one year of probation. Daisy and Walker pleaded guilty to second-degree assault and received a punishment of ninety days in county jail and three years of probation.[69] Showing some leniency, Judge Denoo stipulated that the defendants could serve their jail time on weekends to enable them to continue their studies, assuming that they were allowed to remain students at the university.[70] During the hearing, Denoo expressed further sympathy for the Black defendants, explaining that he was giving them probation because it would enable them to later expunge their convictions.[71] However, other statements by the judge were viewed by the BSU as racially offensive and left the strongest impression from the hearing. In the offending comments, Denoo said,

> Now, if there are some inconsiderate white people, and I am sure there are, and they abuse you in any manner you are just going to have to bow your head and let it drain off, consider the source as not all white people feel that way. Consider the source, let it drain off your back like water off a duck's back and bear it because you now have this extra problem. We don't expect you to be angels, we only expect that you will comport your-

self according to law, that you will not unreasonably violate any law, that you will behave as other law abiding citizens, we expect nothing more than that.[72]

Hearing this, the Black students in the courtroom were especially angered by Denoo's advice to "bow your head and let it drain off" when faced with racial slights. Given the charged atmosphere and Black Power ethos of the time, this was an especially poor choice of words. The BSU interpreted it as ordering them to bow down to white people and be submissive, advice that was antithetical to Black Power.[73] Expressing its reactions, the BSU later declared, "Today's decision by the Whitman County judge against our five brothers proved that the main business of the court was *not* to dispense justice. The business of this court was to insult, intimidate, and imprison our five brothers."[74] Consequently, the BSU resolved to protest the court's decision, viewing the prosecution as a miscarriage of justice.

Following the sentencing, the BSU demanded that Terrell intervene to support the convicted students, urging "that the power and resources of your offices [*sic*] be used to guarantee the immediate suspension of the sentences of our brothers." Moreover, the BSU demanded that no disciplinary action be taken against students and faculty who engaged in protests to support the "five brothers."[75] Terrell rejected the demands and instead suggested that members of the BSU and his office resume regular meetings to discuss the students' concerns.[76] For the BSU, the time for talk had passed. The organization quickly formulated plans for an act of civil disobedience. The weekend jail time for the five sentenced students was to begin on Friday, February 28, and the BSU was resolved to stop it. It contacted Black students at nearby colleges and universities, including Eastern Washington University and Whitworth University, and requested their support.[77] Quickly, a plan emerged to block the entrance of the jail with a wall of demonstrators and thereby prevent the incarceration of the "five brothers."

Reflecting the revolutionary spirit of the era, the plan to block the jail was a toned-down version of an initial proposal to challenge law enforcement with armed resistance and "shoot it out" if needed. Many BSU members had firearms during this time, so an armed standoff was easy to imagine. BSU members carried guns, even before the convictions, due to numerous threats of violence directed at them as Black activists. Ernest Thomas was a particular target for the threats, and they were frequent and serious enough that Thomas received a gun permit from otherwise unfriendly county officials. When going to class and doing other day-to-day activities, he was commonly armed with "two snub-nosed .38s."[78] These death threats to Thomas and others came by phone and by mail; as Thomas recalled, at least one threat was "written in the bathroom in this Chinese restaurant. And the owners told us about it. Told us about it, and we saw it on the bathroom walls."[79] BSU members took these threats very seriously and therefore took precautions, including carrying weapons. Along with the need for protection, many BSU members also believed that revolutionary violence was necessary and inevitable. This sense of impending danger and looming armed struggle was common among activist youth of the time, encouraged by decolonial struggles abroad and icons like Malcolm X and Robert F. Williams. Given this zeitgeist, a gun battle with the county sheriff to thwart the incarceration of the five brothers was seriously considered, but older members of the group, especially Johnnetta Cole and David Covin, persuaded the BSU to accept a less perilous approach. Cole and Covin had families to consider and were less inclined to become martyrs.[80]

At around 4:30 p.m. on February 28, the BSU and its allies gathered in Colfax and put their plan into action. Colfax was the seat of Whitman County and the location of the county courthouse and jail. Approximately seventy-five demonstrators were present. When Sheriff Mike Humphries and the five brothers arrived, the protesters refused to let them pass into the building and a standoff ensued. Adding another combustible element, white townsfolk soon gathered at the scene, threatening the demonstrators, throwing rocks, and unintentionally breaking three courthouse windows. In an ironic twist, the protesters soon asked Sheriff Humphries for protection from the antagonistic locals.[81] To find safety, the BSU and the five brothers first went into the courthouse building, and then took refuge in a nearby Methodist church with Humphries's approval. Johnnetta Cole arranged for this with the church pastor, the Reverend Tracy Manley.[82]

Once the demonstrators were inside the church, their anxiety reached new heights as they heard a radio report that highway patrolmen and police from Spokane and across eastern Washington were racing to Colfax.[83] Fearing a police assault, the protesters began stockpiling wet cloths to put over their faces if tear gas was used. Then, in another unexpected turn, the BSU got a call from a patrolman who explained that he and other officers were coming to Colfax to protect the BSU from "fleets" of armed locals who were also amassing in the town. Looking outside, the protesters saw an alarming number of armed white people in trucks and believed the patrolman's words. Yet they declined the officer's advice to leave the building and remained in the church all night.[84]

Despite the high tensions and the real chance of violence, the group passed the sleepless night without incident. The next morning at about 10:30 a.m., Manley asked the BSU to leave, explaining that he had received threats to his family and church. The group acceded to the request and by noon relocated to another religious facility, St. Patrick's Catholic Church. Their use of St. Patrick's was arranged by James Bell, a BSU member from Eastern Washington University, and Father Stefani. Exhausted and lacking options, the demonstrators soon agreed to be arrested after negotiations between BSU member Mark Williams and Sheriff Humphries.[85] Along with the "five brothers," forty-two demonstrators spent the next night in jail: six students from Whitworth University, nine from Eastern Washington University, twenty-seven students from WSU, and one faculty member, Johnnetta Cole. On Sunday, the forty-two were released due to legal aid from Carl Maxey. Later, in April, each was fined twenty-five dollars for "obstruction of the judicial process."[86] Although no one was injured in the weekend's unrest, the BSU and its allies were clearly under grave threat, and these events highlight again the extreme anti-Black opinion in the region. Although this repression did not worsen to include the serious injuries and death faced by Black protesters in the South, it shows that "Jim Crow North" conditions existed in rural Washington.

On March 3, the Monday following the turmoil in Colfax, the BSU denounced university and court officials in front of a crowd in the Todd Auditorium. The speakers included Eddie Leon and Mark Williams of WSU, and Carl Miller and Larry Gossett of the University of Washington. Three of the five sentenced students, Walker, Thomas, and Smith, also made short statements. Leon described the trial as a "kangaroo court," and Carl Miller criticized Judge Denoo for prioritizing the

AGR's property rights over the issue of racism. Mark Williams added disparaging comments about Sheriff Mike Humphries, especially his indecisiveness and the conditions of the jail. Williams and Larry Gossett both took aim at President Terrell for failing to respond to the BSU's demands. Summarizing the Black students' view, Gossett announced that Terrell, Humphries, and other local officials had been put on the BSU's "whitelist"—a clever appropriation of the term "blacklist." Terrell and the campus administration responded with a statement defending WSU's record on racial issues, and Washington governor Dan Evans made a statement of support for Judge Denoo and local law enforcement.[87]

Tensions remained high on campus as the final Disciplinary Committee hearing approach, scheduled for Wednesday, March 5. Many feared new unrest if the "five brothers" were given additional sanctions by campus officials.[88] Both the politically moderate student government and the leftist SDS expressed concern about potential repercussions.[89] However, shortly before the hearing was set to begin, Terrell announced that he was indefinitely suspending disciplinary action against the five, reversing his earlier position and defusing the situation.[90] When the next weekend came, the five defendants—Thomas, Smith, Henderson, Daisy, and Walker—began serving their sentences as ordered.[91] Looking back, Thomas mused that the jail time consisted of a lot of homework, or, as he put it, "study and study and study." As a consequence, he added, "I got a real good GPA that semester."[92]

The Campaign for Black Studies Resumes

Throughout the AGR-BSU controversy, the effort to create Black Studies continued as BSU members held meetings, researched relevant materials, and drafted documents. The campaign continued to make slow but steady progress; by March, Johnnetta Cole was chair of a campus-wide Black Studies Committee, endorsed by Terrell. Rutledge Dennis and David Covin also sat on this committee, along with William F. Mullen (professor, political science), Alfred Crosby (professor, history), Richard S. Thornton (professor, fine arts), and Dan Barrom.[93] In tandem with this committee's work, the BSU also advanced Black Studies by creating non-credit courses in WSU's Free University, a program, like San Francisco State's Experimental College, where students could develop their own classes.[94] Rudy Martin taught the first such Black Studies course on African American literature.[95]

Around this time, Johnnetta Cole and the Black Studies Committee completed their final proposal and submitted it for official approval, a process that required authorization by a series of administrative units. Approval was needed from T. H. Kennedy, dean of the College of Sciences and Arts, Herbert Wood, acting academic vice president, the Education Policies Committee, the Residential Instructional Staff, and lastly President Terrell and the Board of Regents. Given the extensive hurdles, Cole and the committee expected the process to take several months, but were encouraged by the outspoken support of Terrell and other administrators.

The proposal for Black Studies called for an interdisciplinary set of degree requirements that conformed to the structure of existing WSU majors. Notably, the proposal also anticipated critics by addressing the employment prospects of Black Studies graduates and arguing that majors would be primed for work in the anti-poverty programs of the Great Society.[96] Subsequently, ASWSU reiterated its endorsement with a supportive resolution.[97] Separately, another development undoubtably encouraged WSU administrators to support Black Studies. This was a consensus in favor of the new curriculum among peer institutions, expressed at a meeting of administrators from across the Pacific Eight (Pac-8) Athletic Conference. WSU, one of the Pac-8 schools, hosted the 1969 meeting. The other participants were Oregon State University, Stanford University, the University of California at Berkeley, the University of California at Los Angeles, the University of Oregon, the University of Southern California, and the University of Washington. The general consensus of the meeting was that "universities have neglected the area of Black Studies, which they should have considered earlier." It was also agreed that Black Studies programs should meet general university requirements and be chaired by African Americans who were experienced educators. Of all the institutions, only Oregon State and Washington State did not have Black Studies programs by that point, and both expected to have programs by the fall.[98] Two significant points are in evidence here. First, this is an indication of effective Black Power organizing across the West Coast, as Black Studies was intertwined with the larger Black campus movement. Acceptance of Black Studies by

these universities was a product of struggle, rather than something or-
ganic or inevitable. Second, here we see how relationships between peer
institutions were also a factor in the story of Black Studies because, as
organizational research shows, institutions like universities often adopt
new practices as their peer organizations do in order to maintain status
and credibility.[99]

Despite this momentum, Black Studies faced one more major challenge at WSU. By April 4, the proposal had progressed through several steps of the bureaucratic process and had reached the Educational
Policies Committee (EPC).[100] However, instead of simply approving
the plan as other officials had, the EPC elected to reject the proposal
and draft a new plan, infuriating the Black Student Union. The EPC's
counterproposal replaced Black Studies with an ethnic studies program that included options for "American Indian Studies, Black Studies, and Mexican American Studies."[101] Explaining the decision, Leon
Luck, chairman of the EPC, said that the committee felt that an ethnic studies program would "better meet the educational objectives of
WSU and the needs of the society which it serves."[102] It is not entirely
clear why the EPC took this approach, especially given the absence
of any public statements by Mexican American or Native American
groups at WSU. One possibility was that the ethnic studies approach
was viewed as more inclusive and cost-effective. However, given the
larger context of hostility toward the BSU, lingering resentment about
the AGR incident, and general opposition to Black Power organizing,
it is also plausible that the EPC's decision to remove "Black" from the
new program was an effort to thwart Black empowerment on campus.
Following this logic, the EPC may have changed the name and broad-
ened the focus in an effort to lessen the BSU's influence on the new
academic program.

The EPC's counterproposal was completed on April 8 and the two
plans faced a crucial vote of the Residential Instructional Staff (RIS),
the faculty senate, in early May.[103] The RIS vote would determine which
proposal would go on to the president and Board of Regents, and the
Black Studies and ethnic studies proposals competed for support as the
next meeting approached. Outlining its position, the BSU explained
that it agreed that Native Americans and Mexican Americans de-

served inclusion in university curriculum, but it objected to the EPC's model because each group deserved its own department and degree. As Johnnetta Cole put it, "Each of the three main minority groups in this country, the American Indian, the Mexican American and the Black American is in search of its dignity as a people," and the most dignifying approach would be for WSU to create "a degree reading Bachelor's of Arts in American Indian Studies, Mexican American Studies, or Black Studies."[104]

The debate about the dueling proposals continued with editorials, public statements, and forums.[105] Then, fearing that the RIS might reject both proposals, the two sides began to negotiate and reached a compromise.[106] The new proposal blended the Black Studies and ethnic studies plans by establishing a "Program for American Minority Studies" that included a central coordinator and three independent programs: Black Studies, American Indian studies, and Mexican American studies. Each program would have its own director and grant degrees reading bachelor's in Black Studies, and so on. In the fall, Black Studies was to begin along with a committee to develop American Indian and Mexican American studies.[107]

At the RIS meeting, the compromise proposal was swiftly approved. At under thirty minutes, it was reportedly the shortest RIS meeting in the history of WSU. The BSU was overjoyed at the result. Rutledge Dennis said, "I was very shocked by the reaction and the quickness of the vote in favor of the program." Ernie Thomas added, "This is a beautiful thing in that only a small minority of faculty voted no. This vividly illustrates what needs to be happening on campuses where faculty and students participate together. It's cool, it's a beautiful thing." Johnnetta Cole simply said, "I'm tremendously pleased."[108]

As expected, President Terrell and the Board of Regents gave final approval in June.[109] In the fall, Black Studies began with several new courses: Introduction to Black Studies (Black Studies 101), The Arts of Black America (Black Studies 102), Studies in Black American Literature (English 320), Black Revolution (Philosophy 345), Black Politics (Political Science 324), and The Sociology of Black Americans (Sociology 380).[110] Johnnetta Cole was appointed as the first director of Black Studies.[111]

WSU, 1969–1970

The final high point of the BSU's Black Power activism at WSU occurred during the following year, in May 1970, when the organization boldly announced a boycott of the school by all African Americans. This subsequently ignited a campus-wide student strike against racism. The crisis grew out of a series of new actions by law enforcement that appeared racially discriminatory. For instance, earlier in the spring, Ralph Atkins, a Black student, was accused of an arson attack on the campus football stadium, Rogers' Field, and was also charged in connection with a grape-stomping protest supporting the United Farm Workers.[112] Separately, four Black WSU students were charged with raping a white woman, and two were convicted.[113] Added to these tensions, national developments related to the Vietnam War also impacted the campus. At the end of April, President Richard Nixon announced that he was escalating the war into Cambodia, and soon after, four anti-war protesters were killed at Kent State University. This set off a wave of protests at colleges and universities nationwide, and at WSU students held a nine-hour occupation of the administration building on May 5.[114] The string of national controversies continued on May 14 when police fired on Black demonstrators at Jackson State College in Mississippi, killing two people. This shooting, and the fact that its Black victims garnered less national attention than the white Kent State victims, added to the local and national developments influencing the BSU at WSU.

In the aftermath of the Jackson State shooting, the BSU and several allied groups at WSU decided to channel their frustrations into a new, joint campaign. This coalition included MECHA (Movimiento Estudiantil Chicano/a de Aztlán), the Radical Union (formerly the WSU chapter of Students for a Democratic Society), the Three Forks Peace Coalition, the Young Socialist Alliance, and the Women's Liberation Front. On Monday, May 18, they collectively issued a series of new demands: disarm campus police and ROTC (Reserve Officers Training Corps), create an oversight board for local police, abolish the Disciplinary Board, create an oversight board to curb racism in student publications, hold a mandatory ten-day workshop against racism, increase enrollments of non-white or "third world" students, increase financial aid for students of color, and remove all non-union grapes.[115] These demands reflect the range of concerns and causes that motivated the BSU and its allies by this time.

President Terrell rejected the demands with his usual call for dialogue. In response, the BSU announced that it would organize a boycott of WSU by all Black students, faculty, and staff if the demands remained unmet.[116] Reportedly, the idea for a Black mass withdrawal from WSU was also motivated by continued threats of violence, such as from a local white militia called the La Crosse Nightriders.[117] This BSU announcement of a potential boycott set off a flurry of actions by allies and supporters, and by the day's end a "Strike Against Racism" was called. Lasting from May 22 to May 29, the student strike called on all students to withhold all academic and financial obligations from the university, and to refuse to patronize any local business that did not support the strike.

The struggle gained thousands of participants and reached its high point on Wednesday, May 27. That day, approximately 3,500 to 4,000 supporters attended a mass meeting, during which the steering committee announced plans to march through classroom corridors. Also at the meeting, Marguerita Sugiyama, a MECHA leader, persuaded the group to rally for Chicano studies the following day. It's unknown exactly how many of the attendees were students, but 4,000 people represented approximately 33 percent of the student population, which totaled about 12,000. Thus, support for the strike was significant even though the attendees did not constitute a majority of students.[118]

The tumultuous week also featured a nighttime rally in front of the president's house, but ultimately ended in compromise. The post-strike agreement did not address all the original demands but produced sufficient changes for the BSU to call off its planned boycott. The agreement included the creation of a special assistant to the president for minority affairs; the creation of an advisory council of students of color; hiring of Black, Chicano, and Native students as recruiters; regular diversity training for administrative staff; and a campus-wide racism workshop to be held in the fall.[119] The agreed-upon racism workshop took place on October 7 and 8, 1970, during which twenty thousand participants attended group sessions and listened to speakers such as Dr. Charles Hurst of Chicago's Malcolm X Community College, Dr. Nathan Hare of San Francisco State University, Dr. Ralph Guzmán of the University of

California, Santa Cruz, and Luis Valdez of the United Farm Workers.[120] This strike represented the final chapter in a groundbreaking period of political activism by the Black Student Union and its allies, which forced Washington State University to confront issues of race and ethnicity in unprecedented ways.[121]

Beginning with descriptions of two BSU members, Ernest Thomas and David Covin, this chapter detailed the campaign for Black Studies at Washington State University. After its founding, Black Studies would struggle in its early years due to budgetary challenges,[122] yet the program achieved departmental status in 1970 under its second director, Talmadge Anderson, and continued for several decades.[123] Consequently, the campaign for Black Studies is another illustration of the productivity of BSU activism, and by extension the Black Power movement, during the late 1960s. BSU members worked tirelessly and built support for their vision, collaborated with allies, and navigated bureaucratic hurdles. In addition, this hard-won reform materialized within a hostile and repressive environment that included credible death threats, harassment, racial profiling, hostile law enforcement, and conflict with other students. The racist undertones of the BSU-Alpha Gamma Rho incident, as well as the vigorous response from police and prosecutors, reflected broader sentiments against the BSU and Black Power. The Black activists at WSU faced significantly more opposition and repression than their counterparts in Seattle. This extends scholarship on the Jim Crow North to a hitherto understudied region of the country and unearths the clear relevance of Pacific Northwest history to studies of mid-twentieth-century racial inequality. Overall, this helps uncover a fuller account of our nation's racial past. In addition, this chapter has made it clear that the BSU of WSU deserves high praise for its courageous leadership and actions, which propelled its institution toward greater racial justice.

Conclusion

"Fighting for Our Freedom Was Exhilarating"

Many student activists of the Black Student Union earned their college degrees and went on to distinguished careers as educators, professionals, and community leaders. All are part of the rich legacy of the BSU. Yet, among so many noteworthy individuals, the person who most directly embodies the decades-long impact of the BSU is Emile Pitre. Not only was Pitre a member of the BSU during its inaugural year at the University of Washington, but his lifetime of public service also included decades of professional work at that same university. While other BSU members had successful careers in education, Pitre is the only person to do so at the same institution where he was an activist, exemplifying the BSU's transformative impact on the University of Washington.

Pitre was the fourth son of eight children in a Louisiana sharecropping family. For much of his childhood, he attended only part of the school year because his labor was needed in the fields. However, in eighth grade a teacher recognized his scholastic potential and spoke with his father. After that, Pitre attended the entire school year and eventually became the first in his family to earn a high school diploma. Subsequently, he enrolled at Southern University with a scholarship from the National Science Foundation and graduated in 1967 with a bachelor's degree in chemistry. That fall, he then matriculated at the University of Washington to pursue a master's in chemistry.[1]

Pitre was attracted to UW and the city of Seattle because he had heard that race relations there were better than in his home state of Louisiana. Yet, when he arrived on campus, a racist incident soon dampened his expectations. He remembered, "I was walking across campus one day and a student in braces said, 'Everywhere I go you damned niggers are here.'"[2] This experience added to his inclination to find a Black community at UW, and he became one of the early members of the Black Student Union. Describing his reaction to the racist slur, Pitre said, "That helped me realize that prejudice existed all over, so joining the Black Student Union and being involved in the struggle seemed to me to be an appropriate thing to do."[3] Months later, when the BSU launched its sit-in of the UW president's office on May 20, 1968, Pitre was one of the participants.[4] When asked how he felt during the sit-in, Pitre recalled a mixture of concern and exhilaration:

> I was apprehensive going in because I had an NIH [National Institutes of Health] fellowship and they said that if you got arrested protesting you would lose the fellowship. So I was apprehensive about that. But for me, fighting for our freedom was exhilarating. And I have a saying about [it,] "That's when I feel the most free, is when I'm fighting on behalf of freedom." I was emboldened.[5]

After Pitre earned his master's degree, his professional career took him away from UW from 1972 to 1982, until he returned for a job as a chemistry instructor in the university's Instructional Center (IC). The IC was one of the many retention programs that was created as a direct result of the BSU sit-in, as was the larger unit that coordinated these diversity initiatives, the Office of Minority Affairs (OMA). Thus, Pitre returned to help nurture and grow one of the reforms he helped bring to life, and he remained a steadfast member of the OMA team until his retirement in 2014, after over thirty years of service. Appropriately, Eddie Demmings, another BSU member, described Pitre as "the keeper of the flame" for the way his career at UW protected the legacy and victories of the BSU.[6] Elaborating on this statement, Demmings explained,

> At one point I said, and I wrote, that Emile Pitre is the keeper of the flame. If I go to my grave tomorrow, there would be nothing I ever said in my life more apt than that. Emile Pitre is just an absolutely remarkable person. The way he has sustained through the decades the vision of the BSU, and nurtured it, and nurtured the things that sprung from it and everything. We are so lucky. Not just in the past, but right now to this day, that we have Emile Pitre.[7]

Indeed, after beginning as an IC instructor in 1982, Pitre became IC assistant director in 1985 and director in 1989. During his tenure as director, in 2001, the IC became the first UW program to ever win two of the university's distinguished Brotman Awards, one for instructional excellence and the other for diversity.[8] The following year, Pitre was promoted to the leadership of OMA, becoming associate vice president for minority affairs.[9] Throughout this time, Pitre served as the advisor for the Black Student Union for approximately twenty years and mentored countless numbers of students (including the author of this book). Reflecting on his moniker as "the keeper of the flame" and his longtime service at the University of Washington, Pitre said,

> One of the reasons why I was so attracted to being here [at UW] was to make sure that what the BSU started would survive. And it turns out, not only did it survive but it thrived. And I never let anyone forget how this all came about. And there were times when they would say that, "There was some student activists that ended up causing this to happen." And I said, "No, no, this is how the story really went." And it was a story of what happened with BSU.[10]

Over the years, Pitre pushed his fellow administrators and successive waves of Black students to recognize the importance and legacy of the 1960s BSU, even as some wanted to move on. After this long advocacy, in 2008 the 1968 BSU was awarded the prestigious Charles E. Odegaard Award, the highest diversity-related honor at UW.[11]

The BSU's positive impact on generations of students is undeniable. Between 1982 and 2018 alone, the Instructional Center helped more than twenty thousand students graduate from UW, many of whom were students of color, low-income, and first-generation students.[12] A related tally spanning the years 1968 to 2008 found that some forty-nine thousand students of color graduated from the University of Washington. While not all directly participated in the IC and other OMA initiatives, this total of graduates of color would likely not have occurred without the services initiated by the Black Student Union. The OMA was renamed the Office of Minority Affairs and Diversity (OMAD) in 2002.

At Washington State University, the legacy is less clear, but still significant. Unlike at UW, where an Office of Minority Affairs was established in 1970 and headed by a vice president, diversity efforts at WSU did not have the same level of institutional stability. Programs like WSU's Special Education Program have come and gone, and responsibilities for related recruitment and retention initiatives have been allocated and reallocated over the years. Despite these challenges, programs like Multicultural Student Services (MSS) have continued to serve students. MSS, founded in 1987, provides cultural programming, advising, mentoring, and other retention services to students of color and thereby carries on the legacy of the Black Student Union.[13] Yet MSS has also faced varying degrees of support from upper administration. Thus, at WSU, there is not the unbroken chain of BSU reforms that we find at UW. Yet here too, the BSU deserves recognition for challenging the prevailing priorities of the institution and forcing WSU to acknowledge the needs of Black students.

The current status of Black Studies at both schools also reflects a pattern of persistence despite struggle. At the time of this writing, Black Studies retains a presence at both schools, but has been merged with other units. This often entailed a loss of autonomy and resources, as Black Studies was demoted from being a full, recognized department. As mentioned previously, Black Studies at UW is now part of the department of American ethnic studies. At WSU, Black Studies has been merged and remerged into a series of conglomerated departments: comparative American cultures; comparative ethnic studies; critical culture, gender, and race studies; and now the School of Languages, Cultures, and Race. These reorganizations often occurred over the objections of faculty and students, highlighting long-standing complaints about insufficient respect and resources. Yet dedicated educators at both schools continue to provide curriculum that foregrounds nondominant perspectives and critiques injustice, and thereby carries on the vision of the BSU. Thus, here too, the impact of the BSU's activism lives on.

As detailed in the previous chapters, *Washington State Rising* chronicles the origins, activists, and actions of the Black Student Union at the University of Washington in Seattle and at Washington State University in Pullman. We have seen how members of both BSUs organized, spoke out, built networks of support, mobilized, and demonstrated at their respective institutions from 1967 to 1970. Due to their efforts, advocacy, and agitation, the two largest higher education institutions in the state were forced to create new measures to address racial injustice. Most especially, the BSU won new programs to recruit and retain Black students and other people of color, and won the establishment of Black Studies. These interventions changed the trajectory of these universities, displacing preexisting standards of who and what was welcomed within academia. Given their outstanding efforts and impacts, the Black Student Union of the state of Washington deserves to be ranked among the most consequential groups of the Black campus movement.

Washington State Rising concurs with and extends Ibram X. Kendi's assessment that the Black campus movement revolutionized American higher education nationwide.[14] This text contributes new evidence to this analysis, particularly in regard to how Black students in the state of Washington attacked institutional discrimination against the perspectives and scholarship of people of color, and the ubiquitous white normativity that privileged white people. Through bold actions like insurgent classroom teach-ins and challenges to local law enforcement, the Black Student Unions at the University of Washington and Washington State University carried forward the Black campus movement just as their counterparts did across the country.

While chronicling the trailblazing and intrepid activism of the Black Student Union in Washington, this book makes several further interventions into relevant, historical scholarship. *Washington State Rising* asserts two overarching points, and additional assertions that correspond to the two BSU groups profiled. The first overarching claim is that Seattle and the state of Washington were notable sites of political organizing during the Black Power movement. The second is that late 1960s BSU actions in Washington complicate conventional understandings of the Black Power movement as counterproductive. Furthermore, this study asserts that the BSU at the University of Washington–Seattle is notable for its community organizing and interracial coalitions. Finally, the last assertion is that the experience of the BSU at Washington State University illuminates Jim Crow North in Washington State.

First, *Washington State Rising* locates the Black Power movement and the Black campus movement in the state of Washington. Given that this is the first scholarly monograph to do so, it raises important insights for how the 1960s are remembered. In general, Seattle, the state of Washington, and the Pacific Northwest are not considered important sites of

Black Power or mid-twentieth-century Black student activism. One explanation for this is the reputation of Seattle and the surrounding area as ostensibly liberal and racially tolerant. Another factor is the geographical location of the region, in the far corner of the nation and outside the central focus of national politics. Both factors contribute to the erroneous notion that the state of Washington was peripheral to the Black freedom struggle of the 1960s. Yet, as we have seen here, a closer look reveals that Washington featured highly active civil rights and Black Power campaigns. Moreover, the presence of both in a heretofore understudied part of the country brings into focus the wide impact and transferability of both movements.

This book also complicates conventional notions of the civil rights and Black Power movements, challenging the perception that Black Power was wholly destructive and the view that Martin Luther King's death was the endpoint of all productive activism. To the contrary, we have seen that the BSU was active after King's assassination and continued to win meaningful reforms in the waning years of the decade. In previous scholarship, this has at times been overlooked, as reflected by the characterizations of Black Power in Clayborne Carson's *In Struggle: SNCC and the Black Awakening of the 1960s* (1981) and Charles M. Payne's *I've Got the Light of Freedom: The Organizing Tradition and the Mississippi Freedom Struggle* (1995). Both erroneously treat the Student Nonviolent Coordinating Committee's (SNCC) late 1960s unraveling as indicative of the dysfunction and misdirection of the larger Black Power movement.[15] To Payne's credit, he walked back these assessments in the second edition of *I've Got the Light of Freedom*. Yet this negative assessment persists in the public imagination, despite wide recognition among scholars and historians that Black Power was more than just threats and riots.

One pillar of the declension narrative is the idea that Black Power abandoned the grassroots and community organizing that characterized the most democratic thrusts of the civil rights movement, a point directly addressed by *Washington State Rising*'s discussion of the BSU at UW. Carson articulated this belief when he wrote of SNCC and other Black Power adherents, "Increasingly preoccupied with internal factional disputes and external repression, they isolated themselves from the everyday realities of the black people in whose name they acted."[16]

Again, Carson's assessment was based on his study of SNCC, but he extrapolated this into a conclusion about the entire Black Power movement. To the contrary, what we see from our study of the BSU at UW is that Black Power could, and sometimes did, foster generative relationships with local Black communities. This is the third major assertion of this text. The BSU in Seattle was directly engaged in the community, organizing auxiliary BSUs at local secondary schools and remaining directly engaged with their adolescent mentees. One prominent example was the April 1968 protest at Franklin High School where BSU members from UW were directly involved. Similarly, the BSU at San Francisco State had a robust slate of community projects, as briefly described in chapter 1. The exception here is the BSU at WSU, as it did not have a prominent community service component, likely because its campus was in a location without a significant off-campus Black community. But the ethos of community concern was still visible in, for example, the BSU at WSU's outspoken reaction to the racist treatment of visiting Black high school students. This, in fact, was the event that brought the group to the forefront of campus politics. Thus, the BSU at WSU was also concerned about off-campus African Americans, much like the other BSUs described herein. Some individuals and groups within Black Power were guilty of abandoning local concerns, as Carson and other critics charged, but this reflects the heterogeneity and complexity of the movement rather than a fundamental characteristic of all groups.

Likewise, the BSU at UW employed a noteworthy commitment to multiculturalism and interracial alliances. Several examples illustrate this fact, including the group's non-Black members, and the BSU's reform agenda that explicitly advocated for Native Americans and Latinos. This "Third World consciousness," or solidarity with similarly stigmatized racial and ethnic groups, was a foundational element in the BSU's motivating philosophy. BSU member Eddie Demmings described this central tenet:

I think from the very beginning, in terms of wanting to desegregate the university, we never thought it was something just for Black students. We always thought, always, from the very beginning, that we wanted to see more people of color in general. And we wanted to see more Native Americans. We wanted to see more Chicanos, everybody. We wanted to

see a more diverse student population, and we reached out to other minorities, racial minorities. And we saw them as brothers and sisters, with
the same needs and essentially the same goals. So we were the Black Student Union, but we were never focused only on Black students.[17]

One of many outcomes of the BSU's Third World consciousness was
how the racial reforms won by the group benefited Black students *and*
non-Black students. This was true in the immediate aftermath of the
group's protest campaign in the spring of 1968 at UW, and it was true as
the reforms were institutionalized into the Office of Minority Affairs.
One exception pertained to Asian/Pacific Islander students, who were
not mentioned in the original BSU demands, but they too were added to
OMA's target population by 1969–1970. It is not clear why Asian/Pacific
Islanders were not initially included, but the BSU supported the subsequent decision to include them.[18] Therefore, the Black Student Union
created and advanced a trailblazing vision of multicultural college classrooms that presaged the diversity, equity, and inclusion policies that
have since become mainstays across the country. Moreover, the BSU's
recognition of the grievances of other minoritized groups speaks to its
astute social analysis and expansive ethic of social justice.

The final assertion of *Washington State Rising* pertains to Washington
State University. The small, rural, college town of Pullman did not have
an established presence of Black political activism as was the case in
Seattle and elsewhere. Thus, the BSU at WSU provides an opportunity
to analyze Black Power activism in a particularly hostile sociopolitical context. What is apparent here, along with the courage of the Black
WSU students, is the increased level of antagonism, repression, and violence faced by the group. This included hostile public opinion, fights
with members of a white fraternity, harassment and persecution by law
enforcement, and death threats from local residents. At the University
of Washington and in Seattle, the BSU certainly faced repression and
hostility, but not to this degree. For instance, as detailed in chapter 5, the
BSU at WSU faced gun-wielding locals in a confrontation at the county
jail in February 1969. Fortunately no one was hurt, but this harrowing
scene brings to mind a lynch mob and featured a real potential for violence. All of this underscores the existence of Jim Crow North, policies
and practices that mirrored the racial climate of the South. *Washington*

State Rising contributes to the literature on Jim Crow North by connecting the concept to the Pacific Northwest. This insight brings into focus that all regions share in the culpability of America's racial sins.

Given these contributions to scholarship, *Washington State Rising* illuminates new knowledge of the Black Power movement, the Black campus movement, the Pacific Northwest, and Black politics of the mid-twentieth century.

As a concluding takeaway, *Washington State Rising* offers insights for contemporary and future protest campaigns for social justice. The Black Student Union provides an instructive example to study. A key insight was the way the organization's success was built on relationships between politicized Black students and various allies: local Black community members, progressive white students and faculty, non-Black students of color, and others. Establishing this web of coalitions created political capital with which BSU pressured school officials for change, and this strategy can be an instructive model for contemporary organizing.

The BSU shows that the slow, difficult, often unglamorous work of building allies and winning community support is a key ingredient in a successful campaign. This point is often underappreciated in both historical and contemporary thinking about activism, because often too much focus is directed on mass mobilization. Americans across the political spectrum are prone to associate effective protest with large gatherings of people. Many think, "If we could just get more people marching or voting, we'd achieve our goal." Yet, while mass mobilizations are an important tool, relationships and alliances are a more resilient source of power. In fact, it is often such social and political bonds that enable the mobilizations to happen, and these relationships can live on after the immediate campaign has passed.

This dynamic is reflected in liberal and progressive politics surrounding the Black Lives Matter protests of 2020, when millions of people mobilized in anti-racist rallies and demanded police reform. The months of protest represented a valiant effort to combat injustice, and may yet contribute to future reforms and improved policing, but many of the participants mobilized due to social media or television images and did not have, and did not gain, meaningful connections to networks of activism. Consequently, this moment of racial politics was not as impactful as it could have been. Without the slow, time-consuming, and sincere work of relationship building, mass actions and the pressure they represent can melt away as fast as they can coalesce, and herein lies the problem. In the public imagination and in political discourse, protests are most often associated with rallies and speeches in front of large crowds, but for a movement to be resilient and have the maximum impact, sincere networks are key. Such networks are needed to maintain the pressure on decision makers, and they can provide the comradery and support needed to sustain ongoing struggle and fend off activist burnout. The youth outreach and community organizing of the BSU are great examples of this relationship building; by investing time and energy into supporting local folks, the students created sincere connections with grassroots allies.

Moreover, the cultivation of grassroots connections is particularly useful for any group with a modest membership size that nevertheless wants to push for change. Here, for instance, the BSUs at UW and SF State augmented their political power by leveraging pressure from community-based individuals and groups. Of course, the racial climate in the late 1960s, with the national tragedy of Martin Luther King Jr.'s assassination and related events, added to the salience of the students' calls for change, but having a broad base of support on and off campus made BSU agitation even harder to ignore. This methodology, which can be effectively combined with pressuring school officials through the news media, was particularly suited for a small organization of Black students at a predominately white institution. Furthermore, this is likely applicable to certain situations today. Thus, *Washington State Rising* provides an example of activism, led by everyday people, college students without elite backgrounds or powerful connections, that can inspire and provide strategies for future protest campaigns.

ACKNOWLEDGMENTS

This book, *Washington State Rising*, is the culmination of a research project that began during my undergraduate junior year at the University of Washington, 2002–2003. Thus, this monograph has taken approximately twenty years to produce. Over those years, an undergraduate research paper grew and evolved into several subsequent stages: an article for the Seattle Civil Rights and Labor History Project, a doctoral dissertation, scholarly journal articles, and now this monograph. The research and writing process has been a long journey of countless hours, ups and downs, progress and setbacks, uncertainty and self-doubt, and hope that someday it might actually be finished. I share this to describe my journey, and to hopefully inspire anyone with a long project they hope to complete. It can happen.

Like any book project, *Washington State Rising* was aided by many people and institutions, so let me start off by thanking everyone who supported me and this project over the years.

I am especially thankful for the love and encouragement from my family, without whom I would not be the person I am today. More than anyone else, four people shaped me during my childhood, adolescence, and early adulthood: my mother, my maternal grandmother, my older sister, and my former spouse. Each has taught me so much over the years. Another loved one who has expressed endless faith in my abilities is my son, who happens to be a few years older than this book project. Therefore, *Washington State Rising* is sort of like his younger sibling. I am blessed to have these treasured individuals and many other beloved family and family friends. Please know that you are all appreciated.

When I first started this research project as an undergraduate at the University of Washington (UW), there were several people who provided important, early support on campus. First and foremost was Emile Pitre, who was one of the original Black Student Union (BSU) members, and later became associate vice president of the Office of Minority Affairs and Diversity at UW. One day, when I shared my interest in researching the BSU's actions during the 1960s, Pitre was immediately encouraging. Soon after, he agreed to sit for an oral history interview, and subsequently shared useful documents, both of which set me on the path that eventually led to this book. Since then, he has continued to be a champion and mentor for me and this research, providing additional interviews, documents, and referrals to other interviewees (for more on Pitre, see the book's conclusion). Another source of early support at UW came from the faculty and staff in the history department, especially William J. Rorabaugh, James N. Gregory, and Quintard Taylor. The UW libraries have also been instrumental throughout the decades. Finally, during the time I started this study, I was also part of a multiracial community of student organizations that often met in the Ethnic Cultural Center. My experiences in that collective, and especially my involvement in a protest group called Minority Think Tank or MTT, provided a crucial stimulus for *Washington State Rising*.

During my time as a doctoral student in American studies at Washington State University (WSU), additional faculty members helped me develop and refine this project. They include my dissertation committee: David J. Leonard, chair, Lisa Guerrero, and Thabiti Lewis. Key research help was provided by Mark O'English, university archivist at WSU, and other staff and resources in the WSU libraries.

Along with Emile Pitre, many additional BSU veterans, and others with relevant memories, agreed to be interviewed. Their willingness to share their time and their stories was truly invaluable for this book's creation. Larry Gossett was an early participant. When I first met him in 2002, he was an elected member of the King County Council, yet agreed to let me interview him despite his busy schedule. This led to several subsequent interviews over the years, and his contributions have been irreplaceable. Other individuals who provided interviews that were members of, or connected to, the BSU at UW are Jessie Crowder, Eddie Demmings, Elmer Dixon, James Garrett, Marcie Hall-McMurtrie, Verlaine Keith-Miller, Carl Miller, and Garry Owens. Likewise, I also interviewed former members of the BSU at Washington State University: David Covin, Rutledge Dennis, Rudy Martin, and Ernest Thomas. Others provided useful context on WSU in the sixties: Felicia Gaskins, Jeff Guillory, Les Purce, and James Short. It was an honor to speak with, and learn from, all interviewees. Similarly, much gratitude goes to those who read and provided feedback on the manuscript as it neared completion: Johnnetta Cole, Eddie Demmings, Marcie Hall-McMurtrie, A. Rafik Mohamed, and Emile Pitre.

Admittedly, some interviews are more prominent in *Washington State Rising* than others, and some notable individuals were not interviewed at all. This is due to the limitations of time and accessibility, and the need to craft a concise narrative, all of which required that some details be omitted. No disrespect is intended here; rather, I hope that any points that I have missed will spur future research and scholarship.

Since the inception of this project, I have worked with or within several institutions that have invested in me, and interacted with colleagues who helped me grow as a scholar, a teacher, a writer, and a professional. Forgive me for not mentioning names, but I want to acknowledge the many faculty, staff, administrators, students, and community members who supported me at UW, WSU, Whitworth University, the University of Oregon, and California State University, San Bernardino, my current institution. I also benefited from institutes and trainings by the New York Metro American Studies Association and the Oral History Center of the Bancroft Library at the University of California, Berkeley. The J. Paul Leonard Library at San Francisco State University also provided some key sources and assistance. Several outlets have previously published parts of this research and thereby supported its continuance: Seattle Civil Rights and Labor History Project (SCRLHP), *Pacific Northwest Quarterly*, and *California History*. Their editors and staff are appreciated. Trevor Griffey, historian and co-founder of the SCRLHP, also deserves thanks for directing me to the FBI file on the Seattle BSU that he published on the Internet Archive. Special financial assistance was provided by the Mellon Emerging Faculty Leaders Award, administered by the Institute for Citizens and Scholars.

Several individuals have played a role in shepherding this manuscript through the final stages of publication. I deeply value their work and contributions. The publication of my manuscript with New York University Press was facilitated, first and foremost, by Ibram X. Kendi, series co-editor for NYU Press's Black Power series. I first met Kendi at a National Council of Black Studies conference in 2012, and he has remained the kind, collegial, and unassuming person that I first met, despite his ensuing rise to prominence. Kendi, Ashley D. Farmer, series co-editor, Clara Platter, senior editor, and all others at NYU Press have my thanks.

Finally, any errors or misrepresentations contained in the preceding pages are unintended and do not express malice or ill-intent. As the saying goes, "Charge it to my *head* and not my *heart*." What is contained within *Washington State Rising* is the product of my earnest efforts to interpret source material, recount the facts, and construct a compelling narrative, all to the best of my abilities. Moreover, while striving for historical accuracy, I have also endeavored to express the respect and admiration merited to the Black Student Union. I sincerely believe that the historical record of the group's activities and influence substantiates this high regard. Any statements or passages that contradict this esteem, or any inaccuracies, are regrettable and unintentional. Thank you, dear reader, for picking up this book; I hope you find it worthwhile.

NOTES

INTRODUCTION

1 Dave Doctor, "New Black Image Emerging," *Daily* (University of Washington), February 15, 1968, 6–7.
2 "Negroes Ask 'Why' in Letter to Public," *Daily Evergreen*, May 14, 1968, 2.
3 "Negroes Ask 'Why.'"
4 Peniel E. Joseph, *Waiting 'til the Midnight Hour: A Narrative History of Black Power in America* (New York: Henry Holt, 2006), 203.
5 Hilda Bryant, "A White University?," *Seattle Post-Intelligencer*, June 4, 1969, 14; Dave Ferbon, "Late-Hour Compromise Averts Sit-In Violence," *Daily*, May 21, 1968, 1; Dee Norton, "Agreement Ends Student Sit-In," *Seattle Times*, May 21, 1968, 5.
6 Elmer Dixon, interview with author, July 2, 2018.
7 Craig Collisson, "The Fight to Legitimize Blackness: How Black Students Changed the University" (PhD diss., University of Washington, 2008); Larry S. Richardson, "Civil Rights in Seattle: A Rhetorical Analysis of a Social Movement" (PhD diss., Washington State University, 1975); Marc A. Robinson, "The Black Power Movement and the Black Student Union (BSU) in Washington State, 1967–1970" (PhD diss., Washington State University, 2012); Joyce Yvonne Stephens, "The Historical Development of Black Studies, with Special Reference to Washington State University" (master's thesis, Washington State University, 1976); Dianne Louise Walker, "The University of Washington Establishment and the Black Student Union Sit-In of 1968" (master's thesis, University of Washington, 1980).
8 Charlie Hinckley and Jamala Henderson, *In Pursuit of Social Justice: An Oral History of the Early Years of Diversity Efforts at the University of Washington* (Seattle: UWTV, 2007), www.uwtv.org.
9 "The Black Student Union at UW," Seattle Civil Rights and Labor History Project, accessed April 4, 2022, http://depts.washington.edu/civilr/index.htm; Samuel E. Kelly, with Quintard Taylor, *Dr. Sam, Soldier, Educator, Advocate, Friend: An Autobiography* (Seattle: University of Washington Press, 2010).
10 Robert Cohen, "Introduction: A Prophetic Minority versus Recalcitrant Majority; Southern Student Dissent and the Struggle for Progressive Change in the 1960s," in *Rebellion in Black and White: Southern Student Activism in the 1960s*, ed. Robert Cohen and David Snyder (Baltimore: Johns Hopkins University Press, 2013), 20–21.

11 Cassandra Tate, "Washington State University, Part 2," HistoryLink.org, May 26, 2004, https://historylink.org.

12 Sundiata Keita Cha-Jua and Clarence Lang, "The 'Long Movement' as Vampire: Temporal and Spatial Fallacies in Recent Black Freedom Studies," *Journal of African American History* 92, no. 2 (Spring 2007): 272.

13 Jeanne F. Theoharis and Komozi Woodard, eds., *Freedom North: Black Freedom Struggles outside the South, 1940–1980* (New York: Palgrave Macmillan, 2003); Matthew Countryman, *Up South: Civil Rights and Black Power in Philadelphia* (Philadelphia: University of Pennsylvania Press, 2006), 3–4; Nikhil Pal Singh, *Black Is a Country: Race and the Unfinished Struggle for Democracy* (Cambridge: Harvard University Press, 2004); Robert O. Self, *American Babylon: Race and the Struggle for Postwar Oakland* (Princeton: Princeton University Press, 2005), 11–12; Jacquelyn Dowd Hall, "The Long Civil Rights Movement and the Political Uses of the Past," *Journal of American History* 91, no. 4 (2005): 1–66; Jeanne F. Theoharis, *A More Beautiful and Terrible History: The Uses and Misuses of Civil Rights History* (Boston: Beacon, 2018).

14 Cha-Jua and Lang, "'Long Movement,'" 274–75.

15 Ashley D. Farmer, *Remaking Black Power: How Black Women Transformed an Era* (Chapel Hill: University of North Carolina Press, 2017), 7–9.

16 Peniel Joseph, "Introduction: Toward a New Historiography of the Black Power Movement," in *The Black Power Movement: Rethinking the Civil Rights–Black Power Era*, ed. Peniel E. Joseph (New York: Routledge, 2006), 3–4.

17 Peniel E. Joseph, "The Black Power Movement: A State of the Field," *Journal of American History* 96, no. 3 (2009): 751–52.

18 Matthew Lassiter and Joseph Crespino, eds., *The Myth of Southern Exceptionalism* (New York: Oxford University Press, 2010).

19 Brian Purnell and Jeanne Theoharis, with Komozi Woodard, eds., *The Strange Careers of the Jim Crow North: Segregation and Struggle outside the South* (New York: New York University Press, 2019); Countryman, *Up South*; Donna Jean Murch, *Living for the City: Migration, Education, and the Rise of the Black Panther Party in Oakland, California* (Chapel Hill: University of North Carolina Press, 2010); Josh Sides, *L.A. City Limits: African American Los Angeles from the Great Depression to the Present* (Berkeley: University of California Press, 2003); Genevieve Carpio, *Collisions at the Crossroads: How Place and Mobility Make Race* (Berkeley University of California Press, 2019); Brett Gadsden, *Between North and South: Delaware, Desegregation, and the Myth of American Sectionalism* (Philadelphia: University of Pennsylvania Press, 2012).

20 Countryman, *Up South*, 10.

21 Nancy Beadie, Joy Williamson-Lott, Michael Bowman, Teresa Frizell, Gonzalo Guzmán, Jisoo Hyan, Joanna Johnson, Kathryn Nicholas, Lani Phillips, Rebecca Wellington, and La'akea Yoshia, "Gateways to the West, Part I: Education in the Shaping of the West," *History of Education Quarterly* 56, no. 3 (August 2016): 422, emphasis in original.

22 Beadie et al., "Gateways to the West, Part I," 218.

23 Nancy Beadie, Joy Williamson-Lott, Michael Bowman, Teresa Frizell, Gonzalo Guzmán, Jisoo Hyan, Joanna Johnson, Kathryn Nicholas, Lani Phillips, Rebecca Wellington, and La'akea Yoshia, "Gateways to the West, Part II: Education and the Making of Race, Place, and Culture in the West," *History of Education Quarterly* 57, no. 1 (February 2017): 99.

24 Brian Purnell and Jeanne Theoharis, "Introduction: Histories of Racism and Resistance, Seen and Unseen; How and Why to Think about the Jim Crow North," in Purnell, Theoharis, and Woodard, *Strange Careers of the Jim Crow North*, 5–6.

25 Purnell and Theoharis, "Introduction: Histories of Racism," 9.

26 Richard McCormick, *The Black Student Protest Movement at Rutgers* (New Brunswick: Rutgers University Press, 1990); Donald Alexander Downs, *Cornell '69: Liberalism and the Crisis of the American University* (Ithaca: Cornell University Press, 1999); Wayne Glasker, *Black Students in the Ivory Tower: African American Student Activism at the University of Pittsburgh, 1967–1990* (Amherst: University of Massachusetts Press, 2002); Joy Ann Williamson, *Black Power on Campus: The University of Illinois, 1965–1975* (Urbana: University of Illinois Press, 2003); Fabio Rojas, *From Black Power to Black Studies: How a Radical Social Movement Became an Academic Discipline* (Baltimore: Johns Hopkins University Press, 2007); William H. Exum, *Paradoxes of Protest: Black Student Activism in a White University* (Philadelphia: University of Pennsylvania Press, 1985); Dikran Karagueuzian, *Blow It Up! The Black Student Revolt at San Francisco State College and the Emergence of Dr. Hayakawa* (Boston: Gambit, 1971); Jack Bass and Jack Nelson, *The Orangeburg Massacre* (Macon, GA: Mercer, 1984); Tim Spofford, *Lynch Street: The May 1970 Slayings at Jackson State College* (Kent, OH: Kent State University Press, 1988); "The History of Black Student Activism," special issue, *Journal of African American History* 88, no. 2 (Spring 2003); Stefan M. Bradley, *Harlem vs. Columbia University: Black Student Power in the Late 1960s* (Urbana: University of Illinois Press, 2009); Ibram H. Rogers, *The Black Campus Movement: Black Students and the Racial Reconstitution of Higher Education, 1965–1972* (New York: Palgrave Macmillan, 2012); Martha Biondi, *Black Revolution on Campus* (Berkeley: University of California Press, 2012); Collisson, "Fight to Legitimize Blackness."

27 Biondi, *Black Revolution on Campus*, 1.

28 Rogers, *Black Campus Movement*, 3.

29 Rogers, *Black Campus Movement*, 3; Biondi, *Black Revolution on Campus*, 2; Cohen, "Introduction: A Prophetic Minority," 7.

30 Jack Newfield, *A Prophetic Minority* (New York: Signet, 1966); Todd Gitlin, *The Sixties: Years of Hope, Days of Rage* (New York: Bantam, 1993); Terry Anderson, *The Movement and the Sixties: Protest in America from Greensboro to Wounded Knee* (New York: Oxford University Press, 1996); Kirkpatrick Sale, *SDS* (New York: Random House, 1973); James Miller, *Democracy in the Streets: From Port Huron to the Siege of Chicago* (New York: Simon and Schuster, 1987); Maurice

Isserman, *If I Had a Hammer: The Death of the Old Left and the Birth of the New Left* (New York: Basic Books, 1987).

31 Rogers, *Black Campus Movement*, 4–5.

32 Peniel E. Joseph, ed., *Neighborhood Rebels: Black Power at the Local Level* (New York: Palgrave Macmillan, 2010).

33 Williamson, *Black Power on Campus*, 81–85.

34 Bradley, *Harlem vs. Columbia*, 54–55.

35 Curtis J. Austin, *Up against the Wall: Violence in the Making and Unmaking of the Black Panther Party* (Fayetteville: University of Arkansas Press, 2008); Joshua Bloom and Waldo E. Martin Jr., *Black against Empire: The History and Politics of the Black Panther Party* (Berkeley: University of California Press, 2016); Murch, *Living for the City*; Charles E. Jones, *The Black Panther Party [Reconsidered]* (Baltimore: Black Classic Press, 1988); Judson L. Jeffries, *Huey P. Newton: The Radical Theorist* (Oxford: University Press of Mississippi, 2002); Judson L. Jeffries, ed., *On the Ground: The Black Panther Party in Communities across America* (Oxford: University Press of Mississippi, 2010); Robyn C. Spencer, *The Revolution Has Come: Black Power, Gender, and the Black Panther Party in Oakland* (Durham: Duke University Press, 2016).

36 Bloom and Martin, *Black against Empire*, 272.

37 Aaron Dixon, *My People Are Rising: Memoir of a Black Panther Party Captain* (Chicago: Haymarket Books, 2012).

38 Murch, *Living for the City*, 4, 11, 44–45.

39 Garry Owens, interview with author, June 27, 2018; Eddie Demmings, interviews with author, September 24, 2018, and September 14, 2022; E. J. Brisker, "Introduction to a Black Man," Glenn Terrell Papers: Black Studies 1970, Archives and Special Collections, Washington State University Library (archives 205, box 4, folder 217, pp. 94–96). Doug Merlino and Linda Holden Givens, "Gossett, Larry (b. 1945)," HistoryLink. org, October 3, 2019, https://historylink.org.

40 Ernest Thomas, interview with author, September 1, 2011; Beverly Guy-Sheftall, "Cole, Johnnetta Betsch," in *Black Women in America*, 2nd ed., ed. Darlene Clark Hine (Oxford: Oxford University Press, 2005), 277–78.

41 Lucas N. N. Burke and Judson L. Jeffries, *The Portland Black Panthers: Empowering Albina and Remaking a City* (Seattle: University of Washington Press, 2016), 3–4.

42 Seattle FBI file number 157–680, DocId:59160112, p. 2, accessed September 21, 2021, http://archive.org.

43 Seattle FBI file number 157–680.

44 Carol Burns, *As Long as the Rivers Run* (Salmon Defense, 1971), https://archive. org; Coll Thrush, *Native Seattle: Histories from the Crossing-Over Place* (Seattle: University of Washington Press, 2017); Trova Heffernan, *Where the Salmon Run: The Life and Legacy of Billy Frank Jr.* (reprint, Olympia: Office of the Secretary of State's Washington State Heritage Center Legacy Project, 2013); B. J. Cummings,

The River That Made Seattle: A Human and Natural History of the Duwamish (Seattle: University of Washington Press, 2020).

45 Jerry García, ed., *We Are Aztlán! Chicanx Histories in the Northern Borderlands* (Pullman: Washington State University Press, 2017); Bruce E. Johansen, *Seattle's El Centro de la Raza: Dr. King's Living Laboratory* (Lanham, MD: Lexington Books, 2020).

46 Bob Santos, *Hum Bows, Not Hot Dogs: Memoirs of a Savvy Asian American Activist* (Seattle: International Examiner Press, 2002); Ron Chew, *My Forgotten Seattle* (Seattle: International Examiner Press, 2020); Megan Asaka, *Seattle from the Margins: Exclusion, Erasure, and the Making of a Pacific Coast City* (Seattle: University of Washington Press, 2022).

47 Bob Santos and Gary Iwamoto, *The Gang of Four: Four Leaders, Four Communities, One Friendship* (Seattle: Chin Music Press, 2015); Diana K. Johnson, *Seattle in Coalition: Multiracial Alliances, Labor Politics, and Transnational Activism in the Pacific Northwest, 1970–1999* (Chapel Hill: University of North Carolina Press, 2023); Marc Arsell Robinson, "Black Student Unions to the Gang of Four: Interracial Alliances and Community Organizing from San Francisco to Seattle," *California History* 98, no. 2 (2021): 24–49.

48 Daudi Abe, *Emerald Street: A History of Hip Hop in Seattle* (Seattle: University of Washington Press, 2020).

CHAPTER 1. SEATTLE AND THE FOUNDATIONS OF THE BLACK STUDENT UNION, 1940S–1960S

1 John M. Findlay, "Pioneers and Pandemonium: Stability and Change in Seattle History," *Pacific Northwest Quarterly* 107, no. 1 (Winter 2015–2016): 17.

2 Findlay, "Pioneers," 5.

3 Findlay, "Pioneers," 21.

4 Findlay, "Pioneers," 21; Quintard Taylor, *The Forging of a Black Community: Seattle's Central District from 1870 through the Civil Rights Era* (Seattle: University of Washington Press, 1994), 244.

5 Taylor, *Forging of a Black Community*, 245.

6 Taylor, *Forging of a Black Community*, 160–61.

7 Taylor, *Forging of a Black Community*, 161.

8 Findlay, "Pioneers," 17.

9 Singh, *Black Is a Country*, 123.

10 Taylor, *Forging of a Black Community*, 163.

11 Taylor, *Forging of a Black Community*, 163–64.

12 Karen Tucker Anderson, "Last Hired, First Fired: Black Women Workers during World War II," *Journal of American History* 69, no. 1 (June 1982): 83–84.

13 Heather MacIntosh, "Civic Unity Committee in Seattle," HistoryLink.org, January 1, 1999, https://historylink.org, 1.

14 MacIntosh, "Civic Unity Committee," 3–4.

15 Taylor, *Forging of a Black Community*, 88.

16 Taylor, *Forging of a Black Community*, 170.

17 MacIntosh, "Civic Unity Committee," 3–4.
18 Taylor, *Forging of a Black Community*, 170.
19 David Wilma, "Christian Friends for Racial Equality," HistoryLink.org, April 7, 2001, https://historylink.org, 1.
20 Mary T. Henry, "Campbell, Bertha Pitts (1889–1990)," HistoryLink.org, October 13, 1998, https://historylink.org, 1.
21 Wilma, "Christian Friends," 1.
22 Johanna Phillips, "Christian Friends for Racial Equality, 1942–1970," Seattle Civil Rights and Labor History Project, 2006, https://depts.washington.edu/civilr/index.htm, 6, 11–12, 14.
23 Howard A. Droker, "Seattle Race Relations during the Second World War," *Pacific Northwest Quarterly* 67, no. 4 (October 1976): 168–69; Wilma, "Christian Friends."
24 MacIntosh, "Civic Unity Committee," 2.
25 Droker, "Seattle Race Relations," 171.
26 Frederick Dennis Garrity, "The Civic Unity Committee of Seattle, 1944–1964" (master's thesis, University of Washington, 1971), 13–14.
27 Garrity, "Civic Unity Committee," 13–14.
28 MacIntosh, "Civic Unity Committee," 4.
29 Taylor, *Forging of a Black Community*, 171–72.
30 Andre Wooten, "Charles Moorehead Stokes (1903–1996)," Blackpast.org, January 18, 2007, www.blackpast.org, 1.
31 Taylor, *Forging of a Black Community*, 177, 176.
32 Doris H. Pieroth, "With All Deliberate Caution: School Integration in Seattle, 1954–1968," *Pacific Northwest Quarterly* 73, no. 2 (April 1982): 51.
33 Owens, interview, June 27, 2018.
34 Owens, interview, June 27, 2018.
35 Owens, interview, June 27, 2018.
36 Joan Singler, Jean During, Betty Lou Valentine, and Maid Adams, *Seattle in Black and White: The Congress of Racial Equality and the Fight for Equal Opportunity* (Seattle: University of Washington Press, 2011), 16.
37 Singler et al., *Seattle in Black and White*, 16, 18–19, 20, 27–28.
38 Singler et al., *Seattle in Black and White*, 7, 37, 39–45.
39 Richardson, "Civil Rights," 81.
40 Dale E. Soden, *Outsiders in a Promised Land: Religious Activists in Pacific Northwest History* (Corvallis: Oregon State University Press, 2015), 161, 168, 174.
41 Richardson, "Civil Rights," 81–82.
42 Soden, *Outsiders in a Promised Land*, 158, 161.
43 Walt Crowley, *Rites of Passage: A Memoir of the Sixties in Seattle* (Seattle: University of Washington Press, 1995), 29.
44 Pieroth, "With All Deliberate Caution," 53–54.
45 Soden, *Outsiders in a Promised Land*, 165.
46 Soden, *Outsiders in a Promised Land*, 166–69, 183.
47 Soden, *Outsiders in a Promised Land*, 175.

48 Soden, *Outsiders in a Promised Land*, 177–78.
49 Pieroth, "With All Deliberate Caution," 57.
50 Demmings, interview, September 24, 2018.
51 Carl Miller, interview with author, June 26, 2018.
52 Miller, interview, June 26, 2018.
53 Countryman, *Up South*, 105–9.
54 Countryman, *Up South*, 98.
55 Miller, interview, June 26, 2018.
56 Miller, interview, June 26, 2018.
57 Letter, July 9, 1963, Student Nonviolent Coordinating Committee Papers, 1959–1972, Schomburg Center for Research in Black Culture (Reel 32:107; Sc Micro R-4020); "Harry Belafonte Reception: Edgewater Inn, 31 July 1963," Student Nonviolent Coordinating Committee Papers, 1959–1972, Schomburg Center for Research in Black Culture (Reel 32:107; Sc Micro R-4020); letter, August 7, 1963, Student Nonviolent Coordinating Committee Papers, 1959–1972, Schomburg Center for Research in Black Culture (Reel 32:107; Sc Micro R-4020).
58 Miller, interview, June 26, 2018.
59 Miller, interview, June 26, 2018.
60 Miller, interview, June 26, 2018.
61 Miller, interview, June 26, 2018.
62 Taylor, *Forging of a Black Community*, 214.
63 Miller, interview, June 26, 2018.
64 Central Washington University was then called Central Washington State College. Lane Smith, "Black Community Power Will End Abuses, Carmichael Says," *Seattle Times*, April 20, 1967, 5.
65 Douglas Honig and Laura Brenner, *On Freedom's Frontier: The First Fifty Years of the American Civil Liberties Union in Washington State* (Seattle: American Civil Liberties Union Washington, 1987), 52.
66 "Carmichael Ticket Sales Slow at UW," *Seattle Times*, April 19, 1967, 2.
67 "First Amendment Victory: Prior Restraint Is Blocked and Carmichael Delivers His Speech," *American Civil Liberties Union of Washington News*, May–June 1967, 1, 4.
68 "First Amendment Victory."
69 Robert Cour and Walter E. Evans, "Carmichael Rips into Whites Here," *Seattle Post-Intelligencer*, April 20, 1967, 1.
70 "Carmichael Ticket Sales," 2.
71 Smith, "Black Community Power," 5.
72 Anne Todd, "Black Power Must Grow Further, Says Carmichael," *Daily*, April 20, 1967, 1.
73 Todd, "Black Power Must Grow."
74 Cour and Evans, "Carmichael Rips into Whites," 1, 7.
75 Todd, "Black Power Must Grow," 1.
76 Smith, "Black Community Power," 5.

77 Todd, "Black Power Must Grow," 1.

78 Smith, "Black Community Power," 5.

79 Cour and Evans, "Carmichael Rips into Whites," 1, 7.

80 Cour and Evans, "Carmichael Rips into Whites," 1, 7.

81 Smith, "Black Community Power," 5.

82 Smith, "Black Community Power," 5.

83 Smith, "Black Community Power," 5.

84 Cour and Evans, "Carmichael Rips into Whites," 1, 7.

85 Cour and Evans, "Carmichael Rips into Whites," 1, 7.

86 Larry Gossett, "Stokely Carmichael's 1967 Visit to Seattle Had a Significant Impact on Young People," Seattle Civil Rights and Labor History Project, June 3, 2005, http://depts.washington.edu/civilr/index.htm.

87 Doctor, "New Black Image," 6.

88 Lane Smith, "Black-Power Forum Points to Dissatisfaction with Integration," Seattle Times, May 4, 1967, 3.

89 Taylor, Forging of a Black Community, 213; Smith, "Black-Power Forum," 3.

90 Smith, "Black-Power Forum," 3.

91 Smith, "Black-Power Forum," 3.

92 Taylor, Forging of a Black Community, 214–15, 220.

93 Singler et al., Seattle in Black and White, 200; Lane Smith, "New CORE Leaders Here Set Meeting on Black-Power Goals," Seattle Times, September 14, 1967, 8.

94 Taylor, Forging of a Black Community, 218–20; Dixon, My People Are Rising, 81–83.

95 A significant portion of this section is adapted from part of Robinson, "Black Student Unions."

96 At the time under study, the institution was known as San Francisco State College, and became San Francisco State University in 1972. "SF State Facts, 2009–2010," San Francisco State University, accessed February 24, 2012, www.sfsu.edu.

97 James Garrett, interview with author, July 23, 2018. For more on Charlie Cobb, see "Charlie Cobb," SNCC Digital Gateway, accessed October 15, 2019, https://snccdigital.org.

98 Garrett, interview, July 23, 2018.

99 Garrett, interview, July 23, 2018.

100 William H. Orrick, Shut It Down! A College in Crisis: San Francisco State College, October 1968–April 1969; a Report to the National Commission on the Causes and Prevention of Violence (Washington, DC: US Govt. Printing Office, 1969), 77.

101 Karagueuzian, Blow It Up!, 1–3, 40.

102 Franciscan, 1964 (San Francisco: San Francisco State College, 1964), 189, https://diva.sfsu.edu.

103 "Today at State," Golden Gater, November 19, 1964, 3, https://sfsu-dspace.calstate.edu; "Soulful Sounds," Golden Gater, May 19, 1965, 1, https://sfsu-dspace.calstate.edu; "Today at State," Golden Gater, May 26, 1965, 2, https://sfsu-dspace.calstate.edu; "Africa Must Unite: NSA Talk," Golden Gater, March 29, 1965, 3, https://sfsu-dspace.calstate.edu.

---

104 "'Freedom Fast' Today," *Golden Gater*, December 11, 1964, 1, https://sfsu-dspace.calstate.edu; "Freedom Week Features, Voter Test, Feast, Songs," *Golden Gater*, May 7, 1965, 3, https://sfsu-dspace.calstate.edu.

105 "24 hr. Viet Vigil in Lounge Tonight," *Golden Gater*, May 17, 1965, 1, https://sfsu-dspace.calstate.edu.

106 David Yamane, *Student Movements for Multiculturalism: Challenging the Curricular Color Line in Higher Education* (Baltimore: Johns Hopkins University Press, 2002), 13.

107 Noliwe Rooks, *White Money/Black Power: The Surprising History of African American Studies and the Crisis of Race in Higher Education* (Boston: Beacon, 2006), 38.

108 Orrick, *Shut It Down!*, 78.

109 Karagueuzian, *Blow It Up!*, 40.

110 Garrett, interview, July 23, 2018.

111 Garrett, interview, July 23, 2018.

112 Garrett, interview, July 23, 2018.

113 Garrett, interview, July 23, 2018.

114 Sherri Cavan, John Kinch, Kathy Charmaz, Carol Englebrecht, and Ken Magoon, "Fred Thalheimer, 1929–1999," *Footnotes: Newsletter of the American Sociological Association* 28, no. 3 (March 2000), www.asanet.org.

115 Garrett, interview, July 23, 2018.

116 Rojas, *From Black Power to Black Studies*, 52.

117 Orrick, *Shut It Down!*, 81.

118 Garrett, interview, July 23, 2018.

119 Orrick, *Shut It Down!*, 80; Sam Whiting, "Black Student Union at SFSU Started It All," *San Francisco Chronicle*, February 1, 2010, www.sfgate.com.

120 Orrick, *Shut It Down!*, 78; Whiting, "Black Student Union at SFSU."

121 Karagueuzian, *Blow It Up!*, 41.

122 Whiting, "Black Student Union at SFSU."

123 Whiting, "Black Student Union at SFSU."

124 Orrick, *Shut It Down!*, 86, 90.

125 Orrick, *Shut It Down!*, 89.

126 Karagueuzian, *Blow It Up!*, 41; James Garrett, email to author, June 23, 2021.

127 Orrick, *Shut It Down!*, 81; Rojas, *From Black Power to Black Studies*, 53.

128 Robinson, "Black Student Unions," 28.

129 Whiting, "Black Student Union at SFSU."

130 Orrick, *Shut It Down!*, 83.

131 Orrick, *Shut It Down!*, 85.

132 Orrick, *Shut It Down!*, 87.

133 Orrick, *Shut It Down!*, 97.

134 Black Studies Curriculum, Spring 1968, Black Student Union folder, Item 3, SF State Strike Collection, J. Paul Leonard Library, San Francisco State University, http://digital-collections.library.sfsu.edu, 1.

135 Robinson, "Black Student Unions," 29.

136 Black Studies Curriculum, Spring 1968, 1.

137 Black Studies Curriculum, Spring 1968, 1–8.

138 Peniel Joseph, "Black Studies, Student Activism, and the Black Power Movement," in Joseph, *Black Power Movement*, 251–52.

139 Rogers, *Black Campus Movement*, 5.

140 Rogers, *Black Campus Movement*, 152.

141 Orrick, *Shut It Down!*, 109.

142 Orrick, *Shut It Down!*, 113.

143 Bloom and Martin, *Black against Empire*, 270–71.

144 "Demands and Explanations," November 1968, SF State Strike Collection, J. Paul Leonard Library, San Francisco State University (box 44, folder 326, item 5), http://digital-collections.library.sfsu.edu.

145 Karagueuzian, *Blow It Up!*, 2; Whiting, "Black Student Union at SFSU"; Yamane, *Student Movements*, 13.

146 "SFSC Student-Led Strike Materials in the J. Paul Leonard Library: Additional Page, LibGuides," J. Paul Leonard Library, San Francisco State University, May 11, 2019, https://libguides.sfsu.edu; Juanita Tamayo Lott, *Golden Children: Legacy of Ethnic Studies, SF State* (Berkeley: Eastwind Books of Berkeley, 2018), 2.

147 Rojas, *From Black Power to Black Studies*, 69; Orrick, *Shut It Down!*, 151.

148 Rojas, *From Black Power to Black Studies*, 48–49; Rooks, *White Money/Black Power*, 33; Karagueuzian, *Blow It Up!*, 128, 138.

149 Rooks, *White Money/Black Power*, 34; Karagueuzian, *Blow It Up!*, 8; Orrick, *Shut It Down!*, 41.

150 Rooks, *White Money/Black Power*, 34.

151 Margaret Leahy, "On Strike! We're Gonna Shut It Down," in *Ten Years That Shook the City: San Francisco, 1968–1978*, ed. Chris Carlsson and Lisa Ruth Elliott (San Francisco: City Lights Books, 2011), 24, www.foundsf.org.

152 Rooks, *White Money/Black Power*, 34.

153 Lott, *Golden Children*, 55.

154 Rooks, *White Money/Black Power*, 34.

155 Orrick, *Shut It Down!*, 128–29.

156 Rojas, *From Black Power to Black Studies*, 85–86.

157 Bloom and Martin, *Black against Empire*, 282–83; Lott, *Golden Children*, 55.

158 Yamane, *Student Movements*, 14.

159 "College of Ethnic Studies, History," San Francisco State University, accessed June 16, 2021, https://ethnicstudies.sfsu.edu.

160 Whiting, "Black Student Union at SFSU."

161 Rojas, *From Black Power to Black Studies*, 81, 86.

162 Karagueuzian, *Blow It Up!*, 192.

CHAPTER 2. "YOU DONE *REALLY* CHANGED"

1 Katherine Long, "A 1968 Sit-In by Black Students Led to Big Changes at the UW," *Seattle Times*, May 5, 2018, B1.

2 Collisson, "Fight to Legitimize Blackness," 25; "Black Power at UW," *Seattle Post-Intelligencer*, December 7, 1967, 12.

3 Rogers, *Black Campus Movement*, 3.

4 Demmings, interview, September 14, 2022.

5 Verlaine Keith-Miller, interview with author, July 17, 2018.

6 Keith-Miller, interview, July 17, 2018.

7 Keith-Miller, interview, July 17, 2018.

8 Keith-Miller, interview, July 17, 2018.

9 "OMA&D Mourns Passing of Alumna and Founding BSU Member Verlaine Keith-Miller," Office of Minority Affairs and Diversity, November 15, 2018, www.washington.edu.

10 Merlino and Givens, "Gossett, Larry."

11 Merlino and Givens, "Gossett, Larry."

12 Malcolm X and Alex Haley, *The Autobiography of Malcolm X* (New York: Ballantine, 1999), 42.

13 Merlino and Givens, "Gossett, Larry."

14 Larry Gossett, interview with author, July 13, 2018.

15 Gossett, interview with author, July 13, 2018.

16 Gossett, interview with author, July 13, 2018.

17 Gossett, interview with author, July 13, 2018.

18 Gossett, interview with author, July 13, 2018.

19 Demmings, interview, September 24, 2018.

20 Nancy Wick, "'Elder Statesman' Pitre Helped Plant Seeds of Change in the 1960s," *UW Today*, May 1, 2008, www.washington.edu, 1.

21 Misty Shock Rule, "50 Years of the Movement for Diversity, Access, and Equality," *Columns: The University of Washington Magazine*, March 18, 2018, 33.

22 Hinckley and Henderson, *In Pursuit of Social Justice*.

23 Emile Pitre, interview with author, July 10, 2018.

24 Cathleen Curtis, "The Black Revolution," *Tyee Magazine* 3, no. 2 (1968): 3.

25 Collisson, "Fight to Legitimize Blackness," 25; "Black Power at UW," 12.

26 Gossett, interview with author, July 13, 2018.

27 Gossett, interview with author, July 13, 2018.

28 At the time under study, San Jose State University was known as San Jose State College. "Timeline," San Jose State University, July 1, 2019, www.sjsu.edu.

29 Marc Robinson, "The Early History of the UW Black Student Union," Seattle Civil Rights and Labor History Project, accessed July 23, 2022, http://depts.washington.edu/civilr/index.htm, 2.

30 Larry Gossett, interviews with Trevor Griffey and Brooke Clark, March 16 and June 3, 2005, Seattle Civil Rights and Labor History Project, http://depts.washington.edu/civilr/index.htm.

31 "Olympic Boycott Voted by Negroes," *New York Times*, November 24, 1967, 30; Jeff Prugh, "Negro Group Votes to Boycott '68 Olympics," *Los Angeles Times*, November 24, 1967, pt. 3, 1.

32 Robinson, "Early History," 2.

33 Gossett, interview, Seattle Civil Rights and Labor History Project.

34 Garrett, interview, July 23, 2018.

35 Gossett, interview, Seattle Civil Rights and Labor History Project.

36 Collisson, "Fight to Legitimize Blackness," 26.

37 "Black Power at UW," 12.

38 Hinckley and Henderson, *In Pursuit of Social Justice.*

39 Doctor, "New Black Image," 6.

40 Rojas, *From Black Power to Black Studies,* 100.

41 Rojas, *From Black Power to Black Studies,* 101.

42 Doctor, "New Black Image," 6.

43 Robinson, "Black Student Unions," 33.

44 Marcie Hall-McMurtrie, interview with author, July 24, 2018.

45 Doctor, "New Black Image," 7.

46 Alexis Mansanarez, "Civil Rights Leaders and Former Students Gather to Reflect on 50 Years of Work," *Daily,* May 5, 2017, www.dailyuw.com; Gossett, interview with author, April 13, 2004.

47 Pitre, interview, July 10, 2018.

48 Hall-McMurtrie, interview, July 24, 2018.

49 Kathy Mack, "Black Women Tell Ordeals in Climbing out of 'Cruel Valley,'" *Daily,* April 22, 1969, 16.

50 Keith-Miller, interview, July 17, 2018.

51 Gossett, interview, Seattle Civil Rights and Labor History Project.

52 Mack, "Black Women Tell Ordeals," 16.

53 "The Voice of the UW BSU: The Word Is Now!" *Daily,* February 16, 1968, 3.

54 Curtis, "Black Revolution," 4.

55 Collisson, "Fight to Legitimize Blackness," 31.

56 Elmer Dixon, interview with author, July 2, 2018.

57 Elmer Dixon, interview with Janet Jones and Trevor Griffey, Seattle Civil Rights and Labor History Project, May 17, 2005, https://depts.washington.edu/civilr/index.htm.

58 Collisson, "Fight to Legitimize Blackness," 31.

59 Robinson, "Early History," 3.

60 Gossett, interview, Seattle Civil Rights and Labor History Project.

61 At the time under study, Seattle Central College was known as Seattle Community College, and Seattle Pacific University was known as Seattle Pacific College. "Our History," Seattle Central, accessed May 10, 2021, https://seattlecentral.edu; "Our History: 1970-90," Seattle Pacific University, 2021, https://spu.edu; Gossett, interview with author, July 13, 2018.

62 Gossett, interview with author, October 23, 2003.

63 Collisson, "Fight to Legitimize Blackness," 30.

64 Gossett, interview with author, July 13, 2018.

65 Gossett, interview with author, July 13, 2018.

66 Gossett, interview with author, July 13, 2018.

67 Hinckley and Henderson, *In Pursuit of Social Justice.*

68 Hinckley and Henderson, *In Pursuit of Social Justice.*

69 Gossett, interview, Seattle Civil Rights and Labor History Project.

70 Gossett, interview, Seattle Civil Rights and Labor History Project.

71 Demmings, interview, September 24, 2018.

72 Gossett, interview, Seattle Civil Rights and Labor History Project.

73 Don Hannula, "Non-Franklin Students Led Negro Sit-In, Says Principal," *Seattle Times*, March 30, 1968, 13.

74 Gossett, interview with author, October 23, 2003.

75 Tikia Gilbert, "The Franklin High School Sit-In," Seattle Civil Rights and Labor History Project, accessed October 25, 2011, http://depts.washington.edu/civilr/index.htm, 1.

76 Hannula, "Non-Franklin Students," 13.

77 Gilbert, "Franklin High School Sit-In," 1.

78 "White Racism Critic Calls Franklin 'Sick School,'" *Seattle Post-Intelligencer*, June 29, 1968, 3.

79 Gossett, interview, Seattle Civil Rights and Labor History Project.

80 Gilbert, "Franklin High School Sit-In," 1.

81 Gilbert, "Franklin High School Sit-In," 1–2.

82 Gilbert, "Franklin High School Sit-In," 2.

83 Dixon, *My People Are Rising*, 71–72.

84 Gilbert, "Franklin High School Sit-In," 2.

85 Dixon, *My People Are Rising*, 72.

86 Gilbert, "Franklin High School Sit-In," 2–3.

87 Gossett, interview, Seattle Civil Rights and Labor History Project.

88 Constantine Angelos, "Human-Relations Unit Urged Franklin High," *Seattle Times*, April 1, 1968, 3.

89 Gossett, interview, Seattle Civil Rights and Labor History Project; Gilbert, "Franklin High School Sit-In," 3.

90 Gilbert, "Franklin High School Sit-In," 3; Gossett, interview with author, October 23, 2003; Gossett, interview, Seattle Civil Rights and Labor History Project.

91 Nell Irving Painter, *Creating Black Americans: African-American History and Its Meanings, 1619 to the Present* (New York: Oxford University Press, 2007), 328, 330.

92 Aaron Dixon, interviews with Janet Jones, Trevor Griffey, and Alex Morrow, Seattle Civil Rights and Labor History Project, May 2 and July 13, 2005, http://depts.washington.edu/civilr/index.htm.

93 Crowley, *Rites of Passage*, 114, 253.

94 Gilbert, "Franklin High School Sit-In," 4.

95 Gossett, interview, Seattle Civil Rights and Labor History Project.

96 Gossett, interview, Seattle Civil Rights and Labor History Project ; Gilbert, "Franklin High School Sit-In," 4.

97 Gilbert, "Franklin High School Sit-In," 4.

98 Gilbert, "Franklin High School Sit-In," 5, 6; Gossett, interview with author, July 13, 2018.

99 Crowley, *Rites of Passage*, 114.

100 Louis Massiah, dir., *Eyes on the Prize: Power! 1967–1968*, *American Experience*, PBS, 1990; Terry Kay Rockefeller, dir., *Eyes on the Prize: A Nation of Law? 1968–1971*, *American Experience*, PBS, 1990.

101 Mark Kitchell, dir., *Berkeley in the Sixties*, California Newsreel, 1990.

102 Gossett, interview, Seattle Civil Rights and Labor History Project.

103 Aaron Dixon, interview, Seattle Civil Rights and Labor History Project.

104 Bloom and Martin, *Black against Empire*, 146–47; Gossett, interview with author, July 5, 2006; Linda Holden Givens, "Black Panther Party Seattle Chapter (1968–1978)," HistoryLink.org, October 16, 2018, https://historylink.org.

105 Crowley, *Rites of Passage*, 114; Aaron Dixon, interview, Seattle Civil Rights and Labor History Project.

106 Bloom and Martin, *Black against Empire*, chap. 12.

CHAPTER 3. "WE TIRED OF Y'ALL'S HALF-STEPPING"

1 Irum Shiekh, dir., *On Strike: Ethnic Studies, 1969–1999*, Fifth Floor Productions, Center for Asian American Media, San Francisco, 1999.

2 Crowley, *Rites of Passage*, 114.

3 Crowley, *Rites of Passage*, 253.

4 Crowley, *Rites of Passage*, 254.

5 At the time under study, the school was known as San Francisco State College. "San Francisco State University—A Brief History," San Francisco State University, accessed June 2, 2021, https://budget.sfsu.edu.

6 Dixon, *My People Are Rising*, 218.

7 Dixon, *My People Are Rising*, 21, 24.

8 Dixon, *My People Are Rising*, 6–7.

9 Cour and Evans, "Carmichael Rips into Whites," 1, 7.

10 Givens, "Black Panther Party Seattle Chapter."

11 Dixon, *My People Are Rising*, 28.

12 This same image was also used on the cover of his memoir. Givens, "Black Panther Party Seattle Chapter."

13 Keith-Miller, interview, July 17, 2018.

14 Brisker, "Introduction to a Black Man."

15 Pitre, interview, July 10, 2018.

16 Brisker, "Introduction to a Black Man."

17 Pitre, interview, July 10, 2018.

18 Garrett, interview, July 23, 2018.

19 Gossett, interview with author, July 13, 2018.

20 Pitre, interview, July 10, 2018.

21 Brisker, "Introduction to a Black Man."

22 Glenn Fowler, "John Summerskill Is Dead at 65; Led San Francisco State in 60's," *New York Times*, June 15, 1990, D18, www.nytimes.com.

23 Garrett, interview, July 23, 2018.

24 "University of Washington Senate, Letter to All Members of the Faculty," Charles Evans Papers, Manuscripts and Archives, University of Washington Libraries (accession number 2598–001, box 1).

25 "Office of Minority Affairs History Timeline, Drafted by Emile Pitre, March 6, 2017," University of Washington, Office of Minority Affairs and Diversity records, 1968–2018, Manuscripts and Archives, University of Washington Libraries (accession number 19–018, box 1).

26 Fred Olson, "Black Students Send Demands to Odegaard," *Daily*, May 7, 1968, 1.

27 Olson, "Black Students," 1; Mike Parks, "UW Black Students Ask Reforms," *Daily*, May 7, 1968, 6.

28 Letter from BSU to Odegaard, May 6, 1968, Black Student Union, Manuscripts and Archives, University of Washington Libraries (accession number 71–069, box 1).

29 Letter from BSU to Odegaard, May 6, 1968.

30 Pope's name was mistakenly listed as "Polk" in the BSU list of demands. Emile Pitre remembers Pope as the correct name. Emile Pitre, email to author, September 3, 2022. See also the entry for Byron Pope in the Kearney Barton Collection of Northwest Music, University of Washington Libraries, https://guides.lib.uw.edu; and Pope's own website, http://byronhpope.com.

31 Julie Emery, "UW Black Students Detail 5 Demands," *Seattle Times*, May 9, 1968, 13.

32 "Full Text of Odegaard's Reply to BSU," *Daily*, May 10, 1968, 1–2; Fred Olson, "Odegaard Gives Answer to BSU Demands," *Daily*, May 10, 1968, 1, 3.

33 "Full Text of Odegaard's Reply."

34 Dennis Carlson, "BSU Meeting with Odegaard 'Encouraging,'" *Daily*, May 14, 1968, 1.

35 Carlson, "BSU Meeting."

36 "Full Text of Odegaard's Reply"; Emery, "UW Black Students," 13.

37 Carlson, "BSU Meeting," 1.

38 Carlson, "BSU Meeting."

39 Carlson, "BSU Meeting," 16.

40 Carlson, "BSU Meeting."

41 Gossett, interview, Seattle Civil Rights and Labor History Project.

42 Robert Cour, "UW Negroes Air Demand for $50,000," *Seattle Post-Intelligencer*, May 18, 1968.

43 Letter from BSU to Odegaard, May 16, 1968, Black Student Union, Manuscripts and Archives, University of Washington Libraries (accession number 71–069, box 1).

44 Gossett, interview, Seattle Civil Rights and Labor History Project.

45 Cour, "UW Negroes Air Demand."

46 Cour, "UW Negroes Air Demand."

47 Hinckley and Henderson, *In Pursuit of Social Justice*.

48 Gossett, interview, Seattle Civil Rights and Labor History Project.

49 Gossett, interview, Seattle Civil Rights and Labor History Project.

50 Garrett, interview, July 23, 2018.

51 Bryant, "White University?," 14; Ferbon, "Late-Hour Compromise," 1; Norton, "Agreement," 5.

52 Minutes of Executive Committee meeting, May 20, 1968, Charles Evans Papers, Manuscripts and Archives, University of Washington Libraries (accession number 2598–001, box 1).

53 Gossett, interview with author, July 5, 2006.

54 Norton, "Agreement," 5; Walker, "University of Washington Establishment," 2.

55 Minutes of Executive Committee meeting, May 20, 1968.

56 Minutes of Executive Committee meeting, May 20, 1968.

57 Pitre, email, September 3, 2022.

58 Minutes of Executive Committee meeting, May 20, 1968.

59 Norton, "Agreement," 5; Walker, "University of Washington Establishment," 66; minutes of Executive Committee meeting, May 20, 1968.

60 Pitre, interview with author, May 12, 2011; Office of Minority Affairs and Diversity, Friends of the Educational Opportunity Program, *Celebration* (Seattle: University of Washington, 2008).

61 Minutes of Executive Committee meeting, May 20, 1968.

62 Jesse Crowder, interview with author, July 26, 2018.

63 Hinckley and Henderson, *In Pursuit of Social Justice*.

64 Hinckley and Henderson, *In Pursuit of Social Justice*; Pitre, email, September 3, 2022.

65 Hinckley and Henderson, *In Pursuit of Social Justice*.

66 Hinckley and Henderson, *In Pursuit of Social Justice*.

67 Walker, "University of Washington Establishment," 66. Michael Rosen was an American Civil Liberties Union lawyer who helped win the case to allow Stokely Carmichael to speak at Garfield High School. He was also helping Miller, Dixon, and Gossett in their criminal trial stemming from the Franklin sit-in. See "Four in Franklin Protest Plead Not Guilty," *Seattle Times*, April 5, 1968, 24.

68 Minutes of Executive Committee meeting, May 20, 1968.

69 Minutes of Executive Committee meeting, May 20, 1968.

70 Hinckley and Henderson, *In Pursuit of Social Justice*.

71 Bryant, "White University?," 14; Ferbon, "Late-Hour Compromise," 1; Norton, "Agreement," 5.

72 Hinckley and Henderson, *In Pursuit of Social Justice*.

73 Hinckley and Henderson, *In Pursuit of Social Justice*.

74 Mike Steward, "Senate Applauds Brisker," *Daily*, May 24, 1968, 1.

75 Robinson, "Early History," 7–8.

76 Pitre, interview, July 10, 2018.

77 Hall-McMurtrie, interview, July 24, 2018; Robinson, "Black Student Unions," 37.

78 Demmings, interview, September 14, 2022.

79 Taylor, *Forging of a Black Community*, 223; Walker, "University of Washington Establishment," 73.

80 Bryant, "White University?," 14.

81 Samuel E. Kelly, "Annual Report of the Office of Minority Affairs for the Academic Year of 1970–71," University of Washington Office of Minority Affairs Records, 1970–2002, Manuscripts and Archives, University of Washington Libraries (accession number 16–025, box 2), 3–4.

82 Taylor, *Forging of a Black Community*, 223; Walker, "University of Washington Establishment," 47.

83 "UW Faculty Group Urges Program to Aid Negroes," *Seattle Times*, May 7, 1968, 6; "Negro Opportunity at UW Urged," *Seattle Post-Intelligencer*, May 8, 1968, 42.

84 Curtis, "Black Revolution," 4–5.

85 Kelly, "Annual Report," 4.

86 Pitre, interview with author, October 17, 2003.

87 Wick, "'Elder Statesman.'"

88 "Instructional Center: Brotman Awards," Office of Minority Affairs and Diversity, June 1, 2021, https://depts.washington.edu.

89 Pitre, interview, October 17, 2003. In 2002 the name of the Office of Minority Affairs was changed to the Office of Minority Affairs and Diversity. See "Office of Minority Affairs and Diversity," UW 150th Story Bank, accessed October 27, 2011, http://depts.washington.edu.

90 Kelly and Taylor, *Dr. Sam*, 166.

91 "History," American Ethnic Studies, accessed June 4, 2021, https://aes.washington.edu.

92 Gilbert, "Franklin High School Sit-In," 3, 5.

93 Mike Parks, "Odegaard Aide Testifies at Franklin Trial," *Seattle Times*, June 11, 1968, 4.

94 Larry Brown, "Three Sentenced in Franklin Case," *Seattle Times*, July 1, 1968, 72.

95 Gilbert, "Franklin High School Sit-In," 5.

96 Larry McCarten, "Sit-In Trio Guilty, 2 Free," *Seattle Post-Intelligencer*, June 14, 1968, 1.

97 Brown, "Three Sentenced," 72; "Blacks, Whites Post Bail for 3 Negroes," *Seattle Times*, July 2, 1968, 6.

98 Gilbert, "Franklin High School Sit-In," 5; Crowley, *Rites of Passage*, 118, 257.

99 Mike Wyne and Robert A. Barr, "12 Arrested in Outbreak in Garfield High Area," *Seattle Times*, July 2, 1968, 6.

100 "Police Sealed Area, Brought in More Help," *Seattle Times*, July 2, 1968, 6.

101 "Blacks, Whites Post Bail," 6; Gilbert, "Franklin High School Sit-In," 5–6.

102 Gilbert, "Franklin High School Sit-In," 6.

103 In 2014 Seattle Central Community College was renamed the Seattle Central College. "Our History," SeattleCentral.edu, accessed July 13, 2020, https://seattlecentral.edu.

104 Crowley, *Rites of Passage*, 136.

105 Theoharis, *More Beautiful and Terrible History*, 147.

106 Crowley, *Rites of Passage*, 137.

107 Craig Collisson, "The BSU Takes on BYU and the UW Athletics Program, 1970," Seattle Civil Rights and Labor History Project, 2007, http://depts.washington.edu/civilr/index.htm, 1.

108 Michael Oriard, *Bowled Over: Big-Time College Football from the Sixties to the BCS Era* (Chapel Hill: University of North Carolina Press, 2009), 104.

109 Collisson, "BSU Takes on BYU," 1–2.

110 Crowley, *Rites of Passage*, 170.

111 Collisson, "BSU Takes on BYU," 1.

112 Collisson, "BSU Takes on BYU," 1, 4–5.

113 Collisson, "BSU Takes on BYU," 6.

114 Cal McCune, *From Romance to Riot: A Seattle Memoir* (Seattle: self-published, 1996), 106–7.

115 Collisson, "BSU Takes on BYU," 9.

116 Collisson, "BSU Takes on BYU," 10.

117 Collisson, "BSU Takes on BYU," 5.

118 Collisson, "BSU Takes on BYU," 7.

119 McCune, *From Romance to Riot*, 107; Collisson, "BSU Takes on BYU," 11.

120 Pitre, interview, July 10, 2018; Kelly and Taylor, *Dr. Sam*, 162.

CHAPTER 4. "NEVER JUST A TEA PARTY"

1 "Negroes Ask 'Why.'" Emphasis in original.

2 Purnell and Theoharis, "Introduction: Histories of Racism," 1.

3 Purnell and Theoharis, "Introduction: Histories of Racism," 1–11.

4 Big Bend Community College, Moses Lake, WA; Carroll College, Helena, MT; Central Washington University, Ellensburg, WA; Columbia Basin College, Pasco, WA; Everett Community College, Everett, WA; Fort Wright College, Spokane, WA; Gonzaga University, Spokane, WA; Highline College, Des Moines, WA; Idaho State University, Pocatello, ID; Lower Columbia College, Longview, WA; Pacific Lutheran University, Tacoma, WA; Seattle Central College, Seattle, WA; Shoreline Community College, Shoreline, WA; Tacoma Community College, Tacoma, WA; University of Idaho, Moscow, ID; University of Washington, Seattle, WA; Washington State University, Pullman, WA; Whitman College, Walla Walla, WA; and Whitworth University, Spokane, WA. Source: "News Letter: Black Studies in the Pacific Northwest," Black Studies, 1970, Glenn Terrell Papers, Manuscripts, Archives, and Special Collections, Washington State University Library (UA205 B4 F217 P100).

5 Stephens, "Historical Development of Black Studies," 56.

6 Eric Mathison, "New Left Movement Present on Campus," *Daily Evergreen*, December 15, 1967, 5.

7 Stephens, "Historical Development of Black Studies," 57.

8 Felicia Gaskins, interview with author, April 14, 2011.

9 "Fifty Years Back: Washington State University in 1962," *Washington State Magazine*, May 2021, http://wsm.wsu.edu.

10 Gaskins, interview, April 14, 2011.

11 Eric Mathison, Jim Jones, and Rosanne King, "A Farewell Interview with the Coles," *Daily Evergreen*, July 13, 1970, 4.

12 Tom Curry, "More Than a Prep School," editorial, *Daily Evergreen*, September 27, 1968, 2.

13 Rutledge Dennis, interview with author, June 8, 2011.

14 Curry, "More Than a Prep School"; Stephens, "Historical Development of Black Studies," 57.

15 Mary White, "White Apathy Produces Black Solidarity," *Daily Evergreen*, April 25, 1969, 8.

16 Guy-Sheftall, "Cole, Johnnetta Betsch," 277–78; Guy-Sheftall, "Johnnetta Betsch Cole," in *Notable Black American Women*, ed. Jessie Carney Smith (Detroit: Gale Research, 1992).

17 Johnnetta Betsch Cole, *Conversations: Straight Talk with America's Sister President* (New York: Anchor, Doubleday, 1993), 11–13, 28–29.

18 Guy-Sheftall, "Cole, Johnnetta Betsch"; Guy-Sheftall, "Johnnetta Betsch Cole"; Mathison, Jones, and King, "Farewell Interview," 4; Peggy McGlone, "African Art Museum Director Cole Will Retire in March," *Washington Post*, December 14, 2016, www.washingtonpost.com.

19 Mathison, Jones, and King, "Farewell Interview," 4.

20 Farmer, *Remaking Black Power*.

21 Mathison, Jones, and King, "Farewell Interview," 4.

22 Mathison, Jones, and King, "Farewell Interview," 4.

23 Ernest Thomas, interview with author, June 8, 2011.

24 David Covin, interview with author, June 9, 2011.

25 Covin, interview, June 9, 2011.

26 "Group Observes Malcolm X Day," *Daily Evergreen*, February 21, 1968, 9.

27 William L. Van Deburg, *A New Day in Babylon: The Black Power Movement and American Culture, 1965–1975* (Chicago: University of Chicago Press, 1993), 2.

28 Deloria Jones, "'Black Revolt Inevitable' Attributed to Malcolm X," *Daily Evergreen*, February 23, 1968, 3.

29 "Civil Rights Issue Draws Comments," *Daily Evergreen*, March 19, 1968, 12; Geraldine Pope, "Race Relations Panel Gives Conflicting Views," *Daily Evergreen*, March 5, 1968, 1; Robinson, "Black Power Movement," 112–16.

30 Mary White, "'Barnyards' to AGR: BSU History Created," *Daily Evergreen*, April 23, 1969, 6.

31 Mathison, Jones, and King, "Farewell Interview," 4.

32 Gossett, interview with author, July 13, 2018.

33 Covin, interview, June 9, 2011.

34 "Project 408 Difficulties Compounded by Schedule," *Daily Evergreen*, May 14, 1968, 2; "Students Accept Apology," *Daily Evergreen*, May 17, 1968, 1.

35 "Committee Clarifies Incident with Report," *Daily Evergreen*, May 14, 1968, 1.

36 Neil Felgenhauer, "Negro Visitors Claim Mistreatment, Insults," *Daily Evergreen*, May 14, 1968, 1.

37 Felgenhauer, "Negro Visitors"; "Negroes Ask 'Why'"; "Committee Clarifies Incident."

38 Felgenhauer, "Negro Visitors."

39 "Negroes Ask 'Why.'"

40 "Press Reaction to Incident Mild," *Daily Evergreen*, May 14, 1968, 2.

41 "Negro Footballers Return to Practice after Absentee," *Daily Evergreen*, May 14, 1968, 2; "1967 Washington State Cougars Stats," Sports Reference, 2000–2021, www.sports-reference.com.

42 Oriard, *Bowled Over*, 97.

43 "No Response Yet to Telegram Plea," *Daily Evergreen*, May 14, 1968, 2.

44 "Negroes Ask 'Why.'"

45 Mathison, Jones, and King, "Farewell Interview," 4.

46 Mark Reese, "A Ridiculous Mountain Is Born," editorial, *Daily Evergreen*, May 24, 1968, 1.

47 "Terrell Issues Apology to Offended Students," *Daily Evergreen*, May 14, 1968, 2.

48 "Terrell Issues Apology."

49 "Terrell Issues Apology."

50 "Committee Clarifies Incident."

51 "Terrell Issues Apology."

52 "Social Responsibility Studied," *Daily Evergreen*, May 15, 1968, 3.

53 "Social Responsibility Studied"; Robinson, "Black Power Movement," 127–30.

54 "Social Responsibility Studied."

55 Dennis, interview, June 8, 2011.

56 Rudy Martin, interview with author, September 27, 2011.

57 "Dr. Terrell Assumes Post as New President," *Daily Evergreen*, September 22, 1967, 1; "'A University Must Find Leaders,' States Terrell," *Daily Evergreen*, March 19, 1968, 1; "Terrell Advocates Social Study," *Daily Evergreen*, September 23, 1968, C12.

58 "Social Responsibility Studied."

59 Rooks, *White Money/Black Power*, 38.

60 "Social Responsibility Studied."

61 Louis McNew, "Interim Report and Recommendations on the Education of Disadvantaged High School Graduates, May 24, 1968," Glenn Terrell Records, Committees: Social Responsibility, Manuscripts, Archives and Special Collections, Washington State University Libraries (archives 205, box 2, folder 19).

62 McNew, "Interim Report and Recommendations."

63 Dennis, interview, June 8, 2011.

64 Louis McNew, "Interim Report of the Committee of Social Responsibility, July 23, 1968," Glenn Terrell Records, Committees: Social Responsibility, Manuscripts, Archives and Special Collections, Washington State University Libraries (archives 205, box 2, folder 19).

65 Curry, "More Than a Prep School"; David Mathiason, "BSU Hits Curriculum, Coordinates Program," *Daily Evergreen*, September 27, 1968, 1.

66 Dennis, interview, June 8, 2011.

CHAPTER 5. "WELL, GLENN-BABY, WHAT'S UP NOW?"

1   Countryman, *Up South*, 3–4.

2   Countryman, *Up South*, 10; Purnell and Theoharis, "Introduction: Histories of Racism," 1–11.

3   Thomas, interview, September 1, 2011.

4   Thomas, interview, September 1, 2011.

5   Thomas, interview, September 1, 2011.

6   Thomas, interview, September 1, 2011.

7   Covin, interview, June 9, 2011.

8   Covin, interview, June 9, 2011.

9   Covin, interview, June 9, 2011.

10 Mathiason, "BSU Hits Curriculum."

11 Mathiason, "BSU Hits Curriculum."

12 Rooks, *White Money/Black Power*, 24, 25.

13 Rojas, *From Black Power to Black Studies*, 100.

14 "Social Responsibility Studied."

15 The Social Responsibility Committee made seven recommendations: (1) recruit Blacks into the Athletic Department, Admissions Office, and Residential Instructional Staff (a body analogous to a faculty senate); (2) establish a study center for disadvantaged, primarily Black students; (3) institute a faculty exchange program with a historically Black college or university; (4) create a summer program where underprepared students could live on campus and get ready for college; (5) start a fundraising drive for scholarships for low-income students; (6) grant the Black Student Union office space; and (7) create new academic programs. Source: McNew, "Interim Report of the Committee of Social Responsibility."

16 ASWSU Board of Control, "ASWSU Activities, May 15, 1968, Memorandum," Glenn Terrell Records, Committees: Social Responsibility, Manuscripts, Archives and Special Collections, Washington State University Libraries (archives 205, box 2, folder 19).

17 Curry, "More Than a Prep School."

18 Curry, "More Than a Prep School."

19 Stephens, "Historical Development of Black Studies," 57; Curry, "More Than a Prep School."

20 Tom Curry, "The Wrong Approach," editorial, *Daily Evergreen*, October 1, 1968, 2.

21 Mark Reese, "No Harmony in the Barnyard," *Daily Evergreen*, October 1, 1968, 5.

22 Mary White, "BSU Members Outline Goals of Organization," *Daily Evergreen*, October 18, 1968, 16; Stephens, "Historical Development of Black Studies," 61–62; Mark Reese, "There's No Other Way," editorial, *Daily Evergreen*, October 4, 1968, 5.

23 Dennis, interview, June 8, 2011.

24 "Afro-American Topics Offered by Colloquy," *Daily Evergreen*, October 4, 1968, 7.

25 "Afro-American Course Possible Spring Semester," *Daily Evergreen*, October 8, 1968, 1; White, "BSU Members Outline Goals."

26 "Black Militant Speaks Wednesday in Heald," *Daily Evergreen*, October 16, 1968, 3; "Social Problems to Be Explored," *Daily Evergreen*, October 11, 1968, 4.

27 Nola Hitchcock, "BSU Militant Leader Urges Black Studies," *Daily Evergreen*, October 18, 1968, 1.

28 Brisker, "Introduction to a Black Man."

29 "WSU Tops in Negro Sociology Doctorates," *Daily Evergreen*, December 4, 1968, 4.

30 Sue Prendergast, "Lack of Communication Stalls Action for Blacks," *Daily Evergreen*, November 15, 1968, 1, 5.

31 Prendergast, "Lack of Communication."

32 Sue Prendergast, "BOC Adopts Black Studies," *Daily Evergreen*, November 22, 1968, 1.

33 "Black Culture Needs Special Studies—Dennis," *Daily Evergreen*, December 17, 1968, 3.

34 David Mathiason, "Police Investigation Continues," *Daily Evergreen*, January 17, 1969, 1.

35 David Mathiason, "BSU Issues Statement Supporting 'Brothers,'" *Daily Evergreen*, January 22, 1969, 1.

36 Thomas, interview, September 1, 2011.

37 Mathiason, "BSU Issues Statement."

38 "WSU, Police Investigating Night Battle," *Spokane Daily Chronicle*, January 16, 1969, 7; Mathiason, "Police Investigation"; Mathiason, "BSU Issues Statement."

39 Mathiason, "Police Investigation."

40 Thomas, interview, September 1, 2011.

41 Mathiason, "BSU Issues Statement."

42 Mathiason, "Police Investigation."

43 Mathiason, "Police Investigation."

44 "Fraternity Damaged in Ruckus," *Spokesman-Review*, January 16, 1969, 1.

45 "Shots Fired as Blacks Invade WSU Fraternity House," *Lewiston (ID) Morning Tribune*, January 16, 1969, 20.

46 Tom Curry, "Wednesday Night," editorial, *Daily Evergreen*, January 17, 1969, 2. Also see Yvonne Thompson and Mary White, "One Year Later," *Daily Evergreen*, January 16, 1970, 1.

47 Mathiason, "Police Investigation."

48 Mathiason, "Police Investigation."
49 Mathiason, "Police Investigation."
50 Patricia Hill Collins, *Black Sexual Politics: African Americans, Gender, and the New Racism* (New York: Routledge, 2004), 63–64.
51 Covin, interview, June 9, 2011.
52 John Howard Griffin, epilogue to *Black Like Me*, audiobook read by Ray Childs (Ashland, OR: Blackstone, 2006).
53 "Terrell Issues Statement," *Daily Evergreen*, January 17, 1969, 1.
54 Mathiason, "BSU Issues Statement."
55 Mathiason, "BSU Issues Statement."
56 Thomas W. Campbell, "Church Holdout Ends with Arrest of 42; Blacks Begin Jail Terms," *Lewiston (ID) Morning Tribune*, March 2, 1969, 18.
57 Covin, interview, June 9, 2011.
58 "Terrell Comments on AGR Incident," *Daily Evergreen*, January 24, 1969, 1.
59 David Mathiason, "Discipline Committee Loses Cole in Handling of Hearing," *Daily Evergreen*, February 5, 1969, 1.
60 "Action Pending in AGR Case," *Daily Evergreen*, January 24, 1969, 1.
61 "Assault Charges Filed against Two Students," *Daily Evergreen*, February 5, 1969, 1.
62 "Assault Charges Filed."
63 Students for a Democratic Society of WSU, "White Racism," editorial, *Daily Evergreen*, February 5, 1969, 2; Dave Mathiason, "The Disciplinary Committee," editorial, *Daily Evergreen*, February 11, 1969, 2.
64 Students for a Democratic Society of WSU, "White Racism," 2.
65 Steven Fuson, "Saving Face," letter, *Daily Evergreen*, January 24, 1969, 2.
66 Also see letters in *Daily Evergreen* on January 21 and 24, 1969.
67 "Three Students to Appear for Trial in Superior Court," *Daily Evergreen*, February 12, 1969, 1; "Six Face Assault Charges Following AGR Incident," *Daily Evergreen*, February 14, 1969, 3.
68 Jerrelene Williamson, Spokane Northwest Black Pioneers, *Images of America: African Americans in Spokane* (Charleston, SC: Arcadia, 2010), 104; Dwayne Mack, *Black Spokane: The Civil Rights Struggle in the Inland Northwest* (Norman: University of Oklahoma Press, 2014).
69 Dave Farrar, "Charged Plead Guilty for Clash with AGR's," *Daily Evergreen*, February 28, 1969, 1.
70 Farrar, "Charged Plead Guilty."
71 John A. Denoo, "The State of Washington vs. Tyrone Daisy, Kenny Walker, Richard Lee Smith, Ronald Henderson, Ernie Thomas, Judgment and Sentence, 27 Feb. 1969," Glenn Terrell Records, Black Studies 1969, Manuscripts, Archives and Special Collections, Washington State University Libraries (archives 205, box 3, folder 163), 3.
72 Denoo, "State of Washington vs. Tyrone Daisy," 4.
73 Mathison, Jones, and King, "Farewell Interview," 4; Dave Mathiason and Bruce Housinger, "Blacks Charge Unfair Treatment," *Daily Evergreen*, March 4, 1969, 1, 7.

74 Emphasis in original. Black Student Union, letter to President Glenn Terrell, February 27, 1969, Glenn Terrell Records, Black People 1969, Manuscripts, Archives and Special Collections, Washington State University Libraries (archives 205, box 3, folder 162), 1–2.

75 Black Student Union, letter to President Glenn Terrell; "Terrell Rejects Demands Sought in Trial Aftermath," *Daily Evergreen*, March 4, 1969, 1, 3.

76 Glenn Terrell, letter to Black Student Union, February 28, 1969, Glenn Terrell Records, Black People 1969, Manuscripts, Archives and Special Collections, Washington State University Libraries (archives 205, box 3, folder 162).

77 At the time under study, Eastern Washington University was known as Eastern Washington State College, and Whitworth University was known as Whitworth College. Jim Kershner, "Eastern Washington University," HistoryLink.org, September 12, 2007, https://historylink.org; "About Whitworth," Whitworth University, accessed February 6, 2021, www.whitworth.edu.

78 Thomas, interview, September 1, 2011.

79 Thomas, interview, September 1, 2011.

80 Covin, interview, June 9, 2011.

81 Dave Farrar, "Weekend Demonstration Sees Forty-Two Students Arrested," *Daily Evergreen*, March 4, 1969, 1, 3; Bill Denstedt, "WSU Black Group Blocks Jailing of 5," *Spokesman-Review*, March 1, 1969, 1, 6.

82 Farrar, "Weekend Demonstration."

83 Covin, interview, June 9, 2011; "42 Students Arrested in Colfax," *Spokesman-Review*, March 2, 1969, second news section, 1.

84 Covin, interview, June 9, 2011.

85 Farrar, "Weekend Demonstration."

86 "Students, Faculty Member Guilty after Colfax Incident," *Daily Evergreen*, April 18, 1969, 1; "Colfax Justice Court Judge to Arraign 42 Beginning March 20," *Pullman Herald*, March 6, 1969, 2; Campbell, "Church Holdout."

87 Mathiason and Housinger, "Blacks Charge Unfair Treatment."

88 "Disciplinary Action," *Daily Evergreen*, March 4, 1969, 2.

89 "BOC Gives Proposals to Ease Racial Strain," *Daily Evergreen*, March 5, 1969, 1; "SDS Demonstration Planned for Today," *Daily Evergreen*, March 5, 1969, 4.

90 Dave Mathiason, "Show of Support Cancelled after Discipline Suspended," *Daily Evergreen*, March 7, 1969, 1.

91 One aftereffect was that Terrell held "off the record" meetings with Pullman community leaders and campus officials, where he defended his handling of the BSU-AGR controversy. See "Terrell Meets with Faculty to Explain Recent Actions," *Daily Evergreen*, March 11, 1969, 1.

92 Thomas, interview, September 1, 2011.

93 "President Terrell Appoints Black Studies Committee," *Daily Evergreen*, January 8, 1969, 3.

94 Cathy Monroe, "Registration Begins for Free University," *Daily Evergreen*, January 15, 1969, 1.

95 "Lit to Reflect Black History," *Daily Evergreen*, January 24, 1969, 11.

96 Nola Hitchcock, "Administration to Consider Proposal for Black Studies," *Daily Evergreen*, February 28, 1969, 1.

97 "BOC Passes Resolution on Black Studies Program," *Daily Evergreen*, March 7, 1969, 10.

98 "University Deans Discuss Black Studies Program," *Daily Evergreen*, March 25, 1969, 1.

99 Rojas, *From Black Power to Black Studies*, 9.

100 Dave Farrar, "Black Studies: A Frenetic Evolution," *Daily Evergreen*, April 22, 1969, 6–7.

101 Carol Cummins, "Ethnic Studies Curriculum to Seek Faculty Acceptance," *Daily Evergreen*, April 23, 1969, 1.

102 Cummins, "Ethnic Studies Curriculum."

103 Farrar, "Black Studies."

104 Dave Farrar, "Drop the Ethnic Studies Program," *Daily Evergreen*, April 23, 1969, 2.

105 Stephens, "Historical Development of Black Studies," 70; "Students Back Black Studies," *Daily Evergreen*, April 25, 1969, 3; Harvey Low, "Ethnic Studies Program," editorial, *Daily Evergreen*, April 29, 1969, 2; Dave Farrar, "Ethnic-Black Studies Forum Discussed Detailed Problem," *Daily Evergreen*, April 30, 1969, 1.

106 "Group Discusses Problems behind Black-Ethnic Studies," *Daily Evergreen*, May 2, 1969, 8.

107 Carol Cummins, "Groups Reach Compromise: 'Minority Studies' Emerges," *Daily Evergreen*, May 2, 1969, 1.

108 Carol Cummins, "RIS Okays 'American Minority Studies,'" *Daily Evergreen*, May 6, 1969, 1.

109 Stephens, "Historical Development of Black Studies," 74.

110 Dave Mathiason, "RIS Decision Generates Elation, Surprise," *Daily Evergreen*, May 7, 1969, 1; "An Undergraduate Program in Black Studies," Glenn Terrell Records, Black Studies 1969, Manuscripts, Archives and Special Collections, Washington State University Libraries (archives 205, box 3, folder 163); "BSP's Class Begins in Fall," *Daily Evergreen*, May 16, 1969, 5.

111 "Johnetta Cole Is Chosen as New Program Director," *Daily Evergreen*, May 28, 1969, 1.

112 Mark T. Fiege, "Rebellion in the Palouse: The Student Strike at Washington State University, May 1970," *Bunchgrass Historian: Whitman County Historical Society Quarterly* 11, no. 1 (1983): 16.

113 John Tappan Menard, "W. Glenn Terrell, 1967–1985," in William Stimson, Mark O'English, et al., *Leading the Crimson and Gray: The Presidents of Washington State University* (Pullman: Washington State University Press, 2019), 149.

114 David Mathiason and Eric Mathison, "Terrell Meets Student Demands," *Daily Evergreen*, May 6, 1970, 1; David Mathiason, "Teach-In to Explore Cambodia," *Daily Evergreen*, May 7, 1970, 1; Menard, "W. Glenn Terrell, 1967–1985," 150–51.

115 Menard, "W. Glenn Terrell, 1967–1985," 153–54; Fiege, "Rebellion in the Palouse," 16–18, and n. 2.

116 David Mathiason, "Demands Denied; Strike Results," *Daily Evergreen*, May 26, 1970, 1, 5.

117 Fiege, "Rebellion in the Palouse," 20, 22; William F. Wilbert, "Political Activities during the 1970 Student Strike: Three Recollections," *Bunchgrass Historian: Whitman County Historical Society Quarterly* 11, no. 1 (1983): 31.

118 Robinson, "Black Power Movement," 214–18.

119 Fiege, "Rebellion in the Palouse," 16; Menard, "W. Glenn Terrell, 1967–1985," 155–56.

120 "Weekly News Service," Racism Workshop Papers 1970–1971, Manuscripts, Archives and Special Collections, Washington State University Libraries (archives 277, box 1, folder 2); "Hare Advocates Societal Change," *Daily Evergreen*, October 9, 1970, 1.

121 For more on the 1969–1970 academic year, see Menard, "W. Glenn Terrell, 1967–1985"; Marc Arsell Robinson, "The Black Campus Movement in the Evergreen State: The Black Student Union at the University of Washington and Washington State University, 1967–1969," *Pacific Northwest Quarterly* 103, no. 2 (Spring 2012): 55–66; and Robinson, "Black Power Movement."

122 Stephens, "Historical Development of Black Studies," 74; Fiege, "Rebellion in the Palouse," 18.

123 Dwayne Mack, "Talmadge Anderson (1932–2011)," Blackpast.org, September 2, 2009, www.blackpast.org.

CONCLUSION

1 Misty Shock Rule, "Keeper of the Flame," *Columns Magazine*, March 2018, 37–38.

2 Hinckley and Henderson, *In Pursuit of Social Justice*.

3 Wick, "'Elder Statesman.'"

4 Wick, "'Elder Statesman.'"

5 Pitre, interview, July 10, 2018.

6 Rule, "Keeper of the Flame."

7 Demmings, interview, September 24, 2018.

8 Rule, "Keeper of the Flame."

9 Wick, "'Elder Statesman.'"

10 Pitre, interview, July 10, 2018.

11 Pitre, email, September 3, 2022.

12 Rule, "Keeper of the Flame."

13 "About Us," Office of Multicultural Student Services, Washington State University, accessed October 5, 2021, www.mss.wsu.edu; "Week Celebrates Multicultural Student Services," *WSU Insider*, October 16, 2012, https://news.wsu.edu.

14 Rogers, *Black Campus Movement*, 4–5.

15 Clayborne Carson, *In Struggle: SNCC and the Black Awakening of the 1960s* (Cambridge: Harvard University Press, 1981), 123, 125–26; Charles M. Payne, *I've Got the Light of Freedom: The Organizing Tradition and the Mississippi Freedom Struggle* (Berkeley: University of California Press, 1995), 294–95.

16 Carson, *In Struggle*, 287.

17 Demmings, interview, September 24, 2018.

18 Pitre, interview, July 10, 2018.

INDEX

AAA. *See* Afro-American Alliance

Abdul-Jabbar, Kareem, 66–67

ACLU. *See* American Civil Liberties Union

Adams, John H., 30, 41

AES. *See* American ethnic studies

Afro-American Alliance (AAA), 121–23

Afro-American Life Insurance Company, 120

Afro-American Student Society, UW, 64, 69

AGR. *See* Alpha Gamma Rho

Akwari, Onye, Afro-American Student Society established by, 64

Alexis, Jack, 48

Alpha Gamma Rho (AGR), 143–46, 147–48

American Civil Liberties Union (ACLU), 37, 109; in Pullman, 147

American ethnic studies, UW (AES), 108

American Indian Studies, WSU, 154–55

Anderson, Donald K., 103

Anderson, Talmadge, 158

Apollo Theater, Harlem, 61

army, US, 34

Asian/Pacific Islanders, 115, 166

Associated Students of Washington State University, 142

athletes, Black, at WSU, 126

Atkins, Ralph, 156

Atlanta, Georgia, Morehouse College in, 30, 89

Beadie, Nancy, 10–11

Belafonte, Harry, 35

Bell, James, 151

Bennett College, 121

Betsch, John, Sr., 120

Betsch, Mary Frances, 120

bigotry: in US army, 34; at UW, 59; at WSU, 2, 124, 129, 135

Biondi, Martha, 12–13

Black against Empire (Bloom and Martin), 15, 84

Black and White Concern Organization, 97

Black Arts and Culture Series, of BSU, 50

Black campus movement, 12–13, 57, 115, 163

The Black Campus Movement (Kendi), 12

Black empowerment conference at SF State, 82–83

Black Like Me (Griffin), 145

Black Lives Matter protests, 167

Black Panther Party (BPP): alarmist reports about, 145; BSU compared to, 14–15, 16–17; A. Dixon in, 84, 109; Great Migration relation to, 15–16; in Seattle, 83–84, 87, 89, 90; at Western Regional Black Youth Conference, 65

Black Power Forum, SNCC, 41–42

Black Power movement (BPM). *See specific topics*

Black Power on Campus (Williamson-Lott), 14

Black Sisters Union, 48

199

Black Student Union (BSU), 11, 74–75, 162; AGR altercation with, 143–46, 147–48; for Black Studies, 50–53, 67, 69, 70, 76–77, 137, 139, 141–43, 152–53; BPP compared to, 14–15, 16–17; BPP relation to, 84; Brisker in, 89–90; coalitions built by, 167–68; J. Cole relation to, 119–20; community organizing of, 4, 6, 58, 105, 115, 163, 168; community service projects of, 48–49, 66–67; in CRM, 164–66; D. Evans relation to, 98, 127; King assassination effect on, 164; as network of struggle, 12; NSA as predecessor of, 44–45, 48; Odegaard relation to, 91–96, 97–98, 103–4, 106; patriarchy in, 48, 71; Pitre in, 160; Project 408 incident response of, 126–28; at SF State, 13, 14, 17, 43, 46, 57, 165, 168; SLF relation to, 113; SNCC effect on UW, 64; SRC relation to, 130–31; Terrell relation to, 152, 157; Theater Project of, 49; "ungawa" as mantra of, 3–4, 79, 105; at UW, 1, 6–7, 17–18, 41, 57, 67–68, 71–73, 76–77, 84–85, 90–94, 106–7, 108, 110, 114–15, 123, 161, 168; at Western Regional Black Youth Conference, 65–66; white support for, 96–97, 102–3; at WSU, 2, 18, 117, 123–24, 132, 133–34, 140, 149, 156–58, 165, 166–67

Black Studies, 162–63; BSU for, 50–53, 67, 69, 70, 76–77, 137, 139, 141–43, 152–53; at UW, 1, 69–70, 76–77, 93–94, 96, 106, 107, 108; at WSU, 18, 138–39, 152–55, 158

Black Studies in the Pacific Northwest conference, 117

Bloody Tuesday, 53–54

Bloom, Joshua, 15, 84

Boeing Airplane Company: defense industry jobs at, 23; Negro Labor's Right to Work at, 24

Bottomly, Forbes, 80

boycotts: Montgomery bus, 8; of Olympic Games, 65–66; Philadelphia selective buying, 33; Seattle public school, 31–32

BPM. See Black Power movement

BPP. See Black Panther Party

Bradley, Stefan M., 14

Braman, James "Dorm," 109

Brazil, Joe, 94

Bremerton, Washington, 23

Brigham Young University (BYU), 111–12, 114

Brisker, E. J., 1, 16, 87, 106; in BSU, 89–90; on Carmichael, 41; in *Daily*, 69; on Odegaard, 92; Odegaard relation to, 98; at UW sit-in protest, 100–101; WSU address of, 141

Brotman Award, UW, 161

Brown, Raymond E., 37

Brown v. Board (1954), 110–11

BSU. See Black Student Union

Bundy, Mattie, 39; at Black Power forum, 42

Burke, Lucas, 16

Burton, Philip, 25

BYU. See Brigham Young University

CACRC. See Central Area Civil Rights Committee

California, 48; Los Angeles, 44, 57, 64–66, 89; Master Plan for Higher Education of, 45; Oakland, 83

CAMP. See Central Area Motivating Program

Campbell, Bertha Pitts, 25

CAPI. See Central Area Committee for Peace and Improvement

Cardwell, Dave, 142

Carlos, John, 65–66

Carmichael, Stokely (Kwame Ture), 1, 3, 8, 41; Seattle visited by, 36–40, 87–88; as SNCC chairman, 35; at Western Regional Black Youth Conference, 65

Carmichael v. Bottomly, 37
Carson, Clayborne, 164–65
Carter, Johnnie Evelyn, 60
Cartwright, Phillip, 96
Castro, Fidel, 52
Central Area Civil Rights Committee (CACRC), 30
Central Area Committee for Peace and Improvement (CAPI), 42
Central Area Motivating Program (CAMP), 80
Central District, Seattle, 27, 28; CACRC in, 30; CAMP in, 80; CAPI in, 42; riot in, 109
CFRE. *See* Christian Friends for Racial Equality
Cha-Jua, Sundiata Keita, 9
Charles E. Odegaard Award, UW, 161
Chicago, Black Studies in, 69
Chicanos/Latinos: BSU relation to, 115, 165; UW recruitment of, 102, 107; at WSU, 154, 157
Christian Friends for Racial Equality (CFRE), 25–26
Churchill, Winston, 137
Church of Latter-Day Saints, racial discrimination of, 111–12
Civic Unity Committee (CUC), 26
civil disobedience: at Franklin High School, 77; of UW BSU, 113; of WSU BSU, 133, 149
Civil Rights Act (1964), 114
civil rights movement (CRM): BPM relation to, 6, 8–10; BSU in, 164–66; Covin in, 136; at Morehouse College, 89; in Seattle, 21, 55
Clark, Marc, 16–17
Cleaver, Eldridge, 83
Cleveland High School, 58
coalitions: BSU building, 167–68; CACRC as, 30; interracial, 4, 6, 163; for protest, 156; WACO as, 49
Cobb, Charlie, 43–44

Cohen, Robert, 5–6
Cold War liberalism, 91–92
Cole, Johnnetta B., 16, 117, 119–20, 128, 150; on Black harassment, 127; on Black Studies Committee, 155; at Colloquium on Afro-American History and Culture, 141; Disciplinary Committee resignation of, 147; on Malcolm X, 122–23; on SRC, 129; on WSU Black Studies Committee, 152–53
Cole, Robert, 119; at Colloquium on Afro-American History and Culture, 141; as SDS advisor, 120–21
Colfax, Washington, 150–52
Collison, Craig, 67–68
Colloquium on Afro-American History and Culture, WSU, 141
Columbia University, SAS at, 14
Colville Confederated Tribes, 70
Communist Party, Seattle chapter of, 64–65
community organizing, 49; in BPM, 13, 164–65; of BSU, 4, 6, 58, 105, 115, 163, 168; grassroots outreach for, 13; of SNCC, 66
community service projects, of BSU, 48–49, 66–67
Congress of Racial Equality (CORE): BPM effect on, 42–43; CACRC working with, 30; Covin in, 121; Garrett in, 46; G. Owens in, 28–29
Conrad, Ernest, 98
Cook, M. E., 109
Cooper, Ray, 29
CORE. *See* Congress of Racial Equality
Corr, Linda, 64
Countryman, Matthew J., 10, 33; on racism, 134
Covin, David, 121–22, 145, 150; on Black subpoenas, 146; on King assassination, 123; on Thomas, 138; Watts Riot reaction of, 136–37; on WSU Black Studies Committee, 152

Crespino, Joseph, 10
CRM. *See* civil rights movement
Crosby, Alfred, 141
Crowder, Jesse, 102, 103
Crowley, Walt, 81, 86
Cuba, 52
CUC. *See* Civic Unity Committee

Daily Evergreen (WSU campus newspaper), 125; on AGR-BSU altercation, 144, 147–48; BSU in, 139, 140
Daily (UW student newspaper), BSU in, 69, 71–72
Daisy, Tyrone J., 147, 148
Dakan, Carl, 111
defense industry, racial discrimination in, 23–24
Demmings, Eddie, 16; on BSU, 77, 98, 165–66; on Carmichael, 41; on HUB blackboard, 68; on Keith-Miller, 58; on Pitre, 160; in school boycott, 32; on UW, 63; as UW recruiter, 107; on UW sit-in protest, 104–5
Dennis, Rutledge, 119; on Black Studies, 138; on integration, 141; on Program for American Minority Studies, WSU, 155; on Terrell, 129; on WSU Black Studies Committee, 152; WSU recruiting by, 131
Denoo, John A., 148–49, 151–52
Devin, William F., 26
Dewitty, Gordon, 99
Disciplinary Committee, WSU, 147, 152
Dixon, Aaron, 15, 98; in BPP, 84, 109; Carmichael effect on, 87–88; on death of King, 81; in jail, 81–82; on Seale, 83
Dixon, Elmer, 3; at Garfield High School, 73–74
Dore, James J., 82
Double V Campaign, 23–24
Dr. Sam, Soldier, Educator, Advocate, Friend (Kelly), 5

Eastern Washington University, 149, 196n77
Edison Technical School Building, UW, 111
Educational Opportunity Program (EOP), 107–8
Educational Policies Committee, WSU (EPC), 154
Edwards, Harry, 65
EEP. *See* Experimental Education Program, WSU
Egashira, Pamela, 47
Elliot, Eugene, 78, 95–96; defense testimony of, 109
EOP. *See* Educational Opportunity Program
EPC. *See* Educational Policies Committee, WSU
ethnic studies, WSU, 154–55
Eurocentrism, in US education, 50–51; at UW, 73, 75–76, 97; at WSU, 137
Evans, Charles, 100; on Odegaard, 105; SEP led by, 107
Evans, Dan, 42, 152; BSU relation to, 98, 127
Executive Committee of the Faculty Senate, UW, 100, 104, 106
Executive Order 8802, 24, 26–27
Experimental College, SF State, 49
Experimental Education Program, WSU (EEP), 130; tutoring services of, 131

Fair Employment Practices Act (1949), 26–27
Faris, Phillip H., 146
Farmer, Ashley, 9, 121
Federal Bureau of Investigation (FBI), 16–17
Findlay, John M., 22
First Presbyterian Church, in Seattle, 30
Fisk University, 120
Flavors, Trolice, 78–79, 80
Forman, James, at Western Regional Black Youth Conference, 65

Franciscan (SF State yearbook), 45

Franklin High School, 28, 73; BSU relation to, 165; L. Gossett at, 60; in Project 408, 124; protest at, 77–80, 108–9

Freedom Rides campaign, 29; Garrett working in, 46

Freedom Schools, 31–32

Freedom Summer campaign, 35, 44; Brisker in, 89; Garrett in, 46

Free University, WSU, 152–53

Friel, Wallis, 148

Friends of SNCC, 35

Garfield High School, 37; BSU at, 3, 73–74; Carmichael speaking at, 38–40, 88; in Project 408, 124; WSU visited by, 116

Garrett, James "Jimmy," 43, 99; as Black Studies consultant, 96; on Brisker, 89–90; as BSU architect, 66; on Odegaard, 91–92; in SF State BSU, 46, 48; in SNCC, 44, 47

Garvey, Marcus, 62

Gaskins, Felicia, 119

General Education Elective Program, SF State (GEEP), 50

Glass, Marvin, 111

Golden Gater (SF State student newspaper), 45

Goldwater, Barry, 118

Gossett, Larry, 1, 16, 40–41, 58; on BPP, 83; on Brisker, 90; on BSU, 67, 74–75; BSU outreach effort of, 123; on Dewitty, 99; at Franklin High School protest, 77–80; Harlem effect on, 61–63; in jail, 81–82; Keith-Miller relation to, 60; on militancy, 70–71; at Todd Auditorium, 151–52; trial of, 109; on Western Regional Black Youth Conference, 65

Gossett, Nelmon Bill, 60

Gossett, Richard, 73

Gossett, Sharon, 73, 74

grassroots outreach, for community organizing, 13

Graves, Letitia A., 25

Great Migration: BPP relation to, 15–16; Second, 22–23

Great Society, 153

Greensboro, North Carolina, 33

Griffey, Trevor, 17

Griffin, John Howard, 145

Hall, Lynn, 112

Halley, Kathleen "Kathy" (also "Nafasi"), 65, 71

Hall-McMurtrie (Hall), Marcie, 70, 102; as UW recruiter, 106–7

Halluran, Kathy, 97

Hampton, Fred, 16–17

Hannawalt, Frank, 38–39

Hare, Nathan, 96

Harlem, New York City, 61–63

Harlem vs. Columbia University (Bradley), 14

Hayakawa, S. I., 54–55

Hayden, Sandra "Casey," 35

Hemings, Sally, 76

Henderson, Ron, 143; in court, 147, 148

high schools: BSU outreach to, 67, 73; Cleveland, 58; Franklin, 28, 60, 73, 77–80, 108–9, 124, 165; Garfield, 3, 37, 38–40, 73–74, 88, 116, 124; William Beaumont, 88

Hilliard, Bill, 106

hip hop, youth movement, 19

Hogness, John, 112–13

Hooper, Cliff, 39

housing, racial discrimination in, 31

HUB. *See* Husky Union Building, UW

Human Rights Commission, 80

Humphries, Mike, 150, 151, 152

Husky Union Building, UW (HUB), 68

Hutton, Bobby, 77, 83

IC. *See* Instructional Center, UW

Idaho, Moscow, 118

Illinois, University of, 14

In Pursuit of Social Justice (documentary), 5
institutional racism, 10, 11–12; Carmichael on, 39; in New York City, 61; in Seattle Community College system, 110–11; at SF state, 45–46; at UW, 75–76
Instructional Center, UW (IC), 108, 160, 161
In Struggle (Carson), 164
International Association of Mechanics, 24
Internet Archive, 17
interracial coalitions, 4, 6, 163
I've Got the Light of Freedom (Payne), 164

Jackson, Mance, 30–31
Jackson State College, 156
James, Frank D., 37
Jefferson, Thomas, 76
Jeffries, Judson, 16
Jim Crow conditions, 4; in the North, 11–12, 116–17, 158, 166–67; in Washington State, 151, 163; in Whitman County, 7–8
Joseph, Penial, 9–10, 13; on Black Studies movement, 51
junior high schools: BSU outreach to, 73; Marshall, 74

Kanz, Ed, 103
Karagueuzian, Dikran, 45, 46
Karenga, Maulana Ron, 65
Katagiri, Mineo, 41
Kearney, Joe, 112
Keith, Dan, 60, 89; Afro-American Student Society established by, 64; in *Daily*, 69
Keith-Miller, Verlaine, 58, 59–60; on A. Dixon, 88; L. Gossett relation to, 60; on women in BSU, 71
Kelly, Samuel E., 5, 107
Kendi, Ibram X., 12–13; on Black campus movement, 57, 163; on Black Studies, 51

Kennedy, Robert, 86
Kennedy, T. H., 153
Kent State University, 114, 156
King, Martin Luther, Jr., 38; assassination of, 77, 80–81, 86, 123–24, 132, 139, 164, 168; BPM after, 6; at March on Washington for Jobs and Freedom, 31; Seattle visit by, 30
King County Jail, 80–82
Ku Klux Klan, 39

LaBrie, Aubrie, 50
La Crosse Nightriders, 157
Laducer, Carmelita, 71, 102
Lang, Clarence, 9
Lassiter, Matthew, 10
law enforcement: at Jackson State College, 156; Odegaard relation to, 105; in Pullman, 144–45; in Seattle, 103, 105, 111, 113; from Spokane, 150–51
Leahy, Margaret, 53–54
Leon, Eddie, 151
Lewis, Abraham Lincoln, 120
Lewiston Morning Tribune (newspaper), 144
Little, Gary, 98
Living for the City (Murch), 15–16
Los Angeles, California: SNCC in, 44; Western Regional Black Youth Conference in, 57, 64–66, 89
Lott, Juanita Tamayo, 54
Loving v. Virginia, 58
Luck, Leon, 154

Makah Reservation, 106
Manley, Tracy, 150–51
March on Washington for Jobs and Freedom, 31, 46
Maroon Tiger (Morehouse College student newspaper), 89
Marshall Junior High, 73; BSU at, 74
Martin, Rudy, 129, 152–53
Martin, Waldo E., Jr., 15, 84

mass mobilizations, 167
Master Plan for Higher Education, of
    California, 45
Mathiason, Dave, 147
Mattraw, Harold, 124–25
Maxey, Carl, 148, 151
McIntosh, Les, at Black Power forum, 42
McKinney, Samuel B., 30, 41
McMannis, D. L., 147
McNew, Louis, 130–31
Mexican Americans, at UW, 93, 94
Mexican American Studies, WSU,
    154–55
Mexico City, Olympic Games in, 65–66
Michaux, Lewis H., 61–62
Miller, Carl, 32–33; at Black Power forum,
    42; on Black Studies, 96; Brisker rela-
    tion to, 89; at Franklin High School
    protest, 78–79; in jail, 81–82; on Ode-
    gaard, 92–93, 95; on police violence,
    113; in SNCC, 34–36; at Todd Audi-
    torium, 151–52; trial of, 109; on UW
    sit-in protest, 103
Minnis, Melvin, 125
Mississippi: Freedom Summer in, 44, 89;
    Garrett in, 46–47; Jackson State Col-
    lege in, 156; SNCC in, 34–35; Whitman
    County compared to, 8
Montgomery bus boycott, 8
Morehouse College, 30, 89
Morgan, Bobby, 103
Morgan, Edward P., 78
Mormon Church. See Church of Latter-
    Day Saints
Morris, Arval, 102, 103–4
Moscow, Idaho, 118
Moses, Bob, 44
Mount Zion Baptist, SNCC Black Power
    forum at, 41–42
Multicultural Student Services, WSU
    (MSS), 162
Muñoz, Carlos, Jr., 86
Murch, Donna Jean, 15–16

Murray, George, 50; suspension of, 52, 53
The Myth of Southern Exceptionalism
    (Lassiter and Crespino), 10

National Association for the Advance-
    ment of Colored People (NAACP): in
    Seattle, 25; Thomas in, 135
National Commission on the Causes and
    Prevention of Violence, 46
National Council of Churches, 38
National Higher Education Act (1965),
    124
National Institutes of Health (NIH), 160
Native Americans: BSU relation to, 115,
    165; at UW, 93, 94; UW recruitment of,
    107; at WSU, 154
Negro Labor's Right to Work, at Boeing
    Airplane Company, 24
Negro Student Association (NSA), 44–45,
    48
Negro Voters League, 37, 39
Neighborhood Rebels (Joseph), 13
Newton, Huey, 15–16, 83
New York City, New York, Harlem, 61–63
NIH. See National Institutes of Health
Nixon, Richard, 156
North Carolina, Greensboro, 33
Northwestern University, 120
NSA. See Negro Student Association

Oakland, California, 83
Oberlin College, 120
Odegaard, Charles, 72, 161; BSU relation
    to, 91–96, 97–98, 103–4, 106; defense
    testimony of, 109; law enforcement
    relation to, 105; Terrell compared to,
    129; at UW sit-in protest, 100–101
Office of Minority Affairs and Diversity
    (OMA/OMAD), UW, 107, 115, 160,
    161, 166, 189n89; expansion in 2002,
    161
Oliver, Charles, 78–79, 80
Olympic Games, boycott of, 65–66

OMA/OMAD. *See* Office of Minority Affairs and Diversity (OMA/OMAD), UW

Oregon: Seattle BSU relation to, 68; University of, 65, 153, 171

Oregon State University, 126; Black Studies at, 153

Orrick, William H., Jr., 46

Orrick Report, 48

Owens, Garry, 16, 27; CORE joined by, 28–29

Owens, Jim, 111

Pac-8. *See* Pacific Eight Athletic Conference

Pacific Car and Foundry Company, 23

Pacific Eight Athletic Conference (Pac-8), 153–54

patriarchy, in BSU, 48, 71

Payne, Charles M., 164

Philadelphia, Pennsylvania, selective buying boycott in, 33

Phillips, Johanna, 25–26

Pieroth, Doris H., 27

Pitre, Emile, 63, 71; on Brisker, 89, 90; in IC, 108; at UW, 159–61

Pittsburgh Courier (newspaper), 23

Poitier, Sidney, 46

Pope, Byron, 94

The Portland Black Panthers (Burke and Jeffries), 16

Program for American Minority Studies, WSU, 155

Project 408 incident, 124–25, 132; BSU response to, 126–28

protests: Black Lives Matter, 167; coalitions for, 156; at Franklin High School, 77–80, 108–9; school boycott as, 31–32; at SF State, 53–55; sit-in, 3, 98–106, 108, 160; at UW, 87, 113

Pullman, Washington, 196n91; ACLU in, 147; BSU campaigning in, 18; law enforcement in, 144–45; Seattle

compared to, 7; white homogeneity in, 118, 135, 137

Purnell, Brian, 11–12, 116

racial discrimination: of Church of Latter-Day Saints, 111–12; in defense industry, 24; in education, 110–11; at Franklin High School, 77–78; in housing, 31; lawsuits against, 25; in Seattle, 28–29; Washington State action against, 26–27; at William Beaumont High School, 88; at WSU, 116, 135–36

Racial Equality Bulletin (CFRE), 26

racial justice, at WSU, 2

racism: institutional, 10, 11–12, 39, 45–46, 61, 75–76, 110–11; in the North, 134; at UW, 59, 63, 159–60; WSU BSU strike against, 156–58

Rainier Vista Housing Projects, 28

Ralph, Loren, 77–79, 109

Randolph, A. Philip, 24

Ravarra, Patricia, 48

Reagan, Ronald, 55

Remaking Black Power (Farmer), 121

Renton, Washington, 23

Reserve Officers Training Corps (ROTC), 70

Residential Instructional Staff, WSU (RIS), 154–55

Rojas, Fabio, 47; on Black Studies, 69, 139

Roller, Julius, 102

Roosevelt, Franklin D., 24, 26–27

Rosen, Michael H., 37, 109; at UW sit-in protest, 103–4

ROTC. *See* Reserve Officers Training Corps

Rowland, Jim, 142

Rubisz, Valerie, 64

SABSU. *See* Seattle Alliance of Black Student Unions

Sanchez, Sonia, 50

San Francisco, California, Seattle relation to, 21–22

San Francisco State University (SF State), 48; Black empowerment conference at, 82–83; Black Studies at, 50–53; BSU at, 13, 14, 17, 43, 46, 57, 165, 168; Experimental College of, 49; GEEP at, 50; institutional racism at, 45–46; NSA at, 44–45; protests at, 53–55

SAS. *See* Students' Afro-American Society

Schaefer, Jon, 29

SDS. *See* Students for a Democratic Society

Seale, Bobby, 15–16; in Seattle, 83–84

Seattle, Washington, 1–2, 73–75; Black population in, 17, 21, 22–23; BPM in, 163–64; BPP in, 83–84, 87, 89, 90; Carmichael visiting, 36–40, 87–88; Central District in, 27, 28, 30, 42, 80, 109; Communist Party in, 64–65; CRM in, 21, 55; King visiting, 30; law enforcement in, 103, 105, 111, 113; NAACP in, 25; Pullman compared to, 7; racial discrimination in, 28–29; San Francisco relation to, 21–22; Seale in, 83–84; Sicks Stadium in, 79–80; SNCC in, 34–36; Urban League in, 25, 26, 30

Seattle Alliance of Black Student Unions (SABSU), 74

Seattle Community College system, 110–11

Seattle Liberation Front (SLF), 113

Seattle Magazine, 88

Seattle Post-Intelligencer (newspaper), 40, 68; on Franklin High School protest, 78

Seattle public school boycott, 31–32

Seattle School Board: Carmichael opposed by, 37; Voluntary Racial Transfer Program of, 31, 42

Seattle Schools' Intergroup Relations Office, 80

Seattle Times (newspaper), 36–37, 38; on Central District riot, 109

Seattle Transit Company, 26

SEP. *See* Special Education Program, UW

SF State. *See* San Francisco State University

Shearer, Charles F., 78

Sicks Stadium, Seattle, 79–80

sit-in protest, at UW, 3, 98–106, 108, 160

SLF. *See* Seattle Liberation Front

Smith, E. June, 25

Smith, Richard Lee, in court, 147, 148

Smith, Robert, 52–53

Smith, Tommie, 65–66

Smith, Willie, 126

SNCC. *See* Student Nonviolent Coordinating Committee

Social Responsibility Committee, WSU (SRC), 129, 193n15; for Black Studies, 139; BSU relation to, 130–31

Soden, Dale, 31–32

South Africa, apartheid in, 19

Spearman, Florise, 24

Special Education Program, UW (SEP), 107

Spelman College, 121

Spence, Infanta, 42

Spencer, Robyn C., 15

Spokane, Washington, law enforcement from, 150–51

SRC. *See* Social Responsibility Committee, WSU

St. Patrick's Catholic Church, 151

Stanford University, 112

Stern, Robbie, 96–97, 102

Stewart, Benny, 48; on war of the flea, 54

Stockham, Karen, 35

Stokes, Charles M., 27

The Strange Careers of the Jim Crow North (Purnell and Theoharis), 11–12, 116

student enrollment: at SF State, 45–46; at WSU, 7, 119

Student Nonviolent Coordinating Committee (SNCC), 21, 164–65; Black Power forum organized by, 41–42; Brisker in, 89; Bundy as chairperson of, 39; Carmichael as chairman of, 35; community organizing of, 66; A. Dixon in, 88; Garrett in, 44, 47; L. Gossett in, 62–63; Miller in, 34–36; UW BSU affected by, 64

Students'Afro-American Society (SAS), 14

Students for a Democratic Society (SDS), 96–97, 111; R. Cole as advisor of, 120–21; in Pullman, 147

Sugiyama, Marguerita, 157

Summerskill, John, 91–92

Sweeney, James, 126

Taplin, Ron, 148

Terrell, Glenn, 127–28, 129–30, 153, 196n91; on AGR-BSU altercation, 146; BSU relation to, 152, 157; Covin relation to, 138

Tet Offensive, 86

Thalheimer, Fred, 47

Theater Project, of BSU, 49

Theoharis, Jeanne, 11–12, 116

Third World Liberation Front (TWLF), 53

Thomas, Ernest (Ernie, or "Stone"), 16, 121, 134–36; on AGR-BSU altercation, 144; on Black Studies, 142–43; in court, 147, 148; Covin on, 138; on Program for American Minority Studies, WSU, 155; threats to, 150

Tjokroadismarto, Widjonarko, 29

Todd Auditorium, 151–52

Turner, Willie, 126

TWLF. See Third World Liberation Front

"ungawa," 3–4; at Franklin High School, 79; at UW, 105

United Church of Christ, 41

United Farm Workers, 156

United Negro Improvement Association, 62

United States (US): army of, 34; Eurocentrism in education in, 50–51, 73, 75–76, 97, 137; institutional racism in, 10

University of Illinois at Urbana-Champaign, 14

University of Oregon, 65, 153, 171

University of Washington (UW): Afro-American Student Society at, 64, 69; Black Studies at, 1, 69–70, 76–77, 93–94, 96, 106, 107, 108; BSU at, 1, 6–7, 17–18, 41, 57, 67–68, 71–73, 76–77, 84–85, 90–94, 106–7, 108, 110, 114–15, 123, 161, 168; BYU relation to, 111–12, 114; Carmichael speaking at, 38; Chicanos/Latinos recruitment at, 102, 107; EOP at, 107–8; Eurocentrism at, 73, 75–76, 97; Executive Committee of the Faculty Senate of, 100, 104, 106; L. Gossett at, 60–61; institutional racism at, 75–76; Keith-Miller at, 59–60; OMA of, 107, 115, 160, 161, 166; Pitre at, 159–61; producer of In Pursuit of Social Justice, 5; protests at, 87, 113; racism at, 59, 63, 159–60; SEP at, 107; sit-in protest at, 3, 98–106, 108, 160

University of Wyoming, 112

Up South (Countryman), 10, 33

Upward Bound program, 70

Urban League, in Seattle, 25, 30; CUC partnership with, 26

Us (sociopolitical group), 65

US. See United States

UW. See University of Washington

Van Deburg, William L., 122

Varnado, Jerry, 48, 54

Vietnam War, 39; BSU activism against, 70, 114; NSA against, 45; Tet Offensive in, 86; WSU affected by, 156

VISTA. See Volunteers in Service to America

Voluntary Racial Transfer Program, of Seattle School Board, 31, 42
Volunteers in Service to America (VISTA), 61
Voting Rights Act (1966), 8

WACO. *See* Western Addition Community Organization
Walker, Eddie, 75, 76, 103
Walker, Kenneth, 147, 148
war of the flea, 54
Washington, George, 76
Washington State, 23; Colfax, 150–52; Fair Employment Practices Act in, 26–27; Jim Crow conditions in, 151, 163; Pullman, 7, 18, 118, 135, 137, 144–45, 147, 196n91; Spokane, 150–51; Whitman County, 7–8; Yakima Valley, 107. *See also* Seattle, Washington
Washington State Board Against Discrimination, 27
Washington State University (WSU), 161; Associated Students of, 142; Black athletes at, 126; Black enrollment at, 7, 119; Black Studies at, 18, 138–39, 152–55, 158; Brisker address at, 141; BSU at, 2, 18, 117, 123–24, 132, 133–34, 140, 149, 156–58, 165, 166–67; Chicanos/Latinos at, 154, 157; *Daily Evergreen* of, 125, 139, 140, 144, 147–48; Disciplinary Committee of, 147, 152; EEP at, 130, 131; ethnic studies at, 154–55; Eurocentrism at, 137; MSS at, 162; Project 408 at, 124–28; racial discrimination at, 116, 135–36; SRC at, 129, 193n15
Watts Riot (1965), 33, 34; Covin reaction to, 136–37
We of the Grassroots, 42
Western Addition Community Organization (WACO), 49

Western Regional Black Youth Conference (1967), 57, 64; Brisker at, 89; BSU at, 65–66
White, Joseph, 52
whites: in BPM, 38; BPM anxieties of, 145; BSU support by, 96–97, 102–3; in Pullman, 118, 135, 137
Whitman County, Washington, Jim Crow conditions in, 7–8
Whitman County Jail, 133
Whitworth University, 149, 196n77
William Beaumont High School, 88
Williams, Barbara J., 123, 128; on SRC, 129
Williams, Dorothy West, 24
Williams, Frank, 110
Williams, Hannibal, 49–50
Williams, Mark, 126; at Todd Auditorium, 151–52
Williams, Robert F., 150
Williams, Thomas, 48
Williamson-Lott, Joy Ann, 14
Wilson, James B., 114
Wood, Herbert, 153
Woolworth department stores, 33
World War II: Seattle affected by, 23; Seattle Black population during, 17, 21, 22–23
Wright, Richard, 23–24
WSU. *See* Washington State University

X, Malcolm, 33, 61, 150; AAA memorial for, 122–23; death of, 37

Yakima Valley, Washington, 107
YMCA. *See* Young Men's Christian Association
Young, Andrew, 109
Young, Kenneth, 109
Young Men's Christian Association (YMCA), 141
Young Women's Christian Association (YWCA), 141

ABOUT THE AUTHOR

MARC ARSELL ROBINSON is Assistant Professor in the Department of History at California State University, San Bernardino.